THE GREAT AWAKENING

Volume - I

Sister Thedra

Copyright © 2020 by Halls of Light, LLC

All rights reserved. This book or any portion thereof may not be reproduced or used in any manner whatsoever without the express written permission of the publisher except for the use of brief quotations in a book review.

ISBN: 978-1-7363418-1-0

CONTENTS

Mission Statement iv
About the late Sister Thedra 1
THE ASSOCIATION OF SANANDA AND SANAT KUMARA 7
THE BOOK OF LIGHT 19
LIGHT WORKERS? 28
THE ARYAN 30
THE MIDDLE EAST 38
THE GOLDEN SCRIPTS 53
EVERLASTING FREEDOM 60
A GREAT AWAKENING 88
I SHALL BREAK THESE BARRIERS 134
SISTER THEDRA 148
BEGIN BOOK 168
SISTER THEDRA 194
A BIT OF HISTORY 252

Mission Statement

Give the truth to the world. Let it be received where it will. Many will read the messages. Some will accept the truth, others will read through curiosity, a few will ridicule. Yet to all is the truth given, and to all remains the power of choice.

The hope of the world in these times is in spiritualizing all forms of activity---promoting understanding through love and service. These must be the watchwords if the world is to come into lasting peace. We are trying to influence a world that is going astray and could cause undreamed of suffering. We are trying to overcome the thought of materialists and to bring a spiritual outlook into the earthly life. We need the help of all on earth who can think in spiritual terms. The great battle to be fought now is between the spiritual and the material, between idealism and carnalism. You can help by spreading the word----we are asking that you help because the battle may be long and the victory far away.

Halls of Light is not allied with any sect, denomination, political entity, organization, neither endorses nor opposes any cause. There are no dues for membership. Halls of Light is self-supporting through its own voluntary contributions. Halls of Light has but one purpose: to help through encouragement and understanding...

To contact the publishers or to obtain copies of our other books, please contact us at email: goldtown11@gmail.com

Esu Jesus Sananda

This reproduction is from an actual photograph taken on June 1st, 1961, in Chichen Itza, Yucatan, by one of thirty archaeologists working in the area at the time. Sananda appeared in visible, tangible body and permitted His photograph to be taken.

About the late Sister Thedra

> Since the later part of the last Century the Kumara
> wisdom preserved by Aramu Muru has begun to reemerge
> into the world. This process began with the late Sister
> Thedra, whom Jesus Christ appeared physically to while
> on her deathbed and spontaneously healed her of cancer
> while she was in the Yucatan, where she had gone to
> accept her fate, and the will of our Lord Jesus Christ.
> That is when something miraculous occurred.
> --sus spoke to her saying, "My name is Esu Sananda
> Kumara" and then sent Thedra down to the Monastery of
> the Seven Rays to learn the Kumara wisdom.
> After five years, Thedra was told to return to the
> United States where she founded the Association of
> Sananda and Sanat Kumara at Mt. Shasta in California.
> While heading this organization, Thedra channeled many
> messages from Sananda and taught the Kumara wisdom
> until her passing in 1992.
> While in the Yucatan It is said that while Sister
> during the 1960s Thedra was in the Yucatan, she was
> told a se-ret by her friend George Hunt Williamson,
> also known as Brother Philip, who authored Secrets of
> the Andes, and the SECRET PLACES OF THE LION.
> Williamson, confided in his long-time friend Sister
> Thedra that he intentionally scrambled the
> reincarnational lineages in order to protect this next
> generation when they the Mayan Solar Priests, who were
> the direct line descendants of the Kumara according to
> prophesy were scheduled to reincarnate or return to
> fulfill their missions upon Earth, one of which was to
> relocate these ancient sites where the original records
> of the Amaru were placed for safe keeping.
> Sister Thedra, 1900-1992, spent five years at the abbey
> undergoing intensive spiritual training and > initiations.
> While in South America in the Yucatan, she had an
> experience which changed her in an instant when as it

> is told by her that Jesus Christ physically appeared to
> her and spontaneously cured her of cancer.
>
> He introduced himself to her by his true, name,
> "Sananda Kumara," thereby revealing his affiliation
> with the Venusian founders of the Great Solar
> Brotherhoods. It was by his command that Sister Thedra
> went to Peru where in here travels she met Williamson.
> Sister Thedra eventually left Peru upon telling her
>experience there was complete.
> Even before she returned to the States she met with
> harsh criticism from the church, which she elected to
> leave. (JW That was the church that is in Salt Lake
> City, Utah.)
> She then traveled to Mt. Shasta in California and
> founded the Association of Sananda and Sanat Kumara.
> A.S.S.K.
>
> You ask, Is There A Difference Between Jesus and
> Sananda?
> Our Lords name given at birth by his father Joseph, and
> his beloved mother Mary was Yeshua, thus being of the
> house of David and the order of Yoseph, he would be
> called Yeshua ben Yoseph.
>
> The Roman Emperors placed the name of Jesus upon the
> sir name of Yeshua, after the Emperor Justinian adopted
> Christianity as the official faith of Rome, and ordered
> that the sacred books be compiled, upon approval of a
> specially appointed council, appointed by the Emperor,
> into a recognizable and uniform work titled The Bible.
> Prior to this there never was a Bible per se.
>
> There existed until the time of the Emperor's edict, a
> selection of many Sacred texts, that were employed in
> the Sacred Teachings. Many of which were copies of
> what the Greeks had transposed from the original texts

> in the Libraries of Alexandria, which were originally
> compiled by Alexander the Great, and were destroyed by
> Julius Caesar, fearing that they might prove dangerous
> to the rule of a Caesar, an Earthly God.
> In addition, it kept. (he thought) the knowledge of
> Alexander's Libraries, out of the hands of the
> Ptolemy's, who were said to be descended from his
> bloodline.
> At the time Caesar had no way of knowing the vast
> portions of the Library that were already in the
> Americas, in the Great Universities of the Inca, and
> the Maya.
> Yeshua spent many years in the East after his
> ascension.
> The good Sheppard, upon his appearances to the
> Apostles after his ascension told his Apostles that he
> was in fact going to tend to his Father's other sheep;
> which means, plainly that he was continuing upon his
> sacred journey.
> As the ascended one, Yeshua took to himself the name of
> Sananda, meaning the Christed one, and Sananda was
> thus embraced forever more by the Great Solar
> Brotherhood.
> To many of you this is all new, to others it will be
> received as a welcome easing of the wall that has so
> long separated two sides of the same coin, this is
> being placed into the ethers and the matrix of thought
> at this time as it is the time of the Awakening, and
> the Christos is already emerging into the new
> consciousness, and mother Earth herself.
>
> Sister Thedra and the phenomenon of channeling.
> Authority to use the name of Sananda was given to
> Sister Thedra when Jesus~ Sananda appeared to her in the
> Yucatan, and cured her instantly of the cancer that had
> taken her body over.
> Further, he allowed a picture of his continence to be

> taken at that time that she might realize the
> occurrence was more than a dream. (JW I was told by
> my teacher and Guru Merelle Fagot that Thedra had
> a large format camera called a 620, if I remember right,
> and it had bellows on it and founded out. She used
> this to take the picture of Sananda. Merele said that
> she got some real good pictures with that camera. I
> have seen this picture that Thedra took and Sananda
> didn't look very handsome, he just looked like a normal
> person with not too long of hair and he had very dark
> skin.)
> Sanada's Message to her by Sister Thedra.
> "Sori Sori: Mine hand I have placed upon thine head,
> and I have given unto thee the authority to use Mine
> name. Give unto them the name Sananda, by which they
> shall know Me as the Lord thy God - the Son of God, sent
> that ye be made to know me, the One sent from out the
> inner temple that there be Light in the world of men."
> (The meaning of "Lord God: "The Lord God, for he is
> "Lord" of, and responsible for, that which he has
> brought forth.)
> "Now it is come when ones which have the will to follow
> Me shall come to know Me by that name which I commanded
> thee to give unto the world as Mine "New name."
> There are many that shall call upon the name of Jesus,
> yet, they will deny the new name as they are want to do.
> While unto thee I give assurance that I am the One sent
> that there be Light in the world of men. Now let this
> be understood, that they that deny Mine New Name deny
> Me by any name. So be it I have appointed thee Mine
> spokesman; I've given unto thee the power and authority
> to speak for being that which I AM. And I say unto thee
> Mine child whom I have called forth and anointed thee
> with the Holy Spirit, thy name shall be as it is now
> called, Thedra - that name I spoke unto thee from out
> the ethers, and thou heard Me and accepted that which I
> gave unto thee; and wherein have I deceived thee?

> Wherein have I forgotten thee, or left thee alone?"
> "I say unto thee, Mine hand is upon thee and I shall
> sustain thee and you shall come to know that which I
> have kept for thee. So be it that I have kept thy
> reward, and at no time shall it be dissipated of
> scattered, for it is intact. So let this Mine Word
> suffice them which question thee - let them question,
> and I shall bear witness for thee. For do I not know
  Mine servants from the traitor?
> Do I not reward Mine servants according unto their
> works or merits? I speak that they might know that I am
> mindful of Mine servants, that I am not a poor puny
> priest who has forgotten his servants."
>
> "I say unto them, Mine servants shall be glorified
> above the crowned heads of the nations which have set
> themselves apart, and denied Me Mine part of Mine word
> for they have turned from Me in their conceit and
> forgetfulness."
> "Now let this go on record as Mine Word, and I shall
> give unto them proof, which are of a mind to follow Me.
> So be it as I have spoken and I am not finished; I
> shall speak again and again, and I shall rise Mine
> Voice against them which set foot against Mine
> servants, and they shall be as ones cast out. So let
> them ask of Me and I shall enlighten them. So be it I
> know where of I speak. Be ye as ones blest to accept Me
> and know Me for that which I AM.
> The Final Messages >
. On Saturday, June 13, 1992, at exactly 10.00 PM, at the age of 92,
> Sister Thedra made her final transition from the comfort of her own bed. When the time
> arrived, she simply took one small breath and slipped
> quietly away, without pomp or fanfare.
> She left as she had lived...as a humble servant for the
> greater good.
> The messages that follow were given to Sister Thedra

> shortly before her transition.
> They are compiled here to give you some idea of the
> significance of her passing and of the expansion of the
> work, as she is now free to work unencumbered by the
> physical limitations and by the pain which has so
> encumbered her in the past.
> She has carried on the work here on the Earth plane for
> the last 50 years because that's where the work was
> needed...rest assured that her work now in the higher
> realms will simply be an extension of that work.

THE ASSOCIATION OF SANANDA AND SANAT KUMARA

The Association of Sananda and Sanat Kumara, or A.S.S.K., was established by the one known as Sister Thedra, under the direct guidance of both Sananda and Sanat Kumara. Referred to by Sananda as The Gatehouse, it has functioned as the outer aspect of the work whereby contact is made with those seeking greater spiritual understanding. Since her acceptance into the Brotherhood of The Seven Rays, over thirty years ago, Sister Thedra has recorded the communications, teachings and prophecies given to her by Sananda, Sanat Kumara, and many other Sibors, or teachers of the Brotherhood of Light. Referred to as The **Scripts**, these transcripts represent an in-depth prophecy of the events and changes which the planet shall undergo within this "Time of Awakening." They seek to alert us to these great changes, but more than that, they seek to prepare each of us to grow spiritually with these changes, that they bring a true upliftment to those who truly seek a greater understanding. These are true Spiritual teachings form the very Source of Truth itself.

The Scripts

The Scripts now number over 3000 pages. They have been printed into portions of 24 pages each and are sent out in the order in which they were received.

TheMiddle-East

Sori Sori: This is mine word unto thee this day; We of the host are gathered into the council chambers at this hour for a decision as to that which we shall do concerning the Eastern countries which are within such conflict. This situation has gone so far that it is necessary that we take some sort of action.

This is indeed a grave situation, and we of the council hast debated long and seriously as which action to take. Before we do anything we come to a <u>unanimous</u> and <u>just</u> decision... after every possible aspect or facet of the actions and results of such actions have been carefully weighed.

Now it is the crucial hour, we shall be as the ones to go into action. Action there shall be... of a different tenor... a new compilation shall come upon the unholy holy land. For we have been given permission by the Father-Mother God to execute the plan on which we, the Host, hast set our seal. This shall be a decision of justice for all... and no man shall over turn our decision... for this condition within this part of thy world of man is deplorable and intolerable. Therefore We of the Council have come unto a <u>just</u> and <u>holy decision</u> as to how to deal with an unholy situation.

Be ye as ones prepared to listen, watch and see, that which has amounted to a long and dreadful situation... for we shall allow these ones to give their lives in such fury that they bring to themselves the end of the conflict... they shall destroy themselves... <u>So Be It.</u>

They have set into motion such hatred that we shall do another thing other than bear with their hatred and degradation which is <u>unbearable</u>. We shall allow them to destroy themselves.

Be ye aware of this which I say unto thee, and know ye it is a just decision on our part. Give ye no energy unto this situation... be ye no part of it! For I have given unto ye, mine tried and true chelas/handmaidens, a mission which is very demanding on thy mortal form, and thine time and energy, which shall be conserved. It is necessary that ye rest thine body and keep thine mind free from stress. Give no pity, no sorrow... dwell only on that which is the great plan, which is just and shall be for the <u>good of all</u>, for it shall be quick justice.

We know that which shall accrue from this decision... We make no foolish or unjust decisions. Be ye as ones to bless thine own self by thine understanding our part that we play in this <u>game</u> of "Love and War." Know ye that justice shall prevail!!

It is foreseen that <u>our</u> decision is the greater part of wisdom, for too long hast the conflict gone on... to the point that the planet which gives thee footing is endangered. This is of great concern unto us at this time.

While man of <u>Earth</u> hast gone head long, he hast made his own portion sure and swift. These ones have been warned. Time and time again we have sent our messengers unto these war mongers. We have given them an ultimatum in good faith... many plans we have proposed... yet they heed not our pleading.

While <u>ye of peace</u> shall abide in peace, let not thine mind dwell on the horror, the dark side, which will be unto thee a barrier in, or unto, thine own mission or ascension. For, shall I say unto thee at the present time, that ye might comprehend that which I am saying unto thee "<u>Mine flock</u>", mine chelas, mine ones I have used to bring forth mine words unto the populace... "This, <u>OUR DECISION</u>, and the manifestation, is not of <u>thine business</u>. Be ye not involved in any emotional trauma, for it would have a very detrimental effect on thine assignment or mission... hear ye me in this. I say unto thee again; make ye no pretense of peace within thine self... Let it Be... Let it Be.

Be no part of it! <u>It is not for thee</u> to judge or pity. Let thine time be mine while it is given unto us of the Council to cover thee with our shield, and love shall be thine portion... So Let it Be...

Let it be!!

I Am Sananda

Sori Sori: Ye shall be as one to bring forth this news/information as it has never been given before. The information is of great concern unto us of our realm. When this information is released there shall be a wave of confusion and disbelief... yet there shall be great relief for the ones which have asked for Light - <u>The truth seekers,</u>

It is now come when it is expedient to release such information... it is part of the work of our school (* *see Mine Intercom Messages from the Realms of Light*) For this shall it be seen and understood that We, the host, are not playing second place unto any man of planet Earth. It is now come when such material shall be made available, yet not many are prepared to be mine messenger or scribe. This work of getting these portions out unto the ones which are seeking Truth (*naught else*), is no small task.

While it is given unto few, in comparance with the populace, to ask for this truth which is now available, the populace, or major part of the people of Earth, will have none of it!... reject it as fantasy. Yet it is foreseen that many shall embrace this Truth and give unto 'us' the Host, credit for bringing it forth that they be enlightened... for these have waited long for such enlightenment. They shall <u>know</u> the truth of such information, and accept it with joy and Thanksgiving.

For this it is given unto thee to be prepared to go forth with such as we shall give unto thee for them. While there shall be the bigots... the traitors... the foolish... unlearned, that shall deny thee and bring great stress upon the ones which accept such truth as is brought forth for their sake, one and all... unto the traitors which reject such truth/information I say, it is for thine good that "We" come in love and fulfillment of the law. It is for thine own good that we labor without ceasing or so called recompense. It is for our love that we come into the darkness of thine world that there be Light... that ye be as one enlightened... free from thine bonds of unknowing, the ignorance which is bondage.

Yea, bondage it is. When ye have been presented with such materials as we are prepared to release, it behooves thee to consider well its worth/value and be as ones willing to learn. To lay aside thine preconceived ideas and opinions... to weigh, consider the value of it, unbiased by that which hast been unto thee thine legirons.

Give unto me credit for being that which I am and I shall prove mineself. I am not a traitor. I am come of mine Father... He hast sent me that ye might return unto Him with Me. I am one of the Host which I have brought with me for the purpose of bringing thee out before the great day of sorrow and suffering... <u>this</u> is our <u>intent</u>, our mission at this time.

Be ye as one to open wide thine sleepy eyes, that ye see clearly that which is new unto thee... for each and every day is new unto the ones which have eyes to see clearly that which is new unto thee. For each and every day is new unto the ones which have eyes to see... the ones which have a will to learn.

None other shall move into the "Age of Light," for they shall be as ones <u>which have not the will</u> to learn of me... as one with the mighty Host. What a host it is!!

We have come as the Lighted Ones, sent of Our Father which ye have not remembered in thine days or sojourn within the realm of darkness... which has been thine lot for lo the eons. Now the time is come when ye shall be as ones prepared to receive thine freedom, and there shall be great light within thee which shall lift thee into the realm in which we exist... wherein is no darkness... no sorrow. Be it such as we bring unto thee... present unto thee, this day.

Shall ye give unto me/us credit for being that which we claim to be? Or, shall ye deny thine inheritance and forfeit thine eternal freedom. Ye have been given the gift of freewill... none bring thee against thine will, it is not lawful... we dare not... indeed, it would be an impossibility.

**The school referred to here, is spoken of in more detail in the book, recently, entitled; Mine Intercom Messages from the Realms of Light*

Sori Sori: Mine hand I set to pen for the purpose of bringing Light unto a confused people which have lost their way. This shall be my own testimony unto mankind... and for generations yet to come.

Now that ye have proven thine self prepared to do that which I shall assign unto thee, I shall give unto thee a greater part. That ye have been faithful in small things, I shall give unto thee in greater measure. Mine words shall be simple and the message clear, that the child of little learning, or experience, can understand that which I say unto them. The ones which have the mind the will to receive the Light, Truth, which I am, shall be as ones to give unto me credit for being that which I am.

Now that the time is come to make mine self known, I shall shout it from the Mountains. and it shall be made known unto the ones which are of a mind to be brought out before the day of sorrow. So be it I shall give unto each and every one a warning... and make ye no mistake about that, for I shall be as one which knows them which are of me, and the ones which are of mine enemy.

Now I say of certainty that the enemy is out in full power... therefore I am prepared to do that which is necessary to deliver mine people out. I have said that before, in many ways...yet hast it been heard, or believed?

It is now expedient that <u>I come</u> in full force. I bring with me the whole armor of God the Father Mother, which hast sent me with a mighty host. There shall be a great clash of power, for the dark ones are within the land as the destroyers. We of the Light... the Mighty Host... come that the destroyers be put to their end. They shall come face to face with the hosts of Light, which they shall not be able to stand against, for we are well prepared for this day.

This day hast been foretold for eons of time, yet man hast not believed it to come... Man hast betrayed himself. Yea I say "Man", for mankind is as a whole. When I speak of man I see a portion which are of the darkest densest evil... Then there are ones which are of little light... Then there are the ones which are prepared to go with me into greater light wherein they shall find peace perfect peace.

I see the darkest ones of no light, no will of their own, going headlong into the pit of utter darkness. These are not redeemable... by any means.

This is the time of sifting and sorting, classifying unto their light and class. While I speak of man there is not intent to differ male or female, for we see the light by which they are found, and classified. Then each entity (being) is put into the <u>place</u> for which he hast prepared himself... be it the glory of the highest Light or the pits of the darkest of the pits. Be it such as ye have not dreamed of in thine nightmares! I say unto one and all; each are dealt with as they have willed... with justice and mercy.

There is an infallible law "<u>as ye are prepared so shall ye receive</u>". My words have been shouted from every land of Earth, for every generation that they be prepared to go all the way with me.

Now, the ones which have been determined to destroy themselves, hast gone so far that they have the power to destroy the <u>Planet</u> on which they abide. This power, which they use, is the MISUSED power given unto all mankind for to glorify the Earth and all living creatures. This misused power shall be their ending... their own extinction.., for it is foreseen that which is just and wise for the Host of light to do.

The carnage shall come unto an end... IT SHALL END... for no longer shall an innocent generation/people suffer such sorrow and destruction. Yet, Let it be understood that the blameless victims shall have the respite so earned... even as they have sown so shall their harvest be. Justice shall, and does prevail. By Mine own command shall the day come speedily when there shall be a great and horrible blast which shall be seen from afar. And it shall take <u>with it</u> a great toll of energy which hast been misused.

Then the tenor of the ones left shall be as one of Light. There shall be a portion which have awakened... prepared.... which shall be delivered up before the <u>DAY OF SORROW</u>.

So be it and Selah.

Sori Sori: It is now come when there shall be no light from the sun for three days. Now I say ye have heard this aforehand. Yea, ye have been told this before, for it hast been aforehand seen and known. While no man knows or knew the day; while it is closer, near time, it is easier to calculate the time. I say it is nigh upon thee.

For this I speak that ye be as one prepared for such as shall come upon thee. There is wisdom in preparation. I mean ye shall prepare thine self and give ye heed unto thine time... how ye spend thine hours, even unto the minutes... for minutes make up the hours.

When ye put thine hand to mischief it is given unto thee to go headlong without thought of consequence. Yet each minute is accounted unto thee and <u>how it is spent, for what it is spent</u>... what have ye profited there by. Each act or word is accurately recorded, weighed and balanced... know ye this? Ye have been told... did ye not hear it? Think ye are alone in this little world of Men, forgotten by thine "Source"? I say unto one and all, <u>Ye are never from sight of the Source of thine Being.</u>

While ye have forgotten It/Him, ye know not that which goes on about thee in the Cosmos... <u>yea, throughout the Cosmos</u>... for ye and I are part of this whole of all Creation. This creation of which we are part knows each entity, being... male or female... which lives, breaths and hast his being in Him. "One", inclusive of All life, for all is one in Him.

Ye have called this oneness. "Source". "God", knowing not that which is meant by either expression. For no word in any language, any means what so ever, can convey unto man of flesh that which <u>is the "All" - the All encompassing</u>. Mans mind is not capable of comprehending the totality of "Allness", for he is but part of this "All". <u>Complete in its Perfect Wholeness... Everness.</u>

<u>3 X3 + 9 = 18 YEARS</u>

Sori Sori: By the calculations of man, he hast but three times three plus 9 years to prepare himself for the ultimate change... in which there is no turning back or reversing all that he hast set in motion. I am come that all might know that which is fortuned unto man of Earth through his own wanton and willfulness.

He hast gone so far that peace shall be unreasonable... unheard of... as he hast not reckoned with the law. Therefore Man, as the wanton ones, shall be moved into a corner, wherein he shall have time necessary to prepare himself for a new part wherein he may find surcease, rest and repose from war and bloodshed. He shall atone for his willful ways... cleanse himself... atone... and come with clean hands and a pure heart... then We of the great and mighty Christ Council shall take note of him.

It is the way of the dark robed brothers to give their time and strength in hatred one for the other, in a death struggle... In <u>Mine name?</u> Nay! what blasphemy! Ne'er do they say in the name of mine adversary I do these abominable things.

They, the ones which call themselves Christian are worse than the "pagan" for they blaspheme against the holy spirit, and darkness shall follow them unto the end. I say they shall find no respite, no rest when they have left of the mortal body. This I would have them know, for it is the law as ye sow so shall ye reap.

Was it not said of olden time? Hast it not been repeated? Many which are warring against each other this day are repeating that which they did in years past... Yea in ages past. When they put aside the garment of flesh they are of the same humor or nature... yet they find no peace... no rest. Now it is given unto these to return... return again and again until they have resolved hatred and unholy nature.

While there are ones which have come from afar to assist, "they" (the wanton ones) give little thought unto our part, our <u>existence</u>, our pleading that they turn from their carnage and seek... then Light and peace shall be established within them.

This is the beginning of a New Day when ye shall arise and be about the Fathers business... that ye cleanse thine being of all hatred and malice, greed and whoredom. Turn thine hand to service in the love of thine fellow man in the Light which I Am. I bring the Light, for that I Am. I have prepared a place for thee wherein is only light, and peace abides therein.

Now hear me in this... for I say unto thee, none bring within this place, wherein I am, thine part which ye have brought upon the Earth as a filthy stench within the time of thine waywardness and rebellion. It shall be left unto the darkness... ye with it to haunt thee... for ye shall first divest thineself of the least portion of hatred... selfishness... bigotry... hypocrisy... unrighteousness... uncleanness... before ye find peace within the light. For there is no darkness with the Light in which I abide.

Sori Sori: This is the day of redemption, for it is so written in the heavens. It is now come when ye shall see the Hand of God move. This is that which has been foretold in the ancient records. The Word of the Lord thy God of Truth and Light hast given of himself that there be a plan which is now come to its maturity; the fulfilling of the Word; the promise made 2000 years ago.

Let this be as a reminder of that promise, for it is the way of mankind to forget after a time; it hast been the forgetting which hast brought him all his sorrow and suffering. Now he shall be caused to remember his "Source" and return unto it, for there is a plan for his redemption.

For that hast Mine Father Sent Me. I Am come with a mighty host and a loud shout; I Am Come! I Am Come! Awaken all ye nations of the Earth! So shall they hear this cry. Yea, I say this Call hast gone forth throughout the Cosmos. There hast come from the farthermost parts of the heavens, answer to the call. For this plan of redemption is formulated within the Light. Yea I say it is formulated by the very Source of the [symbol], the All, the Cause of thine Being, in which ye are Eternally living. Yea in which ye live and have thine Eternal existence.

Ye have wandered long in thine lethargy, the deep and terrifying sleep wherein ye have dreamed, yet ye thought these dreams <u>real</u>. I Am come that ye might come out of thine dream state and come to know thineself as I know thee. I say I know the child of Earth as I know Mine self, to be one with the Father from which ye have been given Being. Ye are One in Him, for He, It, which is the All-Inclusive of All that lives and breathes, we call Father, for ye, Man of Earth, can comprehend that word.

We of the Mighty Council bend low before thee. We find ways and means to formulate words, language that might convey our mission, our intent. We find ones of thine realm which can and will assist us in this, our greatest mission unto Mankind. While that is our mission we have volunteered for, we shall see it unto its completion.

It is now written in the heavens that Mankind shall awaken unto his true estate, arise from his slumbers and return unto his Source. While it is a task assigned unto the ones which have come forth as ones prepared for such a mission, by their own effort they have been prepared for this the greatest of missions.

Can ye, O Man, possibly realize from thy lowly places wherein ye labor for a poor pittance, that which we of the Host are prepared to do? I say with love and self-sacrifice, that we are come also with the intent to awaken thee unto thine true Identity! How this is to be accomplished depends partly upon each one of thee within the Earth environs. For ye which have taken upon flesh bodies have a responsibility... know ye this? Yea even unto the ones which have no knowledge of his being, the imbecile, for he, the imbecile, is within the All, and he is playing out his illusions. So as we see the whole of him, we know him as he is; therefore he is responsible for his part. This I would have thee know.

While there are ones which have, and are, bringing into flesh bodies unwanted beings; and before the entity hast taken a breath they are torn from the flesh womb as so much UNWANTED TRASH; yea trash to be relegated to the 'can' or to the scientists-chemists lab. What think ye O man-woman shall be done about this? As we see the horror of thine ways shall we keep silent? Shall we, the ones sent in concert, as one body of Lighted beings, stand by at this thine time of great decision when ye stand on the brink of destruction, and keep silent? This is not our intent.

Let this be understood, that we are not come to coddle the sleepers; we are come to awaken them. We are speaking unto the ones which know not that they sleep. Yet we say Awaken! O Man, Awaken! And ye shall hear, for this is the purpose of our mission which shall not be aborted! While ye shall choose thine method of awakening, ye shall either come as one willingly with hand outstretched, that we lead thee gently... or resist our invitation and prove thine self a traitor unto thine own self.

It is said many times, many ways; come as one clean of hands, pure of heart and willing to learn, and We of the Host shall attend thee in love and wisdom.

Seek ye the Light and be ye fearless in thine seeking. Remember from whence thine blessings, yea thine life, so precious is given.......

THE BOOK OF LIGHT
BOOK TWO

Excerpts of prophecies from other planets

... And it is said there shall be winds, and there shall, and they shall be in the time when it is winter. And the trees shall bow down their boughs, and the winds shall sing with the cold, there shall be great suffering among the people and they shall fall down and cry for mercy.

And there shall be a mighty earthquake and it shall split in twain the country of North America, and it shall be as nothing the world has known before, for it shall be that there shall be a great part of the great land of the north continent go down, and a great sea shall form within her center part from the Dominion of Canada into the Gulf of Mexico.

And there shall be great ocean liners, liners which shall travel within its waters, which shall be propelled by solar energy of the next age, and with this they shall be unable to travel east to west or from west to east, through what is now the Atlantic Ocean, for it shall have a mountain range which has been thrown up from the bottom of the Atlantic, and it shall be extended into the air to the altitude of 18,000 feet. And it shall be as the Sittur of old (Atlantis-Lemuria), for it was the Light of the world that this land once took her place in the sun. And she went down amid a great shock and a great wave, and it shall be that she shall come up the same way as she went down.

And the west side shall be as the sheer side of granite, and it shall be without foothold; and the way shall be as the eagle flies from the place which is Upper Virginia three hundred miles due east; and at this point it shall be one thousand and eight hundred feet from the waters; and not an entrance through the land shall there be unto the east, for it is not for them which are to be the remnants to communicate by water; for it shall be with a new science, and a new method shall be given unto them. For there is not a place which is that shall and remain the same in its present state.

And not a person shall be left which is not prepared for that which shall be. And there are many called but few are chosen, for there are none which have been chosen which have not been carefully prepared; and they have been unto themselves true, and they have given credit where credit is due. And now it is given unto them to be the seed of the New Civilization which shall come upon Earth.

And within the time which is left before this shall come upon the Earth, it shall be that many will be called. And they shall doubt, and they shall fear, and they shall faint, and they shall fall by the way. And they shall be in no wise wise, for it is given unto man to fear that which he does not understand -- and for that does he wait.

And now the time is upon him when he waits no more. He either moves on or he is left unto the elements of the earth, and they shall consume him as the pore (flesh). And that which is eternal shall take upon itself another bound, and it shall be sealed, and he shall have no memory of that which has been, and the experience of the past shall be blanked from his memory.

And not a person shall be as he is, for he shall take upon him a new garment and a new name, for it is given to man to be as the little ones. And he shall grow into that which he knows not of, for he has not yet become as God, and he shall be within the law when he proclaims that which he shall become!

And within the time which is allotted unto things, he shall become God and he shall be as God, and he shall declare (symbol) and he shall know whereof he speaks, for it is given unto man to mutter the mutterings of the unlearned and that which is full of spurious spores, and it profit nothing.

Yet he shall learn that which he has said shall be as his bound. And he shall be bound by his words until they have been fulfilled unto every jot and tittle. And he shall be as one which has in his hand the scales whereupon he may weigh them - word for word shall he weigh them.

And not another shall be responsible for the words of another, nor shall any man take upon himself that which is done by another, for it is the law that no man atones for another. Yet it is the law that each shall "love his brother as himself, and he shall not be his sice, nor shall he be his grouse", for it is given unto man not to know one from the other while in the time of <u>thinking</u>, for he is under a spell -- and it shall be removed, and he shall awaken.

And he shall find that he has descended into the Earth which is dark, and he has taken upon himself the garments of the Earth, and he has lost his identity with the Father which has sent him forth. And he has not only been dreaming, but he has been worse than asleep -- he has been dead. For it is given unto man to believe that which he sees, feels, and touches to be real, and yet he knoweth that which he cannot see to exist, and without question does he enjoy the benefits thereof. Yet he has not been in the least concerned with that which shall profit him most, for it is for his own good that these things have been given him, yet he has not looked for that which is eternal, for it is given unto him to be as the pore (flesh).

And the pore sees, feels, tastes, and hears that which is of the Earth, and that which is eternal and without the pore he sees not, neither does he hear. And so shall he be blind and deaf unto reality until he has grown to the age of accountability whereupon he shall receive his inheritance, which is sight and sound.

And ye shall see and hear that which is and shall remain ever of the eternal verities. And not a person shall deny that which he does not under- stand, for therein is the greatest of folly. For it is said that "There are none so foolish as those which think themselves wise." And it is so!

And now within the time which is near they shall learn many truths -- which is new unto them. And they shall say that it is the ravings of the foolish, and they shall say that it is not possible, yet they reckon not with the law, for it is in no wise the work of men -- which shall be as nothing -- that shall bring about these things. For he has been un (the animal mind, or the mind of man -- goat mind) and he knoweth not that which he doeth. For he has been within the darkness, and he is not accountable for the things which he has said in his sleep.

And yet he stirs within his sleep, and he stirs within his slumbers. And he has but begun to stir, for in the days which are to come, he shall awaken from the deep sleep which has fallen upon him. And he shall stand within the place wherein he shall go as one come alive! And he shall walk knowing whither he goeth and from whence he came! And not a place shall he fall nor shall he stumble, for it shall be his inheritance to talk with surety, and he shall not be afraid.

And within the time which is allotted him upon the Earth, he shall prepare himself for that which shall come unto him. And he shall be as one in the dark. Yet there shall be beacons of light which shall appear unto them.

And they shall learn much which is new unto them, and for that has there been many among them which have been sent for to be the beacons. And they shall be as my lamp unto the feet of the weary, and unto the world shall they light my lamps where they find them from the tapers which I have given unto them.

And it is said that "I am the Way", and it is so! And none can come save by me, for I am the keeper of the gate, and I guard my secrets well.

And not a person is so foolish as those which plunder my secrets...for it is given unto man to take that which he can pilfer without paying the forfeit. And therein is folly! For it is the law: That which is earned is for the best part worth the effort, and that effort is within itself that which is most profitable.

And for that reason is much kept from man's grasp -- that he might wain and wax strong and that he may learn to stand alone within the time when there is no help. And yet there is no time when help is denied, but the wisdom of withholding it is the greatest of all good deeds.

Within their wanton would they purchase their fare into a place called heaven where they might have a life of ease which should profit them nothing. And that which is not profitable unto eternal life is denied them by the Father, for He knows before they call that which they need and that which shall profit them.

And it is now time that they arise from their sleep and shake the dust off their garments. And they shall awaken, and they shall become alive. And they shall learn that which is within the law. And they shall become aware of that which is real. And they shall not be bound by the garments of the flesh, for it is the law: That which is eternal surpasseth that which is flesh. And that which is eternal is not bound within the flesh, and it has never entered into the flesh -- yet flesh has its being in that which is eternal, without beginning and without end. So it is that the pore shall pass, and the ONE WHICH IS shall be no less for its passing.

And so shall it be in the days which shall come. For it is said that there shall be great famine and great pestilence and great suffering, and yet it shall be as nothing seen before. And not a place shall be left untouched -- but that is but the outward manifestation of that which shall be, for it is the law: That which goes out must come back. And it is given unto man to be the part which has gone out from the Father, and to the Father he must return.

And in the days which shall come there shall be a great gathering in. And they shall be separated one from the other, and they shall be as the ones of old -- they shall be as the sheep and they shall be herded into places as the flocks of the fields, for it is given unto men to follow.

And there are few which dare to be their own carter, and the carter is one which can say for himself that way which he shall go. And he shall find his own way, and therein is wisdom. For there are none so foolish as those who wait for the herd; therein is folly!

So in the days which are to come they shall be gathered together as the flocks, and they shall await one who dares assume responsibility for them. And it is a poor poison, for there is not a person which has profited thereby.

And when it is given unto him to prove himself, he has not the metal to withstand temptation and the tribulations which come. And he has been unto himself traitor by passing on unto another the responsibility which is rightfully his.

So shall they learn the hard way, for it is the law that each in his time shall become that which he was created for to become. Yet there is no time, for it is not within the law -- that which ye calculate as time -- for it is an illusion of man, and therefore unlawful.

And within the place wherein the Earth shall move shall be a new solar sun and a new orbit shall the Earth have. And she shall have no darkness, for it shall be a new field within the firmaments. And a new berth shall she have, and the time element shall be new unto her, for there shall be no shadows within her, for she shall have a new sun and a new moon. And she shall have no pains, for she shall be as young again -- for she shall have rest.

And she shall shine in all her glory, and she shall be peopled with the ones which have awakened and those which shall remember that which has been. And they shall know that which shall be, for they shall be one with the Father. And they shall know that which is of the Father and that which is of the Earth.

And therein shall they abide within the law which is of the eternal verities. And they shall not be bowed down with the pity of the Earth as it is now upon the Earth, for it is indeed pity to see them which stirs not. They walk with eyes which see not, and they are deaf unto the call of the Clarions, which have been sent unto them for their own sake.

And within the time which is near they shall see and they shall hear, and they shall be as one which knows not what he sees. Yet he shall call out for learning, and it shall not be denied him. For many are among them for the purpose of bringing the light, and it shall not be denied them, nor shall it be forced upon them, for it is unethical for them that would be so foolish.

And within the time which is come they may be as the children of the Father, yet they have forgotten the way unto the Father's house. And they shall cry for help, and it shall be given to freely and without price.

And not a person can comprehend the fullness of the Brother's love, for from the Father have they come, and to the Father return.

And now it is come upon the Earth that which man has feared and that which he understands not, and he cries out in his delirium that there is no place for to hide. And so is it that there is no place wherein he can go that he cannot be bound nor a place wherein he can hide.

For the Father has sent them which have guarded the Earth for her duration, and they have not been asleep...nor have they forgotten their identity...for they are trustworthy and they have been entrusted with the guidance of the Earth and her destiny. And she has not gone awry for naught, nor has she been on an orgy, for she has gone the way of her ORDAINED course. And it is for the good of all that she shall move out into a new berth; for from her solar sun shall she run, for therein is danger within the future; for it is given unto the orb which ye call Sun to explode within its orbit. And therein is wisdom, for he has fulfilled the cycle which was ordained unto him.

And not a person shall say it is not so! For therein is foolishness. For it is the law: That which is created shall fulfill its cycle and return to its native state. And it is so! And so be it that the time is come when the Earth shall move out into a new berth, and she shall have a new course and a new sun and a new moon. (ref. Mine Intercom Messages)

And so shall she rest for three thousand years. And she shall again be peopled, and she shall be as new.

And there shall be a new people, and they shall know that which is of the Father. And there shall be a new Garden of Julian, and therein shall be the Father's Kingdom upon the Earth. And it shall be for the good of all that there shall be one who shall reign supreme, yet they shall work as one man.

And there shall be peace. And each man shall be peace unto himself, and he shall be as the keeper of the peace. And he shall be as the lawgiver and the keeper thereof, for he shall know that which is ethical and he shall abide thereby.

And there shall be none among them which shall covet another's possessions, nor shall they know hatred.

For it is established that the new Kingdom shall be established upon the Lotus which now lies within the bed of the Pacific Ocean.

And it shall be that there shall be peace and harmony, and it shall reign for the cycle which shall last for twelve thousand years. And again she shall be in a new cycle which shall bring another order -- and therein is another story...

And for the time being we are interested only with the next decade which shall bring about many unbelievable changes, and they shall be as tragedy at the time. Yet considering that which is eternal -- has no beginning nor no end -- what is there to fear? And why is there anything of thy apportioned lot that ye shall fear?

And blest is the man which can be his own carter and say: "Thy will be done. I am as thou art, and I am not of the Earth, yet I am in it." And he shall see the glory of the dawn, for it is given unto him to know wherein is his strength. And not a place shall he seek to hide, but he shall go forth to meet that which is apportioned unto Him. And he shall know the truth and it shall make him free. And not a person shall set foot against his door. And not a person shall keep him out of the Father's house, for by his own hand shall he open all the doors which have been closed unto him.

And so shall he find his way unto the Father's house from which he went forth, and so be it that he returneth triumphantly. And the Father shall be glad, for it is given unto Him to wait, that His offspring go out and return. And therein is wisdom. For it is the law: So above, so below... and for this do they wait that they fulfill the law which has sent them forth. And it is the fulfilling of such law that they return and that they be made new and groomed for another new day. And in that day they shall know peace and they shall have rest from the turmoil which has beset them.

LIGHT WORKERS?

Sori Sori: There is not time to loose, yet there is wisdom in taking time to learn well, that which we bring unto thee, or present unto thee.

There art many times that we speak unto the ones which are willing, to be brought in, yet they give unto us no ear. They talk, talk, thinking themselves wise. They are as children playing games... with their prattling they reveal their foolishness. They close us out, therefore they know not that we have for them.

These are the ones which find a "crumb" and cry, I've found... I know!! Yet, they have but the crumb... they are ones satisfied. Even so they bring such confusion as to invite the enemy in.

Now I say, the ones which pick up the crumb and rush out crying, "Look, Look, see that which I have, come partake with me"... these are the ones which think themselves wise. They are satisfied with the crumb, while we bring the loaf. We have called unto them also; "Come to the Feast!" They are too busy going hither and yon with the crumb.

I ask of them, Prepare thine self, for greater... greater and stronger food which shall enrich thine soul, and make ready thine self for the Banquet. Has thou heard mine call or received mine invitation to the feast?

Blest art they which have received the invitation... for it is the last call.

* * *

Sori Sori: For this hour let us speak of the 'Light workers.' Now I ask of thee, who are these which call themselves Light workers? Know ye these? I say unto thee these which speak so glibly of themselves know not that which Light is... neither that which is the reflection of Light. They but make mock of that which they do not understand.

It is come when they shall see themselves as one unknowing, for many things shall be revealed unto them within the next year of your 3rd dimension. They then shall stand as ones in awe of the new understanding, and be as ones humbled by the new found learning. I say be ye as one blest to be prepared to accept the new revelations, for it shall come... IT SHALL COME!.. and all shall be blest which accept it, for it shall be as nothing they/ye have known.

Things are moving across the cosmos which ye have not even dreamed of, which shall change thine Earth, the planet upon which ye dwell... yet it shall be as one with the law of the Cosmos.

We, thine benefactors, know for long this day shall be the fulfilling of the prophets, for it is our part to foretell of such things, yet it is not given unto man to understand such as hast been foretold so long ago.

It is written in stone, on parchments, in the skies, yea even into thine cosmogony for anyone so prepared to read. These hast given forth such information for the ones of this day to find and learn. The day hast come when the Heavens shall reveal her secrets. So be it the Earth on which ye stand shall give up her secrets and it shall be a time of learning, and great joy shall be upon her, the Earth, for there shall be war no more. So be it and Selah.

THE ARYAN

Part 6

Was it not told thee that the Mother Sarah, from whom ye were sent out, shall walk among thee? And it is come that she shall, for she is prepared to give of herself that ye shall come to know thyself and thy oneness with her and the Father. And return unto them -- and for that does she come into the world of men that all may partake of her love and mercy. Give unto the Father-Mother thanks for this day and ye shall come to know the wisdom of giving thanks, for it is by <u>their</u> grace and mercy that ye have been kept for this day in which ye shall receive thy liberation. Be ye as one who can hear that which I am saying unto thee, for in the time which is near it shall serve thee well. And ye shall remember that which has been said, for it is said for a purpose, and it is said in a manner which shall serve to awaken thee.

It is given unto the child and unto the one who shall heed, and not as a work of art alone, for there is no pretense to your academic art. And ye shall be as little children who are seeking of the Father, that which shall satisfy thy hunger. And ye shall be fed, and ye shall be satisfied, for the food which shall be given unto thee is manna from heaven which shall be unto thee all things. And ye shall learn that which is meant by "manna" from heaven. Ye shall create within thyself, ye shall speak the word, and it shall appear, ye shall control the elements, and ye shall command and it shall be done. And ye shall be as the Father, perfect, and ye shall create like unto Him, and for that do ye wait. While it is thy inheritance, ye have to be prepared to receive it in His Name and in His Grace and Wisdom.

Ye shall not be deceived, for it is given unto the Father to know and to stand ready to give unto thee as ye are prepared to receive, and He is not deceived by appearances for He has given unto thee thy being and He knows wherein ye are prepared. Ye shall learn to say "Father, thy will be done in me, through me, by me and for me", for it is "thy passport" into the inner temple and be ye not deceived, for there are none so foolish as they who think themselves wise. Now in the day of thy seeking, the black dragon shall seek thee out -- he shall endeavor to ensnare thee and ye shall be alert and wise, and ye shall be silent and ye shall ask no man's opinion -- and ye shall give unto the Father credit for thy being -- and for thy oneness with Him, and ye shall look to Him for thy salvation and ye shall keep thy own counsel. For blest indeed is the one who keeps his counsel -- it is thy defense against the black dragon and ye shall not be in any wise deceived by him, for he revealeth himself for what he is. And thy sword of light shall be thy only weapon, and ye shall carry it by day and by night. And nothing shall prevail against thee. And so be it that ye shall know such peace as ye have not known since thy going out from the Father-Mother, and ye shall receive the blessing of them from the inner temple which await thy coming. And so be it and Selah.

Part 7

Be ye as one who has upon thy head a crown and walk which way it tilts not. For ye are the children of the most High Living God, and ye shall come into thy inheritance, and ye shall walk with dignity and ye shall know as ye are known, for it is thy birthright that ye shall receive thy sonship even as they who have gone the Royal Road. And ye shall be in the place wherein ye are prepared for, that which shall serve to groom thee for thy coronation. And ye shall sit upon the High Holy Mount and ye shall see the earth pass out of her berth into her new one and ye shall watch the events as they occur, and ye shall know that which ye see and ye shall know that which ye see and ye shall remember them and ye shall be given the wisdom to comprehend the law of these things which ye shall see -- and for that shall ye wait, for it is given unto thee as ye can comprehend and as ye are prepared.

And so be it that the day of preparation is come, and ye shall be given as ye ask, and as ye are prepared to receive. The place wherein ye are shall serve as a school and ye shall be alert unto that which shall be given unto thee, for it shall serve to give thee strength and wisdom. And ye shall realize the wisdom of thy seeking, for as ye seek, ye are given in greater capacity. So be it as ye will it. Prepare thyself to receive and one shall be sent out from the inner temple that shall point the way, and ye shall receive them in the name of the Father, Son and Holy Ghost.

And be ye as the wise and give unto them as ye would have the Father give unto thee, for as ye receive them, have ye received the Father. And will it not profit thee to be alert that ye may know them? For it shall be given unto them to lift the dead, to heal the sick and to make the blind to see. They shall be unto thee all things, and they shall unbind thee in the name of the one who has sent them unto thee. And as it is given unto them of the Father, they shall give unto thee in His name and by His grace, and of His mercy shall they administer unto them who believe and give them credence. And be ye prepared to receive them and so be it that ye shall be lifted up, and ye shall know that which I have said unto thee is given unto me of the Father, for they shall touch thee and ye shall be quickened and ye shall know and ye shall see and hear, and ye shall be given comprehension and wisdom, for the veil of Maya shall be parted and for that have many been sent unto thee. Now ye shall be prepared to receive of the Father of thy own account, and ye shall be made ready for that. So be it and Selah.

Part 8

Blest are the hands which do the will of the Father, for they shall be lifted up and they shall be unto Him his light and his glory made manifest within the earth. For now it is come that He shall endow many with His gifts and His riches, to partake of the fullness of His riches, for it is not yet apparent what manner of man ye shall become. And so shall ye receive in abundance that which has been kept for thee. And ye shall be brought into the secret place of the Most High and ye shall be given thy sonship of the Father. And there shall be great rejoicing throughout the Cosmos. For it is decreed that everyone shall partake of the Father's riches -- of His estate, so be it as ye are prepared. In no time of the earth's history have so many come to her aid, that she and her children be lifted up -- be brought out into the light. Ye shall be gathered in as the grain from the field, and ye shall be put into the places which are made ready for thee. For each and every one shall be classified according to his preparation. Ye shall choose in which place ye shall go, for it is given unto thee to have free will and as ye will it, so it is.

Before thee is a part of that which shall be revealed unto thee. When ye are so made ready, the fullness of the great plan shall be revealed unto thee. And now ye shall be given that which ye can comprehend, and as thy capacity is increased, ye shall be given more and of greater strength. For it is the better part of wisdom to give as ye can consume.

Part 9

Be ye at peace and poise, and give unto thyself credit for strength to pick thyself up and walk within the light which never fails. For it is given unto thee to be thy own porter, and ye shall be the one to bring thyself into the inner temple, and to prepare thyself. And there shall be many hands that shall reach out unto thee that ye may be made ready to enter. And will ye not be glad for thy preparation? So be it and Selah. Bring thy whole self, thy heart, thy hands, thy will, as thy living offering, as thy sacrifice unto the Father, for <u>none other can he use</u>. Be ye as wise as a serpent and silent as the sphinx, for it is between thee and the Father, that which ye are doing. For in the temple ye speak not to any man -- ye are prepared in silence. It is said that "the tongue is man's pitfall." He has not learned to master the tongue! But in the inner temple he has mastered it. When he speaks, it is with wisdom and prudence, and there are none so foolish as to partake of the seeds of Satan, which are but the idle words which lead to waste and wanton. So be ye as one who says only that which is inspired of the Christ, and that which shall lift up thy brother.

And for thy sake shall ye be given that which ye shall fortune unto thy brother, for ye shall learn that which ye send out, shall return unto thee, and it is the law which no man escapes. So be ye forewarned for it is the cause of thy sorrow and thy suffering. That which ye have sowed, ye are <u>now</u> reaping. As ye turn thy face unto the light and see thy source within the light and the cause of thy being, thy leg-irons shall be cut away, and ye shall be free from thy bondage. It is given unto me, the wanderer, to know how heavy thy leg-irons are, for I have had them cut away. I have cried for mercy and wisdom. I know from experience that which ye have experienced. I have been a fellow wayfarer for many centuries and I have watched thy going out and thy coming in for I have not lost my memory. It has been given unto me to remember thee, and to know wherein thy weakness lies and, too, wherein is thy strength. For nowhere have I been unto myself traitor. I have watched diligently for the coming of our Lord and Master. I have wandered upon the mountains, I have waited by the rivers, I have searched the sands, I have gone into the valleys in search of Him. I have cried out as a motherless child. I have longed for His return -- I have hungered for His presence. And at last, my waiting is ended and I am free. It is with love and prudence that I now reveal myself as a fellow wayfarer. I have seen within thy face thy longing and thy sorrow. I have given unto thee of my love and of my mercy, and understanding, that ye, too, may know the Master as I know Him. For He now walks the earth within the garment of flesh, even as you and I. And ye shall be given comprehension to know him if ye but seek Him out, for it is decreed that every man shall come to know Him, and for this has the world of men waited. So be it and Selah.

Part 10

Be ye of a mind to seek out them who are sent of the Father to deliver thee out of bondage, for the day is come when they are seeking thee out.

Ye shall seek them, and as ye seek them, they shall reveal themselves. Blest are they who are so ready to receive the brothers who are come into the earth, for to fulfill the plan which is given unto us. For it shall now be revealed unto them who are prepared for such a revelation, and it shall profit thee to ready thyself that ye may partake of the great plan. Be ye foretold, that which shall be given unto thee and as ye are of a mind to receive, so shall it be given unto thee in the name of the Father, Son and Holy Ghost. Will it not profit thee to be alert unto the things which are about thee? Was it not so with the children of the Lotus (Atlantis)? Were they prepared? Some were, which had been true unto themselves and which had held fast unto the Light which was their inheritance. They were the ones who set up the altars in Egypt, and of the New Land (North America), and within the Orient. And unto this day have they guarded it with their being and they have given of themselves, that this age might come into its fullness.

Were some of us not among them? And were some of us not the traitors? And is it not given unto us to partake of the harvest which is now ready for reaping?

Blest are they who have guarded the light upon the altars of the earth, for it is now time for the gathering together and the bringing in, and there shall be great joy and much gladness. Be ye as one who shall stand in the light of the Christ, and know thyself as ye are known -- see thy source and thy memory shall be given unto thee. And blest is the one who has his memory. Be it the law that as ye are prepared, so shall ye receive and as ye receive, so shall ye give unto others, that they may be blest of thy being. In like manner shall the earth be lifted up. So be it and Selah.

Be ye foretold that there shall be many changes within the earth and that there is wisdom in thy preparation, and so be it that ye shall be made ready to receive them who are sent unto thee and them who are ready to groom thee for thy new part. And as ye receive them in the name of the Father, Son and Holy Ghost, have ye received the Father who has sent them. So be it and Selah.

Part 11

Was it not said there shall be great winds and is it not so? For it is given unto them who have revealed these things unto them, to know whereof they speak, for it is given unto them to have the greater vision, and they receive of the Father. And they know as He knows. So be it that there shall be great floods within the borders of the land to the North and to the South. For it is given unto the elements to be as one gone drunk, and it is given unto them to return unto man, that which man has sent out. For great shall be the suffering which shall come upon this earth. For the lakes shall know no bounds, and the rivers shall become as lakes, and the rains shall come out of season. The fires shall consume the places wherein there are many people. Sorrow shall follow them which shall be rescued! And they shall remember the words which have been given unto them. Man shall be given much torment by pestilence and disease, for his science shall be aught against that which shall come upon him. Blest indeed are they who shall be ready for that which shall come upon them.

For the mountains shall afford no hiding place, for they shall tremble and quake beneath their feet. And will it not be so within the land to the east? For it is given unto the lands to change and shift, and to go under as one baptized, and some shall shake and dip and arise -- some shall remain beneath the waters to the east. Was it not said that the hot desert of Africa bloom again (Refer Prophecies from other planets) and that the land of Turkey shall give up her secrets and that she shall become the light of the east? And so shall it be, and so be it. And as such shall she arise glorified to take her place within the sun and to fulfill her destiny. For a new people shall inhabit "the Emerald" and she shall be a garden with tropical flora and with fauna not known to man of this age.

And the waters of the Mediterranean shall wash over the land to the north unto the polar zone and it shall return unto its place, and the Black Sea and the Mediterranean shall become one sea. And there shall be great changes within the borders of the continent of Asia. Africa shall be changed -- her shoreline shall be broken to the west, and great rivers shall flow within the desert.

As ye have been told time and time again -- that the earth shall shift upon her axis and so shall she -- there shall be a change of climate. That which is now the barren north shall become semitropical -- bear semitropical fruit and the fauna shall be that of a new species. And that which is the impassable barrier of the south pole shall be penetrated and man shall discover a new continent within. And that which he has in legend as the paradise of the ice region. And therein is a revelation for it is given unto me to know the secret places within the impassable barrier of ice. It has been kept for this age and now it shall be opened up. They who are prepared to enter the secret places and they shall be blest. From this place shall come some records which have hitherto been concealed, and so be it such as shall be revealed unto thee. And so be it that the Father has deemed it wise that ye be given this. So be it that ye may be prepared to receive it in His name. So be it and Selah. (This is recorded in the Lake Titicaca region of the Andes Mountains of South America.)

***

THE MIDDLE EAST

Sori Sori: Mine beloved, I say unto one and all, that it is now come when the end of the 'man of terror' shall be put to an end, for it is written that he shall meet with his end even as he has meted out unto his victims. He shall reap his reward... the agent of his ending lies in wait.

There is such emotion and hatred abounding in many places, among many peoples, even unto "The land of the free and the home of the brave" (that) the unrest shall bring about great hardship and unrest/anxiety. The end is not yet in sight.

It is so written that 'All their talks of peace, their peace pacts, shall be of no substance', Too, it is written that this, the greatest of terrorists, shall meet his fate as he hast created by his own hand/will to destroy and terrorize his subjects...

* * *

Sori Sori: Mine beloved, I say unto thee at this hour, there is a mighty power which shall be manifest upon the Earth, and it shall be as nothing that the unholy land hast experienced, for it shall be that which comes from out the ethers in connection with that which comes from within the Earth. The two powers shall become as one... the action shall be combined in one great and fearful quake.

It is written, and rightly so, that the so-called terrorist which is without recognition shall be the one which causes the two known elements to attract one strange, new and unknown unto any man, to be drawn together in his attempt to make a devise which would destroy the oppressor of his people. As it is written within these papers aforetime, so shall it be the greatest mystery unto mankind. This shall be of such nature that man shall come to the conclusion that he hast been the victim of his own rebellion, and the greater power over which he has no power has been the cause... the unknown source.

This shall awaken the ones which survive. From this shall a new Order come forth in which mankind shall sup from the same cup, and break bread together as brothers, one and all.

* * *

Sori Sori: Mine beloved, I say unto thee this hour, that it is come when there shall be a great blast which shall change the shape of things now existing in the near east... FOREVER! When it would appear to be as a chance for a settlement, it is not as this body of men/women have asked for or imaged.

We of the 'Great Tribunal' see the results of their many years of greed and hatred now swallowing them up. In a moment shall they be as <u>ones removed from the planet.</u> For the plan hast been set into motion and no power shall stop it. It is not possible at this moment to avoid the results of that which they have set into motion. Even thought they are not aware of the higher law that covers all which are involved in any manner what-so-ever, the Law of Justice covers all and sundry. Give ye attention... heed that which I say unto thee, and ye shall do well...

* * *

Sori Sori: Mine beloved, it is now apparent that the man of sin is biding for time in which he can find a way out of his dilemma. He has set a trap for himself. He has made for himself a very sorry portion... now he shall drink it, as it is written. He shall leave behind him a black day in the history of man.

His children shall be as no more, for they shall go with him... for they are of the same nature as the father of them. Sananda hast spoken aforehand that it might be recorded for the days ahead when there shall be great confusion...when men shall lose their reason and be unable to give an account of the events as they have occurred, or how they have occurred. It shall be as no man hast experienced...

* * *

Sori Sori: Be ye consolate, for it is now come when the going out is at hand. And the ones which are crying out for bread and water *(the Kurds which have been driven into the mountains of Iraq and are now starving)* are those which have refused it unto others in ages past. Be it so... SO it is given ye as one which knows the Law, and grieve not that it is the wages of the Law. "Cast thine bread upon the water, and it shall return".

Behold the law... it never fails... be it in one day, one lifetime, or aeons... the penalty heavy or light. I say the Law is sure and exacting!

* * *

As the tribunal sees it

Sori Sori: Beloved, I say unto thee this hour, that it is come when this matter of war is now increased to the point of no return, no win. It is truly spoken as it is written, that there shall be the destruction of many by the secret agent, and that which it brings forth from the inner part of the Earth.

The Earth is a breathing Soul...she is in a precarious condition. She carries within her the seed of a new generation... a generation of lighted beings which shall know peace and bless her as she hast not been blest. There shall be a place in which she shall rest, and no more shall she give footing to a laggardly generation. She shall be a shining Orb within the firmaments.

It is so written that it be afore noted, that mankind prepare for the "New Day", which shall be the day long awaited and spoken of in many places, in many ways, yet not understood by man.

The cry for 'Peace' shall be heard. While the cry for war goes forth, there shall be the great blast which shall bring forth the end of war forever upon the Earth... Then Peace...

First the carnage, for it is at hand... a cumulation of hatred and greed sown within the soil of Mother Earth for many, many, generations! Now the end is in sight, as we of the Great Tribunal see it as done...

* * *

"The asylum of the laggards"

Sanat Kumara

Beloved Ones: "Thou hast placed thineself upon the altar of the Most High Living God that He might glorify Himself in thee, thru thee... SO let it be! I Am Come that it be... for this do I lend unto thee mine hand that ye might be lifted up.

So be it that I have revealed mineself unto thee as the Most Worthy Grand Master of the Inner Temple. I am that and more, for I am that which ye know not, neither do any others know me for that which I am.

I am the one which hast held the Earth for this day. I have brot her thru many crises as an ailing child. I have watched her and her fortune that she might not perish, for great is her part within this day. She shall undergo great strain and stress, yet the pain which she bears is obvious unto them which have eyes to see and a mind to learn. She reels and rocks as one given unto drunkenness, and she gives forth great pain and convulsions, for the reason that she hast taken upon herself the suffering of mankind.

She hast been the asylum of the laggards, and few know wherein she hast given of herself. For long have they come and gone, leaving behind them the debris which they have created, caring not the results thereof. They refuse their own responsibility for such filth, such suffering, such a creation as they have brot about.

While I say unto them, "CLEAN IT UP!" they hear not. They are as ones which have not accepted their own responsibility. Now it is come when they shall be removed into yet another place, and they shall learn well their lessons. For it is come when there shall be a great onrush of Spirit, and they (the laggards) shall not endure the Light thereof. They shall perish, and then they shall be given a place liken unto their own kind. And it shall be a new place, wherein they shall be strengthened and brot to accountability.

Them which are not capable of these things which shall be the fortune of the laggards, shall be cast out even as the chaff. These shall be no more seen upon the Earth, neither within the Realms of Light, for they shall be no more. These shall be cast out and BE NO MORE!

It behooves me to give unto thee this word, and for this hast thou accepted it, that it be given unto them which lament the fortune of these which are not capable of eternal Life. There are ones which deny this mine word, yet I ask them to examine the records which are want (believe) to be complete, which are far from complete... for they have deleted and scrapped much of the record which hast been given unto them. Yet it is within the same (records) as they have that "these shall be cast into outer darkness." When they know the meaning thereof they shall understand that which shall be done this day.

So be it I have touched upon this subject, and it is for the good of all mankind that I give it unto thee at this time. So give it unto them as I give it unto thee. Be ye blest of me and by me, for... I AM Sanat Kumara

* * *

Sori Sori: Mine beloved. This is a day to remember, for there shall be great changes in many places, in many lives. Children shall be born this day which shall be as ones remembering their previous existence in flesh forms. These shall be as the Prophets, the Seers, the Peace Makers.. These shall KNOW themselves and that which they came to do.

It is the beginning of the "New Day" when this generation shall be as the ones to clear away the ruins of this day of carnage. While it is for the greater good of mankind that it is left, or hast been laid waste, as a testimony of man's folly.

Give ye credit where credit is due. Waste not thine energy on the foolish, their preachments, their plans for the next generation, for it (the next generation) shall be its own council and ruler.

This generation shall be as none yet born of Earth woman, for the day of redemption is nigh.

I Am come that it be so... So shall it be. I am the one sent of the All Power, the one and only Father of All, the Cause of Being which makes of all men Brothers.

* * *

Hast thou set thine borders strait?

Be ye as one filled with the Spirit for I say unto thee, the Spirit shall be poured out upon thee, and ye shall be as one prepared for the word which shall go forth. And it shall be given for the good of all, yet ye shall receive it.

For their sake shall it be given unto them, yet there shall be witnesses of the Spirit which shall be poured out upon thee, for they shall know that it is the Spirit which giveth the word.

Now let it be said that they shall receive it according unto their preparation, according to his own understanding. And it shall be no less for their lack of understanding. Yet it shall profit them to ponder that which is said herein, for there shall be given many things which they are want to know.

Many things shall be revealed unto them which see that which is said herein, for there shall be hidden up from the profane many things which shall be shown unto them which hath eyes to see. For hast it ever been that the "word" is hidden from the profane, and the eye of the pure in heart shall be opened and they shall see.

And many shall give unto them a part, and the parts shall be placed together, and these parts shall comprise the Whole. And for this do I give unto thee mine part which shall be added unto the other parts, for I am one which hast awaited this day when I might speak out for the good of all.

It is now come! And yet I find them asleep... eating, drinking, and indulging the senses... making war upon their brothers, and bowing down unto their idols. While I am speaking unto thee and while thou art recording mine words, I see them as demon-possessed, waging war on their fellow men, and therein is their own downfall, I say unto them, he which take up arms against his brother shall perish... It is the law! I say, it is the law, and the law shall not be set aside for any man, nation, country, or the punishment thereof be escaped... be he of any color, nation or creed, for the Just takes not arms against his brother.

Let him which bears arms against another say unto himself, "This is mine brother, this is mine BROTHER, and I am his". And let him consider well his cause, for it is said, "Ye shall not kill". Ye shall neither buy, sell, or carry arms against thine brother... So be it!

It is said, and it is given unto me to know whereof I speak for I know the law... and man comes under this law of which I speak.

It is said, "Bear ye no malice, bear ye no hatred." And unto them which are filled with hatred, I say unto thee, "Thou art as guilty of the crime as tho thou carried the weapon". Yet thine hatred and malice is more poisonous than the armaments... I say, a thousand times more dangerous, yea, a thousand times!

Hear ye me and be ye thotful therefore of thine own closet, or thine garment... is it spotless? ask of thee, art thine hands clean, art thou clean? Satisfy thine own self and answer me... art thine hands clean?

Point not thine finger unto them... (for) art thou his keeper? Hast thine house been set in order? Hast thine borders been set strait? Hast thine obligations been met? Hast thine part been met? Hast thine part been without question?

Hast thou stood as one spotless before men? Hast thou stood as the one without blemish while thou hast blasphemed against the word?

Hold thine tongue and ponder these words, and stay thine hand ere thou hast cleaned <u>well</u> thine dwelling place. Hold thine tongue until thou hast washed thine own hands and removed the blemish from thine own garments.

I have spoken unto them which have ears to hear, unto them which have eyes to see, for none other shall hear or see.

* * *

Each one shall read his record

Let them which would deny mine word come forth and speak, for I shall hear them. Let them which would deny that which I say, speak, and I shall hear him.' For I am aware of them, yea, before they have spoken.

Yet it behooves me to warn them, that which they say shall be as the open book, and they shall be faced with their foolishness, their folly. I say, each and every one shall read from his (own) record. And he shall stand face to face with himself and he shall see wherein he hast denied the Word, and that which he hast brot upon himself. For he shall be as the Judge, and the law shall deal out justice. The law shall be the law, and none shall set it aside or make restitution for him.

It is said that there are none so sad as he which betrays himself... So be it! It is given unto me to know, for I am ever watchful... I am not in anywise in lethargy. I have been at mine work for many a time, and therein is a greater time than thou canst calculate.

Thine time hast now come when ye shall come to know wherein thou art bound, I say, thine limitations are many... Why? Thou art bound in the Earth for a reason, for a season, and thou hast not known wherein thou art bound, wherein thou art, neither by what thou art bound.

Wherein art thou bound? Knowest wherein thou art? O man, I say unto thee, thine limitations árt many! Thou art limited in thine unknowing... thou art limited _for_ thine unknowing... (and) there is the story which thou art want to know.

I say, thou fearest to know the story. I hear ye say, "I do not want to hear, for I believe not." Unto thee I say, thine unbelief hast been thine own undoing... thine unknowing changes not the law. Be ye as one prepared to learn of me and I shall give unto thee a part which I have kept for thee... it shall profit tree to receive it. So be it and Selah.

* * *

The order of man - the order of Melchizedek

◇ : This be the symbol of the manifestation called man as a specie. Be ye as a whole with whole with this Order which shall arise and come forth as One, for the time is come when man shall come into his fullness and his fortune, which is his inheritance.

He hast wandered long in darkness and the shadows hast frightened him. This is the time of the end of such darkness, for it is come when there shall be a great awakening. For this are "We" sending messengers forth with the news of the glorious day of freedom... "It is nigh upon thee."

Be ye glad it is now come that ye are brought forth as one prepared to be delivered from all bondage. For this shall ye be as one to bring forth the glad new day of enlightenment, for long hast man labored. In his illusions he hast given forth many untrue volumes and stories of me and mine work, where upon I walked as man. This shall be part of thine assignment, to set straight, once and for all time, these 'false records' which hast brought chaos among men of no knowledge of truth.

It is come when I shall go before 'man' as I Am. I shall prove mineself unto them which are prepared to receive me, the ones with the will to learn of me or accept me. This is the day when I shall send forth mine Envoys, mine Ambassadors, mine servants, with the good news,

"<u>Thine deliverance is come</u>", for there shall be as ones to accept it. There shall be understanding of that which they are given to do, (and) no longer shall they walk in fear or darkness.

I am come that they might know the truth of their being. I shall speak as man, I shalt walk as man, and be no less for being as One with him, for I know mineself to be one with the Father which hast sent me.

Give ye (Thedra) me thine hand and I shall bring thee forth as one to be as one prepared to bring forth a mighty work of Light, that man should learn of the word which he shall find profitable unto him. Give unto me credit for being that which I Am. I Am the one come to bring thee in. So be it and Selah...

* * *

"The order of Melchizedek

Beloved of Mine Being: Let it be recorded for the record that the Order of Melchizedek is that which is. Before the world wast fashioned it WAS. And in no wise wast it fashioned in the way of man of Earth, for man hast not fashioned such a School, such an Order.

The Order of Melchizedek is that which was from the beginning of man's going out, as fashioned by our Father which is the Designer and the Author of its Laws. I say, the Order of Melchizedek is the highest Order known upon the planet of Earth.

And for that matter, few know it or of it, for it is for the Initiate which hast learned the Law, and for the ones which hast applied the Law unto himself and obeyed all the Laws set forth, as stated in the Law of the Order of Melchizedek.

This is stated simply and wisely, for it is not by design that the Law be complicated. Man complicates, and we are not the complicators... of man's opinions/confusions we are no part.

It is by design that the Law is simply stated, and at no time do we force the opinions of man upon thee, for they are as the legirons which we would but cut away that ye be free. For this have we given unto thee the Law, that ye might be free from all bondage.

So be it that I shall speak at length on the Order of Melchizedek at a later time. I am one sent that this be... So let it be.

Such is mine word unto thee this day... I Am Sananda

"The school of Melchizedek"

The School of Melchizedek hast been established upon solid ground. Upon the Earth hast it taken root. It is established, and I say unto thee, it shall put out roots into far places. And it shall be as none other, for the School of Melchizedek shall be liken unto no other School upon the Earth, for it shall have its roots within the Rock which I AM.

And it shall not give any quarter; neither shall it take any quarter. It shall be self-contained... sufficient within itself. It shall go not out seeking affiliation with any other... it shall be as the self-contained School that it is. It shall bring forth great and glorious fruit, for it is now time to bring out the fruit which hast lain dormant.

It is the time to bring forth the harvesters, for the season is upon us. It is the end time, and the harvesters shall be as ones prepared to go forth to gather in the harvest. Let it suffice that I have said unto thee: "The time is come to bring forth that which hast lain dormant." I shall speak unto thee again of the end time, the harvest, the Plan. So be it I shall lead thee, and I shall give unto thee in abundance and to spare.

I Am Sananda

* * *

Sananda

Obedience

Sori Sori: For this time let us speak of obedience, of loyalty. This is for the most part the greatest of the training of the neophyte, for he has to first learn obedience unto the law, he has to learn from whence his blessing cometh. He gives himself in honest preparation and service, asking no reward, no glory, no honors, for his honor cometh from his honest service rendered selflessly, without thot of self.

For when a man works for self, he is as one on whose head rests the crown of thorns... he hast placed his hand upon the scales that they balance in his favor. He hast been in no wise aware of his fellow's welfare. He thinks to deceive his fellows and gain favor in the sight of his neighbor... for this hast he betrayed himself and his trust. He has betrayed himself, hast he not? Let us say he hast short-changed himself, for it is so.

Now it is said, he shall walk upright and obey the law; he shall do unto others as he would they do unto him. He shall walk as he would have them, for he shall find that they are but the image of himself. They shall too betray themselves, and he shall be as the recipient of that which he hast sent forth, for it shall boomerang upon him and he shall find that he hast profited naught by his deceit.

So be it that he shall learn the way of the neophyte... then when he hast proven himself worthy, he shall be given Greater things to do, greater parts, greater responsibility.

This is but the beginning, for it is seen that they have not as yet comprehended the fullness of the plan. They have not been as the one with the greater vision. They have not been as one which stands on the summit and sees with the greater vision. They see that which they see as but partly, in part. They know not that which they see is but the manifestation of that which they see not.

Now it is said, "Seek ye the Light and it shall not be hidden". Knowest thou the meaning of this? I say, seek ye that which is back of the manifestation, the cause of the manifestation... that which is the cause of ALL manifestation, the FIRST CAUSE.

"Seek ye first the Kingdom of God", knowest the meaning of this? Wherein is the Kingdom of God? I say it is not of man, man's world, the material world, not of Earth... it is of the world which ye shall come to know. Then ye shall know as I know. Then there shall be no mysteries, no ties, no boundaries, no impenetrable walls or barriers, for ye shall be one with the Law, One with thy Cause of Being.

And ye shall stand shorn of all thy preconceived opinions and ideas of the "Father's Kingdom" which shall come on Earth as thou hast prayed. Yet it shall not be a Kingdom such as thou hast imaged.

I say, man, O Man, thou hast imaged vain imaginings, vain indeed, for thou hast been as ones putting thine own words into mine mouth *(sayings attributed to Jesus)*. Thou hast written them and given unto me credit for speech which I have not uttered, for I am not of a mind to speak that which is not of TRUTH, not of the LIGHT. For I say, I am responsible for mine words, and I have never given unto thee that which I now deny.

For I say unto thee, I am accountable unto The One which hast sent me forth. I am accountable unto the Law, even as thou art. Yet I come under the Greater Law, under the Divine Law which is yet above that of nature, yet it (the law of nature) is not without its part. But the laws of "Nature" are natural laws which govern the seen world as it is seen, yet it (the Law) is unseen. The law only brings into the seen that which is not seen, while the unseen is ever Greater and more potent than the seen. Therefore it is said, "Seek ye the Kingdom of God"... that which is back of the manifestation.

That which is back, the cause of the "Natural" manifestation, is of the Father, The Cause. It is said, "See the Hand of God move"! I say it moveth... See it... Behold it moveth. It causeth the axis to spin, thy Earth to rotate thereon, therein, within its orbit. It brings the seasons, the Sun to rise, to set in the appointed time. IT causes the unseen to be made seen. Therefore I say, "Seek ye the Kingdom of God", for hast He not created the Heaven and the Earth?

Wherefore cometh thy knowledge? I ask of thee, wherefore cometh thy knowledge? Thinkest thou, O Man, that thou seest that which causes thy being, which hast held thee fast in the hours of thy unknowing?

I ask thee, Whence goest thou? Whither come thou? It is not a small foolish question I ask of thee! I ask thee to ponder well that which I have put before thee. See that which is written in the "Book of Life". Open up thine eyes... behold the things placed before thee. See the Works of God, for His finger hast power. His finger hast power to move the planets, for He is the Creator, He is the Planner, the Architect, the Husbandman. He hast the Power, the Authority, for He is eternally The Father of His Creation. He creates well, good, according unto the Law which is eternal. Therefore HE IS THE LAW. And He is the First and the Last, Alpha and Omega... He hast the First and the Last Word. He sends out... He brings back that which He send out. And it follows as the night the day, ye shall return unto the place of thy beginning, so be it and Selah.

Yet I say, this is the hour of thy calling. This is the Day! I say, ye shall heed the call and answer. Come forth in this day, or ye shall wait long, and thy waiting shall be long indeed... sad indeed shall it be. For the word hast gone out, "COME HOME, COME HOME", and ye shall come of thine own accord, or ye shall wait!

It is of the greatest concern unto The Mighty Host that ye hear, yet none shall impose upon thy free will, for it is _thine_, thy own precious gift. Do with it as ye will. Yet it is said, fashion for thyself no legirons, for we, The Host, come that ye be free. Come as thou will... stay as ye will... for it is for thy sake that we come.

We of The Host have won our freedom thru obedience and dedication unto the Will of God Our Father. So be it that we speak of things profitable unto thee. So be it we stand by to assist thee in the hour of need. Ye have but to accept us for that which we are and obey the Law.

We have won Our freedom, even as ye shall win thine, by adherence unto the Law. Fear not that ye be misled when ye obey the mandates laid before thee. It is the Law of The One, the Law of The Eternal Shining One of which speak. Ye shall remember thy blessings. Count them one by one, then two by two, then by the dozens, for they shall be multiplied a thousand fold! So be it and Selah.

* * *

THE GOLDEN SCRIPTS

- by William Dudley Pelley -

Many people have never heard of William Dudley Pelley, yet in the 1930's he brought through one of the most eloquently written series of teachings ever given by the Christ Spirit. Because of the richness of these writings, we are reprinting here chapter 91 of one of his books entitled <u>The Golden Scripts</u>, that you might become aware of these writings. All of the Pelley books are listed in the 1991 ASSK book catalogue and may be ordered through ASSK.

****

Ye do have two rulers - Chapter 91 - The Golden Scripts

1 Know that men have often said that I am the son of God, meaning a literal father dwelling in a literal heaven, surrounded by his messengers and judging all men according to their deeds.

2 I bid you to behold that such is a compromise between the truth and what they would believe of their own pictures in form, not knowing how to picture the abstract.

3 But this is important: There are those amongst you, in flesh and out of it, who have seen what no man ever hath seen. They have made their penetration to vast distances of spirit, they have found there sights and sounds beyond earthly comprehension;

4 Behold they have returned to earth to tell of those experiences, to relate what happened to them of their mental senses;

5 They have pictured unto those below them on the earth plane, a series of dramas, apparently occurring within their inspection at the times of their visitations;

6 These have taken form and become apparent to earthly brains as the expression of theology.

7 Now let me tell you the truth about these things, that ye may be wise above your generation,

8 And yet I say unto you, repeat it circumspectly, for verily it transcendeth men's knowledge of the present.

9 The Father, who rendereth unto you a picture of divine paternity, is vaster than men think... in that out of the infinite cometh reason, by a process that hath in it Creation as ye know it;

10 This Reason is the Voice of Creation telling men, born and unborn, of vast mysteries.

11 These mysteries, beloved, are choice of selection... by that I mean they encompass circumstances that cannot be interpreted, except as man compareth them with the knowledge which he hath in his own experience.

12 But this voice of reason is more than argument; it hath in it potencies that take form in thought.

13 I speak unto you with wisdom when I say that all of us are thoughts manifesting in so-called matter, which itself is Thought. Not a projection of the intellect, but a conceiving of things as they might be, wherefore they are.

14 By this I mean, thought is of eternity, before matter, being all that there is in the Cosmos.

15 The Cosmos in turn is Thought... it began to manifest in matter trillions of millennia ago in earthly time for a reason.

16 It was impossible to conceive, even emotionally, without form of some kind to give thought character and measurement.

17 When I tell you that the earth-plane and mortal life are but types of thought measurement, I explain life closer to truth than in any other way any other measurement.

18 Life is projection of Thought indeed, but it is Thought projecting in terms of quantities for measurement of itself, for evaluation of its own attributes.

19 To utter it differently unto you; Life hath in it the essence of Thought, while at the same time it is Thought... this I perceive ye do know.

20 When I speak then of the Father, I speak verily of one who ruleth the Host of all Thought Streams... a Spirit so aged that no man knoweth its antiquity.

21 This Spirit in power is beyond even my conceiving, even as I was temporarily beyond your conceiving whilst in mortal flesh.

22 This Spirit existeth and endureth... older I say than any known to the host of those of whom I have knowledge. He is not God as men conceive God, nevertheless He is so wise in His conceiving that His power transcendeth that of any spirit projected onto any plane of which we have wisdom.

23 When I say that I am Son of God and refer to the Father, invariably I refer to this Spirit, because with Him I am in touch and know no greater beyond Him.

24 I tell you, beloved, I believe others to be beyond Him, but of them I have no knowledge and probably never will have knowledge... they ever receding as we approach them.

25 When therefore I say that the Father existeth, and yet I say there is no God but Thought, I do not speak a paradox, neither do I fabricate. We have spirits here with us upon the Higher Side so powerful of knowledge, concept, and constructive emotionalism, that they do transcend even myself who am given the earth as my temporary ruling place.

26 These spirits are known unto me intimately and unto you when ye are out of your flesh.

27 These infinite Spirits, for I call them such, greater in power than any known to mortal men, have control of the universe as men know it. They are Omnipotent and Omnipresent in the world and in the universe, ruling it by thought projection and enabling it to function.

28 I have come amongst men for this purpose time and time again... not to manifest omnipotence, for omnipotence is always relative, and strictly speaking even the Ruler of the Host hath it not;

29 But I am come among men to teach them something higher than that which they perceive in their earthly travail.

30 I have come as instructor, not as ruler... although by mine instruction do I rule. I have come into flesh times beyond count, manifesting unto men what they may attain even in blinded and handicapped concepts of the present.

31 I have shown them the way, the Truth, and the Light... particularly the light. Now we are come into this situation:

32 Man hath said. There is no God; I say unto you, God in truth is Thought Incarnate... but in men's saying they have meant, There is no ruler unto whom we are accountable.

33 In such concept their erring hath been grievous.

34 Truly there are twenty million rulers unto whom they are accountable, for each species and kind hath its rulers unto whom it is accountable, whether on planes of earth or planets afar in decimal space.

35 Know ye that humankind, as it is beheld by men, is not the only manifestation of morality, although humankind hath a state unto itself. Planets beyond your ken have their species and races and cohorts and potentates, dwelling in all sorts and conditions of livinghood, and making practice of their talents according to their development of intellect.

36 Verily animals are some of these, although far, far down on the scale of intelligence... so far down that whole groups are sometimes required to express one psyche.

37 What I would tell you this hour is this: There is one God in respect that there is a Ruler of the planetary systems. This ruler, I say, is an old, old Spirit, older than any of us have a knowledge.

38 His comings and goings are marked by vast cataclysms, so that stars do perish and reassemble in His presence. Verily is He incarnate in the universe as ye do know the universe of sight and sound, yet doth He dwell in presence upon a far, far planet, greater in extent than your minds can encompass.

39 Behold I do go unto Him for instruction at intervals... a Living Entity who hath so great a power that for Him to speak is for creation to consummate.

40 Gods hath He in turn beyond Him, of similar structure, vastness, and incomprehensibility, for the universe hath no end in majesty.

41 These things we must conceive to get our errands clear.

42 Mayhap the day arriveth when we too shall be so great that whole world systems are born at our speaking, but that altereth not the fact that there dwelleth in Infinity a Creature and a creation of such vastness of concept that He knoweth the comings and goings of planets as doves in a cage that is hung in a casement.

43 Mark this well, my beloved: He hath knowledge of you, even as I have knowledge of you. He saith unto me nightly: What of thy fellowship with those who dwell with thee on the planet Earth, and the concepts thereof in thought? Have those who compose it kept faith with thee? Is it so that they please thee... for great shall be their reward in knowledge if they perform at thy desire, and in fulfillment of thine instruction.

44 I say unto Him: Verily it is so, Father of us All in Creative Wisdom; report I progress day unto day. Night unto night seeth the action advanced whereby the Man Spirits cleave unto my principles and advance in knowledge of spiritual evaluations.

45 Make no mock of this, beloved: a Spirit watcheth over me even as I watch over my friends and compatriots in the work of raising humankind to knowledge, that it proceedeth upward, millennium by millennium.

46 Now mark this well: When it cometh time that we have completed our labors and man no longer hath need of this planet, this thing happeneth; the world as ye do know it disintegrateth in Thought.

47 Out of the mouth of the Father cometh thunderings, declaring a newer a more nearly perfect location for humankind... a better prepared planet, where men do dwell in fleshly concept that nearer perfection than that which now prevaileth, that they may learn other lessons not addicted to the pleasure-pain experience.

48 The time cometh when men shall say, There is no God as we have known Him, not even celestial ruler of our group... we have no use for rulership, for verily we do rule ourselves. Hoaxed have we been by ministers and priests... all, all is theological vanity and humor wrongly placed in our concepts. We have knowledge only of essences; these we rely on; teach us not blasphemies of ourselves.

49 Say unto them, beloved: Lo, it is not so, for verily ye do have two rulers: He who was Jesus of Nazareth ruling you immediately, and He who ruleth over the Order of Which Jesus of Nazareth is a member and in whose household he standeth well.

50 Transcribe this, my beloved, in pictures of gold within frames of silver; tell it with diamonds as your pigments, for so important is it that man should know this that it transcendeth every debacle of reasoning whereof men stand convicted.

51 We have known of old of this ancient ruling Spirit, but man hath conceived of Him wrongly... I tell you: Man hath called Him God of Wrath and Torture, of unpleasant utterance and divine malediction;

52 Verily, verily, it is not so!

53 Greater is He in beauty than I have ever shown myself unto man... greater in understanding, greater in toleration, greater in infinite compassion, for verily hath He not encompassed the world within His bosom, and doth He not encompass it daily and hourly?

54 My beloved, we have an immediate Father so intimate that to think of Him is to know Him, and to live in flesh is to be part of His substance... for verily His incarnation is in the universe itself as ye perceive it: that is His body and His flesh, although He dwell in addressable Spirit a trillion miles afar.

55 I would have you take this literally, no lesson being greater that I have taught you.

56 All up and down men's ages have come those saying: We see not this God, this Ancient Ruler, this Omnipresent One... and in that we cannot point Him out, we deny Him.

57 Verily, my beloved, they speak as children who have not received wisdom from logic and experience....

***

*From; The Golden Scripts
by William Dudley Pelley*

EVERLASTING FREEDOM

Sori Sori: Mine beloved, I am come at this hour that all mankind be awakened, for it is now come that the sheep shall be separated from the goats The ones which are prepared for to come with me shall be as ones lifted up. These shall no more go in to bondage... freedom shall be their portion forever! *(Note: Sheep will follow a Shepherd... Goats just go where they please).*

I have said, many are now come unto me as mine flock, for they have listened to mine speaking and direction. These are the ones which are the greater Light which shall go where I go, and we shall rejoice that the day of deliverance is come. By thine own will ye shall be brought out.

I am declaring unto mankind, that I am come for the purpose of finding the lost and delivering them into their rightful estate. I have given unto mankind much.., many gifts that they (mankind) might see and know that there is a greater Source in which they are part, or have their existence. This is mine intent... to give unto each and every one which has a will, the mind, to accept mine gift of <u>total</u> Freedom.

While I come as man, man has given unto me many names, and fought for their right to bow down before their images of their gods... yet they have given their little gods power to destroy and leave them in desolation. I see and know their plight. I Am the "Living Light" they seek. While they profess to know me, they have looked in the dark shadow World for signs and miracles, which are but the lesser manifestation. It is now come when they shall see, hear, and feel the Power of the Greater Light in which they have their Being".

It is said many times, that there shall be great and sudden changes, which shall be as the will of the Father. Many shall be as ones come alive and remember mine words... yet there shall be the laggards which have stood steadfast and declared <u>their</u> "god" the only one. These which have denied me as the One sent of the Source shall find their Images shall fail to give unto them that which they had imaged, or hoped for.

They shall find that they have been hoodwinked, misled... that they have been as puppets of the lesser gods to whom they have built great and impressive Altars and prayed for their enemies destruction!

I Come! I come not to bring peace! I am come bringing with me a host of Lighted Beings. We carry with us the Light of the Living God. We need no metals, no armor other than that of "Light", in which All have their Being, their Eternal Being, which is indestructible.

This is that which I would have all mankind know. For this I come, that mankind, mortal man, see and know himself to be as I... ONE with his Source, even as "I". I come not to bring unto thee great and fraudulent speeches to deceive thee, that enhance thy greed, thy gluttony, thy hatred for thine Brothers with which ye are bound.

I find that ye are seeking solutions for thine woes and failures to accomplish that which they <u>think</u> the answer to Peace. Peace, my dear ones, rests not on peace pacts designed by man's mortal mind. These so-called solutions are but appeasements... even so, he, man, is better for the effort.

Many a one hast been sent from the lighter/higher realm to teach and direct/lead him as a Nation/Country as a whole, in Unity/Brotherhood... one for All, All for one, in Love and Harmony. This is the basis for "Peace", which is not insight at this late date.

I come crying, "COME! COME! I have for thee a great gift, <u>Everlasting Freedom</u>, when ye are prepared to receive it". I give unto thee in the many ways, formats, etc, the only sure way for lasting peace... "<u>Love Ye Thine Brother As I Love Thee</u>" This shall be thine code of Arms. Art thou prepared to walk with me?... or are ye content with thine lot? So be it as ye choose!

We shall not impose upon thine Sacred Gift... Sacred indeed it is!

I Am the Wayshower

* * *

Unto thine own life

Sori Sori: Mine beloved, I am speaking for the good of all mankind. This is the word I would have them accept unto them self as the personal word directed unto them alone:

Many take mine word and run unto the neighbor or friend to give unto them some news which will benefit <u>them</u>. I say, first take mine word unto thine self... test it... taste it. When ye have found it savory and trustworth, True, then apply it unto thine own life\self, thine life style. When ye are sure of it (that which I have proffered thee), then share it with any one which is prepared to receive it.

Yet I say, it is the better part of wisdom to know that which I say is of great value, yet unto the one which passes it unto another without first putting it to the test in their own life and affairs, are as the "foolish virgins" found without oil for their lamps.

I would have thee study well mine words and understand mine meaning, for they are designed in such a manner that each one might find great value, which will strengthen them in their future progress.

Be ye thoughtful of thine daily life... <u>thy</u> daily life... the goings and comings... thine association with others... that which ye say and do... thine attitude. Examine well that which ye say! Speak only words of value which ye shall benefit by, as they return unto thee three fold, either for weal or woe. Consider these mine words! They are simple, that all might understand and profit by the application.

O, man, I say ye are not wise. Ye know so little 'for sure'. What do ye know of sound, sound waves... that which ye send out in the Ether each day... yea, each hour? For ye are a noisy lot!

I might say a careless and uncouth lot, for ye are unaware of that which ye do with the gifts ye have been endowed with. I would have thee think long and soberly upon these simple words, for they are designed to assist thee in thine assent unto greater things.

Mine plan is not complicated... it is the verity of thine "silence", based on the Word of the 'Source' of Life... passed down from the Source through the medium of Vibration in various means.

Have ye, mine friends, found the source of these vibrations that ye are creating daily? Have ye heard/heeded the word I have been sending forth on "Mine Intercom"? Be ye blest to answer mine Call! Tune in! Ye might hear!.. when ye clear the channel of all unnecessary and excess "Vibes' ye so carelessly send forth to clutter our communication waves. 'Vibes!' By this unnecessary clutter ye are losing great and valuable information, for the Light makes way for greater learning which would assist thee in thine evolvement.

May I give unto thee a parable? A man has three sons. He gives one a message for the King... but this one falls prey unto the guard of the evil one, which hast lain in wait for the first messenger.

The second son was sent out by a different route... he carried no portfolio, no written word. He was accosted, yet the assailant found nothing. This second son has not been true unto himself, for as he had nothing upon his person to be pilfered by the assailant... thus he turned back.

The third son goes forth with the message fully imprinted within his mind. Word for word he repeated it unto the designated one which was to receive it. This third son was clear of mind, free of fear... so too was the receiver of the message sent by the third son. Each so played his part... Which one received the greater reward?

This is but the beginning

Sori Sori: Mine beloved, I come in this time of dire necessity, when your World is in a great turmoil of hatred and unrest. It is the greatest yet which hast come about in the history of mankind... it multiplies daily!

Ye see not that which goes on behind closed doors... ye would not understand the plans set into motion for total destruction,

Now it is imperative that greater powers intervene. Be ye as one which has the will to go forth as a guard, as a forerunner, or as a Messenger which shall stand against the onslaught. I say, there shall be great and sorrowful times in the days ahead, for the fray in the desert was but the beginning.

I am the one sent to give unto all mankind warning and assistance in this dark hour. We of the Higher Realm see with clear vision, while ye see the smog. The plans of men are but puny... some are simple and reasonable, while that which hast been done by the unwise dark one hast now rebounded upon them (Iraq). The Law of Justice shall be justified and no man can stay the hand of the Reaper.

I come not to frighten or cause great fear... I come simply to alert and make straight the way before mankind. Yet, I see that many shall turn their hand unto greater destruction. Men of good will (in their unknowing) will mock me in unbelief and turn traitor unto themselves. They shall follow the ones of the dark brotherhood", and ridicule mine flock which follow me. Yet I say unto all and sundry: I Am come that ye be spared the fate of destruction.

Now ye shall gather up thine household and prepare thineself for sudden changes... for changes there shall be! It will profit thee to give thine hand unto me, and I shall lead thee safely o'er the dangerous places. I see them (the dangerous places) and desire to give unto thee sate passage. I do not coerce or come as an intruder... I shall seek out the ones which are of the mind to obey mine mandates and come with me of their own will. <u>I kidnap no one!</u>

I have heard it said that I set a trap for the unwary, I say unto these unknowing ones: Be ye sure of thine speech! Take note of that which i have said unto mankind! Measure thine steps! Walk softly O, man of little wisdom, thou art walking on shaking sand... I would not have ye caught unaware!

Behold ye that which ye have put aside, for the winter comes surely. I say unto thee, that ye shall remember mine words e'er winter comes. Be ye as one wise and give unto me credit for knowing that which I do or say. I am the one which is sent to find mine "Lost Sheep", (and) I am prepared to accept all which are prepared to come with me.

Be ye blest to come out from the darkness and learn of me, for I am the "Lord God", made man. I Am all things to the ◇ Light which I Am. No impossible situation do I encounter, for I Am the **0**, One with the Law of the ONE. I come not to fail in this mine mission... Let it be said, it is a rescue one.

Are ye ready to join with me? I ask thine wholehearted permission to fetch the out!

* * *

The day of accounting

Sananda Speaking: This is mine word unto all mankind at this hour: "Be ye as one prepared, for there shall be great and sudden changes. Ye shall be as ones perplexed and confused, and ye shall wonder what has transpired while ye have slept.

Now is the time of sifting and sorting. The sleepers shall be the last to awaken... they shall be as the sluggish foolish ones which have thought themselves self sufficient. These changes shall be part of mine plan for the cleansing of the Earth and the freeing of the captives therein.

Let it be understood that I am at the wheel of this mighty ship on which ye have booked passage. I know mine part well. I know the course and I deviate not from it, for it is well defined. While some have mutinied and fallen overboard, they shall find they are yet to go out again for to learn the hard way. Be ye not concerned for those which have mutinied and fallen overboard... be ye watchful of thine own part which ye have asked for.

Ye are the recipients of thine own fortunes which ye have stored away... yea, "for a rainy day", perhaps! Yet, are ye aware that it is now come? This day of the rain is come when mankind shall not have control over the elements. He shall see that he is helpless over his own creation, for he has thought himself wise. He has spurned the word of the Lord of Lords and the Envoys sent in the light of the All-knowing One. Now is the day of accounting when the record shall be set straight.

The record hast been well kept. It shall be seen, and each shall read his own which he shall not deny. This is the Law of Justice! Art thou, O, man, aware of this... this Law of Justice... of which I have defined for thine sake, that ye might know that which ye do?

Ye have said, and I have heard it said: "I Am God". Oh, yea <u>ye are god over thine own creation</u>. Ye shall own it... be it that as it is. Whatever it is ye shall know it for thine own.

Now let us give unto thee a new part, a new day of cleaning out, a sorting of the old, making way for the new. Are ye prepared to go out into the vineyards to gather that harvest which has been prepared for this day of decision? I have said time and time again, "The day of decision is upon thee". Are ye ready to take note of the "Word" given from the Light Source, in the Light for <u>thine sake</u>, that ye be aware of thine Benefactors which are ready to assist thee in Wisdom and Compassion? For they know thine weakness, and for this do they give of themselves that ye be lifted up before the day of great sorrow.

Let thine eyes be opened, that ye might see that which awaits thine preparedness... thine ears be trained to hear that which is said unto thee for thine awakening, thine deliverance.

Yea, thine salvation! Know ye the meaning of that word? Let it be as 'Salvage'. Know ye what is worth salvaging? What is that which is salvageable?

Be ye blest by mine own hand, to give thought unto mine simple word... that ye come as a little child, willing to be lead by the Father, for he/she (the child) knows and trusts his (Fathers) word, and feels his Love and Security.

Let it be as the Father wills... Amen

* * *

The messenger

Thedra: (4:00 a.m.) A knock came on my door... A voice called "Sister"...

I answered...

The one responded: " A'mandex message for Sister"

The Message

Beloved: I bring with me great news such as nothing ye have had. It is imperative that ye give unto me thine hand in the hour of the dawning of light (4:00 a.m.) for a period of time. Let us give the people time to give their energy unto their preparation, for I come as one which is sent as a responsible and trusted messenger.

I come as on wings of light... no tide or wind can stay mine flight. I give unto thee the responsibility of delivering this unto the ones which hast waited for news from the "Source".

Let this be understood by all and sundry... that I am the one which hast been chosen of\by the Source to bring forth this communique. I now deliver it, this special word, which carries within it great import. Let it be received with great and respectful adoration, for it is as the Word of "Life".

It is most necessary unto each and every one which receives this unto him\her self that he\they take this "precious word" unto heart, and give unto it serious thought, credence, and be mindful of its source. I shall give unto this one (Thedra), a trusted servant of long standing, the responsibility of giving unto each one which hast given thought and credence unto the source of these many messages given forth for to awaken the sleepers. For it is no time for lethargy... sleep time is over mine dear ones!

We of this place in space, (which ye know not as it really is... for ye have given very little credit unto us as being 'real', real as ye, thine own self, made flesh and bone...) are as ones of a higher, greater, vibration, dimension, which ye have not seen or touched. While many seem to <u>think</u> they have, I say, they are but imaging vain things... and some are as the ones which would deter thee from thine course and turn thee aside, cast thee aside, and leave thee lonely and in despair.

Now, my dear friends all: I speak as a Brother that ye be as ones prepared to receive the one which comes swiftly, as on a beam of great Light such as ye have not seen. Think not that this is some of thine propaganda for to amuse thee or afford thee a new interest for a short while. Thine interest in things of great import is short lived indeed! Ye are a restless people, looking for <u>New Things</u> of greater concern.

What can I do with this information?

Can it be true?

Is it what I have been taught?

Would my friends agree, or turn from me?

I might loose my job and every thing that I have and love...

I'll think it over!

* * *

Mine brothers\Sisters, I tell thee of a surety, there is an expediency in mine mission, for the time is upon thee when there shall be no time to "<u>think it over</u>".

We of the Host of Light have been thine guardians and councilors for many many ages, yet ye are not, on the whole, prepared to come out from the darkness of despair and sorrow. Now it is come that ye are filled with confusion... dissatisfaction... false hopes... misgivings... for ye have not heeded the Word of Truth... for ye have not had the Full Truth... (partial, yea!)

While ye were too restless, to doubtful to test it out, ye ask of others opinions, and verification of thine own opinions). Now it is come that ye shall trust thine own heart and intelligence endowed unto thee of the 'Source'. Trust the Source of thine Being. Be not afraid to reach out thine hand for help... yet, I say, it is wise to know <u>what</u> to ask and <u>whom</u> to ask.

First: Ask the 'Source', the fountain head of Truth and Light.

Be ye as one faithful in little things and ye shall be entrusted with greater. Be trustworthy in all thine dealings what-so-ever.

Watch thine speech, for it goes before thee to greet thee as a host at the door before thee.

May I, for thine sake, use a metaphor of thine realm: Thine spoken word/language is as your calling card which goes before thee... Look, Watch, See, and remember that which ye have sent on before thee, which shall take form to greet thee at the next door\portal or day to come. <u>Be ye not slothful of speech</u>...

The message I bring at this hour of the dawning of a new day is: It is the hour of great activity in the Higher Realms, in preparation for the greater work to be made known as it is so planned for the good of all. Blest are they which hears and heeds. I am the swift messenger, sent of the Light which never fails...

* * *

False prophets

Sori Sori: Mine beloved, I say unto thee this hour, that it is now time to give unto these which are awaiting the words of mine, this communique, for it shall be timely and purposeful. For it is come when there are many false profits about the land, therefore I say again, it is the time that they shall be put to the test... they (these ones which think themselves wise) shall be brought to account.

The time is come when there shall be a great cry go up for TRUTH and KNOWLEDGE of that which is being done in the Inner Circle of Light.

I say, the Higher Realms shall be as open unto the ones which see the Light of Truth. This is mine part, to bring unto all which are prepared to receive of me and mine "Host" which I bring with me.

It is now come when the time is "Shortened for the Elect sake". It is expedient, for the time is come that the cleaning and cleansing shall be severe... Yet very necessary. For the good of Mankind shall it be.

Mankind hast been as slow to awaken, while there are many which hast answered the Call, which still yet reverberates through the Cosmos: "Awaken All Ye Which Sleep". These which are awakening are crying for Truth/Knowledge, from the Source of Light, from the Ones sent of The "Source", the Light, wherein is no darkness or greed, malice, avarice, hatred, or blaspheming.

Many (false ones) use great and impressive names, and repeat well-known phrases to send forth unto the unknowing ones, which are as weaklings, the unlearned of the Greater Truths. I have sent forth Messengers from mine place of abode into the World of confusion, and yet dis. cord abounds. I am crying from the heights: Come ye out from the darkness... Learn ye of the things necessary for thine upliftment, that ye be spared the fate worse than death.

It is said many times, that it is lawful and necessary that mankind (the whole of it) shall be warned before being destroyed. I have called for volunteers to assist mineself and mine Host in this our greatest mission unto the Earth and her population... the Whole of it! Unto each volunteer which hast chosen Me and the Host with Me, shall find their reward Great. These shall give of themselves in Truth and Justice for all! No longer shall these volunteers be side-tracked by the dark ones which uncover more of the pitfalls to entrap the so-called innocent which are ever anxious for new experiences. I say, the ones which have baited their traps with their own morsels which look and sound so tempting to the unwise, the unlearned, shall fail to hold them pound.

These ones which <u>ask sincerely</u> for Truth, and follow the Law which is set before mankind, shall be as the inheritors of the new Earth and the new heaven. These shall not tire of serving the 'Forces of Light' sent unto the Earth at the propitious time. These shall be as Warriors of Light, Truth, and Justice. Their battle cry shall be "Come ye out from the darkness and learn of the Light in which ye have thine being, wherein ye shall find peace and Love".

These volunteers shall be well equipped to fight such a battle as now consumes the Light, so overshadowed by their unknowing... which in other words is their own ignorance of that which we of the Host of Light bring unto the realm of Earth at this time.

These volunteers shall carry the Armor of the Imperishable Truth, the Sword of Truth. They shall be known by the Light they carry... the work they do! No guile shall be found within these servants of Light. These shall make no pretense of wisdom, of greatness, nor shall these pick thine pockets.

These, which I have called "The Army of Light", overcome the darkness by their Light. They fear no man or beast... they bow to no false god... they ask of no man his opinion. They are prepared to go where sent... when called they murmur not of their lot or ask for rewards.

These ones rush <u>not</u> out to make battle as man is so prone to do. These see with greater, clearer sight, therefore they are fearless and trustworthy. Blest are mine servants which have proven themselves... Blest shall they be...

I, the Lord of Lords, the Host of The Host, the Lord God, hast spoken for the good of all. So be it and Selah.

I Am known here in the Light as Sananda

* * *

Make no mystery of me

Sori Sori: Mine beloved, I speak unto thee at this hour for the good of all, that there be understanding of the time and the Plan as it is given unto thee. The time is propitious... the plan is three fold.

First: The plan hast long been made and is beyond thine comprehension. While ye are given bit by bit, or a portion at a time as ye can comprehend, it is an ongoing program. It is designed (this great and grand plan of mine) that it fit into the whole of it, all the bits and pieces.

Ye see not the greater part, therefore I say, Look! See! Listen and Hear! Learn... Then Do!" For there are many which think themselves wise which claim great wisdom. Now these are causing great confusion among the populace. These take the "crumbs" and run to share with the hungry and curious, which know not that I have the "whole loaf".

Now it is given unto me to be the overseer of mine plan, which hast been given unto me of mine Father, that this day be as the end of all of the old decadent misinformation and lies. Now it is come when I am calling for the tried and true ones which have the will and wisdom to follow where I lead them. Yes, I lead steadily and surely into the greater Heights where the greater Vision and Peace abides. Be ye as one in the care of mine own light that ye might, at all times, see the next step that ye not loose thine way. I Am thine Light.., let no one, man or woman, turn hee aside with their propaganda, for I say, there is no need to make a Mystery of me, an unapproachable idol thing of me.

I Am as ONE with the ALL. I have given unto thee the SIMPLE LAW which shall be revealed in all its purpose and glory as ye are prepared to receive. Be not anxious or fall into lethargy. Be one at peace, for I am the Porter at the Gate. I know thine needs... yea, thine intention... Be ye blest this day... I Am the Wayshower

Freedom!

Sori Sori: Long have I waited this day, this hour, when I might come unto thee bearing witness of The Host of The Living God. Long have I waited... long indeed,

While the time hast not lain heavy upon me, it hast been the time of great preparation when we of The Host have been preparing for this time, the time of the awakening, the time of going forth that each and every man might be enlightened, and that none be forgotten.

There are ones which know not of our existence, the existence of The Host... neither the Host of The Host which bears witness of us, of The Host. These are as ones which have been the fortune (the product) of ages past, wherein they forfeited their gifts, misused them, or denied them. They did not accept that which was proffered them in ages past... they betrayed themselves. Now they are again come into flesh for the purpose of learning and giving of themselves unto the Light which cometh in the darkness.

While the darkness comprehends not the Light, we of the Host shall go forth as One Man, as One Voice, as One Mind, One Mighty Hand... as one Great Surge of Power and Light. And great shall be that Power, that Hand, and nothing shall stay it, for it is the Will of the Most High Living God that this day bring forth the harvest (resurrection). So be it and Selah.

This is the day long foretold, and for this do we go forth that the way be made strait, that they be prepared for the greater part. So be it that we know each and every place, everyone by their number, their color, their sound, their light. So be it and Selah.

This is the word I would give unto them which have a will to learn and to be delivered out of bondage: There is but One Father, which is called "God", the Cause of thy Being, the Source of thy Being... and he is The Creator Supreme. He hast created eternally, and it is Good. He creates perfectly! None other creates eternally perfect, for He is the Perfect All-Wise Living God.

Born of Him art thou, o man. Born of HIM art thou! Eternal art thou! Not of a moment, not of a score, neither a century, but ETERNAL! The Spirit which thou art is not born of woman for a span of time to decay and return no more.

While I bear witness of the Father and His Word, I say unto thee: Greater hast man been... Greater shall he be than he hast imaged. For "Man" hast been as the Spirit, free from flesh, free from bondage, free from darkness... yet he chose to enter into the dense world of flesh as flesh, and to walk as "man-of-Earth". And thru the womb of flesh came he as the animal, bound by the law of flesh, even as the animal is bound.

Now it is given unto him to be both man and animal. The animal is but the flesh... (while) "Man" as created by The Father is perfect, is the Spirit Eternal, for the Father created of Himself thru the Spoken Word and it was perfect in every respect save none.

The part which man hast chosen shall be unto him his "Book of Life" which he hast written upon the pages of Time, which shall bear testimony of his travels, his travails, and his wanderings and wonderings, upon the periphery of Time and Space... flung afar upon the horizon of the Universes of eternal space, and the timeless parapets whereupon there is written his records without error, with the precision of the gods which are appointed the keeping of the records.

I say, Behold ye the vastness of The Father's Domain which He hast created for Man... the Man of His creation... that which He created from Himself, from out His own Being. This He called Good... it wast Good... therefore it is to be given unto this Eternal Being to be brot back, even as it went forth, perfect in every respect.

Therefore the Host shall go forth to awaken the "Man" which slumbers within the animal form. For man lies asleep within the form of flesh, flesh of Earth... and as such he is bound by flesh. Therefore he shall come to know that he is eternal, and that he hast an inheritance, not of Earth, but of the Eternal Heavens... that which is his freedom from bondage, the inheritance kept for him from the beginning.

And for this do we of The Host bear witness of the Eternal Man, the "Spirit of Man" which is the part which is FREE! Free from the animal world.

We speak of "Freedom", of "bondage"... and it shall be understood that bondage is of man's (making). Freedom is of The Father, offered unto thee at this time when the sleepers sleep, knowing not that they sleep. They shall be as ones fully aware that they are in bondage. They shall seek the Light... they shall find... they shall be freed. So be it and Selah.

For this do we go forth as The Father hast willed it. So be it His Will that all be prepared to come forth and accept their inheritance. So let it be Amen and Selah.

* * *

The great day of decision

Sori Sori: Mine beloved, I speak unto thee at this hour for the good of all. Mine word shall be as healing balm unto the Souls of the ones seeking relief from bondage... a light to their feet to guide them on their sojourn into the everlasting freedom and peace. Let each one which has a will to learn of me, mine plan, mercy, and love, find me as one sent to deliver them up. No more suffering or want for anything.

I am he which is sent to bring them which have the will to come out, no more to cry from oppression and bondage. The ones which are prepared shall be caught up with me, as ONE with me. These shall be as new born... they shall remember all things, which shall be for their good. No more shall they cry in darkness and ignorance, for I shall reveal unto them that which they really are... their inheritance willed unto them of the Source. No man shall rob him them of this inheritance, which hast been kept for this day. These which arise with me shall be as the "Prodigal Son" returned. There shall be great rejoicing, and love shall abound.

The time is now come when mankind shall find he hast been hoodwinked... led down the primrose path, to be left desolate and sorrowful, as one which has betrayed himself.

I am come that all mankind Awaken and be as ONE with me, I Am the Light, 'sent' to rescue thee from the darkness which is ready to swallow thee up! Ye know not that which is about thee which is of thine own creation, which thou hast brought about by thine rebellion and ignorance of the Truth of All things, which ye have forgotten. Now I say unto all, that ye shall have thine memory restored, and with this ye shall cry for joy and praise the Eternal source for His grace and mercy. Yet ye shall be as ones willing to come. Freely ye shall come, as One with me, (for) none are brought against their will.

I have called long and loud: Come ye out! Learn of thine self! "<u>Man, know thine self</u>", as one of free will, self-responsible for self and all thine acts and decisions. Ask with a contrite heart, sincerely, for deliverance. Prepare thine own self to come out of the darkness which hast bound thee in suffering and sorrow. Know ye, O, man, what ye have done to bring ye to the edge of destruction, (for) this is the great day of decision... the day of deliverance!

I am not a traitor... I make no idle speeches or false promises. I speak in simple terms that all might understand mine meaning. I am not beholden unto anyone whatsoever for the manner in which I awaken mankind. It is mine intent to do so, therefore, I use any means I feel necessary... even unto turning back upon mankind that which he hast created. It is lawful that it be done, for as he hast sown, so be his reaping. Just is this law.

*　*　*

Man's journey

Sori Sori: By mine own hand I shall lead thee and ye shall be led aright, so be it and Selah. Fear not them which would be unto thee a "poor priest", them which would instruct thee in the way of the unknowing ones. They speak of "The coming of the King of Kings", "that he shall set up a kingdom of God on Earth". Yet it is said, "The Kingdom of God is within"... so be it!

And too it is said, "None enter in save thru the Gate", the strait and narrow, the Light... and it is for this that I am come, that they find the Kingdom within.

Yet the story begins not with man, neither does it end with man. The journey of man is the way of man back unto his place of going out. His journey is but the twinkling of an eye in Eternity, and yet he sees himself as but the beginning and the end.

The totality of man is not that which he sees or knows... he is but the fragment of the Whole. He is not Whole of (by) himself, he is but a fragment of the Whole! Man (mankind), as such, is but the fragment of the whole, the creation of The Eternal Solen Aum Solen... the "ALL"... the ONE.

This is but the beginning of man's sojourn in time, for his time endeth not with the Earth. He is a traveler thru "Time and Space", thru eternity, worlds without end, for he is Spirit... born of Spirit is he.

There is but One Father Eternal, Solen Aum Solen, from which cometh ALL things... eternal, without end, without beginning. Yet man, as such, shall be the fragment... and as the Man made perfect, he shall return unto his Source as ONE with IT. And then he shall know his Source and he shall be ONE with IT. And no more shall he see himself as fragments, for he shall be Whole... Whole in word and deed, for he shall KNOW that which he is, and he shall no more go into darkness as a wanderer upon the periphery of time. So be it and Selah.

Give ye some time unto me

Sori Sori: Mine beloved, I speak unto thee that all might be profited, for as I speak unto one, mine word goes forth as vibration upon the ethers. The ones which are prepared shall be quickened and take unto themselves that which I have sent forth upon the waves of "Mine Intercom".

I have asked thee to look up and ask for comprehension, for I come unto the one which has a mind, a will to be mine "associate". I am prepared to go all the way to the end with thee, through all trials and temptations, storm and suffering. Take mine hand when ye are week and anxious, when ye are lonely or fearful, for I am thine shield and buckler. I shall shield thee from all evil, and NO man shall say me Nay! I ask only that ye accept the hand proffered in Holy Light and Love for all creatures great and small.

Give ye some time unto me; listen for mine voice... yet, ye shall clear the way for me. By thine own effort ye shall clear the channel of all clutter. Rid thine self, thine mind, of emotions which distract thee from the contact with me." say, ye shall be as one prepared to receive me. I shall meet thee half way, yet ye shall do thine part.

I am the Wayshower... I have made strait and safe the way before thee. Thave set thee apart from the ones which deny me and mine counselors, which are as ones prepared to bring thee out of thine bondage. I have likened mine self unto thine "Bondsman"... I come on thine behalf that ye may go free!

Are ye ready to come with me? For my arm is strong, and mine intent is to bring thee out of the chains which hast bound thee, such as: Slothfulness... indifference unto thine own inheritance, thine "Source".

Mine many gifts I have bestowed upon thee, which ye have taken without thought of the giver or their source. Ye have given unto the lessor gods credit for these helping hands, yet, while ye suffer ye make thine self subject to receive of mine Love and generosity. Many ask for healing in time of helpless news... (yet) when they are healed, they forget their <u>Benefactor</u>, and return unto <u>their</u> way, which hast been their own, not mine.

I desire that all be healed, set free and supplied of all good things. I have enumerated many times that which has been thine own chains which ye have forged for thine legirons. I shall name these one by one:

Indifference, is not one of the least links in the chain... it can be clarified as lethargy, spiritual blindness.

Denial of a power greater than mankind hast awakened unto.

Ego... negation of the "Word", the plan for thine release. In thine Ego ye <u>think</u> thineself Wise and self- sufficient. Ye spurn that which hast been given as a safeguard for thine safe passage... thine "Passport" into mine place of abode.

I have given forth individual invitations to join me in this the greatest celebration ever! Are ye ready to join with us The Host?

The Host of the Hosts stands ready to receive one and all which are prepared to come in. I have called this readiness thine "Passport". This, mine beloved children, is no pitiful fabrication of man's... for it, this Passport, is nothing more or less than thine own record, which ye have created.

Do ye remember that which I have given unto thee aforetime... the system of, and in which, ye keep thine own account, even unto every act and deed... and the result, the intent thereof? This is presented unto the 'Bar of Justice', where each and every one which comes forth from out the material World, that he might read, and from which he can make his own assessment. He cannot deny his own record, for before the Bar of Justice nothing can be hidden... <u>All is Light</u>!

So be it I Am the guard, the Porter at the Gate. I point the way... I give directions for thine <u>safe passage</u>. I am the One Sent that ye be brought back unto the place from which ye went out to take up human form for a time. Thine days are numbered... the time is come when ye are called: "Come Home, mine children". "Come Home!"

* * *

Sori Sori: "Let the light shine in!... Let the light shine in!" This shall be my sweet sonnet this hour, for 1 say unto thee, the Light shall shine forth as never before. There shall be great Light which shall be seen by many.

And there shall be some which shall go into the next realm knowing not that this day is come, the day for which they have waited. They shall be as the sleepers and they shall sleep on... while the Light shall be the Light, unseen by them which sleeps. So be it that they shall have their awakening in another "School", wherein they shall learn well their lessons, wherein they shall find themselves.

This is the word I would give unto thee at this hour. So be it and Selah.

* * *

Watch thine speech

Sori Sori: Mine beloved, I speak for the good of all mankind... yet unto each one which has a will to hear, by mine own hand I shall touch them, and they shall know mine touch and be quickened... then, they shall come to know that which have forgotten. They shall be as ones made new.

I say unto the ones which have eyes to see, that they shall see strange and new things. They shall hear and wonder, yet they shall be given comprehension of these new and strange things. While some shall fear and hide themselves, I say, it is the beginning of the new day, when the old shall pass away and all things shall be made new.

Ye shall be as one alert, and Look, Listen, and See. And learn that which ye see! Question that which ye hear! Ponder well that which is set before thee! Be not concerned what thine neighbor believes...be no part of gossip or their beliefs! First, examine that which is designed to make news, sensation, or fear, for it profits ye not. Let go of all thine tendencies to discuss that which is gossip, or repeated from an unhappy experience for to make conversation... it profits no one!

I have reminded thee aforetime, yet what do I hear? Have ye herd mine admonition given for thine <u>own sake</u>?

I need no other motive or incentive to warn thee of thine careless slothful ways, which is not productive unto thine grooming. I speak unto thee in this simple manner that ye might take note. Under no pretense do I make literary style to prove mine self... I need no critique!

So be ye as one ready to take mine simple words of wisdom, simply for the reason that they are intended for thine upliftment. For that have I spoken unto these ones which have a will to learn and be profited by such as I bring, in what-so-ever order i present it... for I speak for the benefit of ALL.

I repeat again! Yet again shall I repeat!... "WATCH that which comes out of thine mouth... WATCH the rebound action... and learn valuable lessons which will be very valuable in the days to come.

Think not that ye are so wise that ye refuse to accept my admonition. Betray not thine own self, for the day of accounting is at hand.

By mine own hand I have penned this simple admonition that ye might be aware of thine state of lethargy, or carelessness. I see... I hear... I speak in this manner for mine Love for each one of mine precious lambs which have wandered far afield. I now make it possible for thee to return unto my fold, where ye may be as one welcome...

* * *

The braggart - the fool

Sori Sori: For this hour let us share the joy of our communion, of our coming... and the joy of being received, and the joy of receiving. So be it such that others shall come to know.

So be it that I go forth with great joy, great anticipation, knowing that there is a great number which are with me, that they might come to know that they are not alone. It is said: Man walks not alone! It is so, for he is not alone... he is NOT alone! Nor is he hidden from our sight. We know where he is, where to find him, for there is no hiding place.

There is a part which hast been withheld for this time, and it is now come when man shall come to know what is meant by the "Host". When they shall walk and talk with us as ONE, when they shall differentiate between the Light and the dark.

It is said: There are ones which would lead thee astray, ride thy back, yet these have not come as ones prepared to lift thee up... they have come to do mischief, to enslave thee. It is now come when they shall know the one from the other. They have been told that which shall prepare them, (and) they shall know them by their "fruit".

They which come bearing witness of the Light ask no favors, set no traps, and give of themselves that others be blest. They give of themselves in selfless service, asking no reward. While the ones of darkness come in their own name, bearing witness of themselves, their "good deeds"... and they strut themselves before man, and boast of their greatness. I say, Behold him in his conceit... know him for that which he is.

See the one who stands watch... he which stands in silence, asking naught but to serve in the name of the Most High. These are the Servants of the Most High. These are the "Avatars", the ones which have made the supreme sacrifice of Self. They serve selflessly, and with joy. Know ye them by their fruits.

It is said that a tree which brings forth no fruit is better than the one which brings forth bitter and poisonous fruit, for it shall be up-rooted and cast into the fire. For it is no longer profitable for the poison to be about, and it shall profit them to know one from the other.

Take ye note of the BRAGGART, for he IS as the braggart. He is mighty in his own eyes, and powerful in his own words, for he hast a good opinion of himself... he THINKS himself wise indeed. Yet he makes a fool of himself, for he is known for that which he is. He is seen as a fool, and a fool knows not that he is foolish. He <u>thinks</u> himself wise, therefore he is wont to see his foolishness. He is wont to know his foolishness. He sees himself as great, and proud is he of his own portent, of his own part, which he hast portioned out for himself. For he is not aware of the Great fortune which awaits him when he is prepared to receive it. Let it be said: He shall be brot face to face with his foolishness. His folly shall be unto him a mockery, and he shall turn away from it in shame. So be it he shall learn the way of the Servant of the Most High Living God. So be it profitable unto him.

For this do we stand by... that he might come to know there is a plan by which he may be brot out of his bondage, and be forever free. So be it and Selah.

So be it as The Father would have it.

* * *

The churches vs the true foundation

Sori Sori: We shall continue our communication, for it is with communication that we are concerned now, at this time. The ones which have (falsely) builded upon mine foundation, upon mine name, shall fall, and they shall be as ones exposed for their fraudulent sayings and their pillage. They shall stand shorn of their self-glory, and then they shall cry out for mercy, for they shall be exposed. They shall stand naked!

Wherein is it said, "'There is no hiding place"? There is no hiding place! I see them which are want to cover themselves with mine name as fraudulent, as traitors, for I builded mine foundation on honor and integrity, on the just Law of Service... while I see them placing their yoke upon the neck of the workmen, the servants, making them subservient unto the plan which is designed to hold them slaves. I shall stand before them as the accuser, as the one which hast come to bear testimony of their evil doing. They shall cry for assistance, and their cry shall be heard, and they shall do that which shall justify the assistance... then it shall be given with wisdom and in Love.

Now it is said that they shall cry out for assistance... then when they have made proper restitution, they shall be assisted in the way in which they should go. I have said that they shall do that for which they came to do... that which they came to do was to be unto their brethren assistants, stewards of a great wealth, which was to assist the ones which were in need, the ones which had <u>earned</u> the assistance so properly provided by and thru the foundation (the Church). This foundation, of which I speak, was given over to them which are now within the world of men as provided by law, and they have not provided for them which were the ones which have earned their assistance. They have gone far afield that they glorify <u>their</u> name, and do honor unto themselves. They are prone to seek of man recognition that they might be glorified.

So be it I say, They shall be brot low. They shall cry out for the assistance of the Host, and they shall come to know the meaning of "Assistance". They shall be as ones <u>prepared</u> to accept our assistance... therefore they shall make restitution and come with clean hands, and bring themselves as ones prepared to receive their assistance.

It is said, "Ye shall have no false gods before thee"... yet I see them bowing before their false gods, their altars of great charm and of great price. Yet wherein do they profit thereby? They have sold their birthright for a poor penny; they have betrayed their trust. I say, they have betrayed their trust, and it behooves me to raise my voice against them, for I am the predecessor which built up the foundation on which they have amassed their fortune.

So be it they shall be as ones responsible for their folly, for they shall stand in judgment as ones adjudged and condemned, for they have been like unto the traitor. They have bound themselves by the law of justice to be adjudged... they have perjured themselves. So be it they shall find themselves unprepared; they shall find they have closed the door on their own fingers. So let it profit them to learn of me, for I shall bear witness of their wickedness, their transgressions. So be it and Selah.

* * *

Sori Sori: Again let us speak of the foundation which is built upon mine name, and they which have perpetuated the name which I have bequeathed unto them.

They, which are the custodians of the name (Jesus/Christ) and the wealth which hast been accrued thru the foundation which is founded upon mine name, have been as weak of Spirit. They are poor in Spirit; they have lost the spirit in which the foundation was formed/laid. They have been as ones taking credit unto themselves for <u>their</u> spirit, <u>their</u> generosity.

Wherein have they been as ones giving of themselves as a sacrifice, the self-sacrifice? They have lost sight of the Spirit in which I labored that others might be blest and profit by my experience. They have been as ones borne of the wind... they have passed this way and shall be known no more, for they have left not anything of themselves that men remember them. They stand stript of all their pride, self-glory, self-styled glory, for they shall face the Tribunal which deals out justice.

I come that they which may read might know that their conceit, deceit, and power which is pilfered, shall avail them naught save misery and humiliation. Humility is no part of these, mine heirs, for they know not humility. Yet they shall see the humble stand in their places, glorified, arrayed in fine linen, and wearing the Breastplate of Righteousness. So be it they shall see the humble sit with the righteous, and they shall find themselves as ones unprepared, unfit to enter in.

So be it I speak that which is necessary, that which is expedient and profitable, for it shall go down in history that I have spoken out in behalf of Justice and Truth.

Now ye shall enter into thy record this my word, and it shall stand as a testimony for them which shall read. I put not mine finger upon them, yet unto them which have eyes to see, let them see... them which have ears to hear, let them hear. And be ye not curious, for it is not of thy concern. Let it be revealed unto them to whom it is of concern. Be ye not concerned for that which is of no concern unto thee, yet that which IS of thy own concern shall be revealed unto thee. So be it and Selah.

* * *

The divine system is perfect

Mine beloved, I am come! I am come even as I said I would. I am the Wayshower... I am the Provender, without stint or lack. I give and I take... I provide as it is expedient and lawful. I know when to take and when to give for the good of every living creature, for I am the overseer of Mine Creation. Each receives as it is lawful, according unto his account. His balance is clearly recorded on his record, his <u>imperishable</u> record.

I Am the record keeper. It hast been said "I Am the ALL", therefore I am aware of Mine Creation, which is subject unto me, the Father of All that I have made to walk, fly, or creep. All are subject unto mine Law of Everlasting Life, the Law of Cycles... motion, rest, and balance. Mine creation is subject to the Law of Change, ever changing. There is no mistakes within mine Law.

While I have given unto Man custody, dominion over the Earth, he is yet subject to the 'Law of the **O** One. He has been bequest a "Free Will" that he learn the Law, and become as aware of this Law in which he hast his being. He shall come to know himself to be ONE with the ALL, for there are untold realms of Light in which every one of mine created Souls shall move and learn. Nothing is impossible... nothing is foolishness in Me. I have purpose in All Mine "Being".

I have a plan that man of Earth has not fathomed, for he is as subject unto the Law of the dimension in which he now exists. The everlasting man, the "Soul", the imperishable life of him, is subject unto the dimension or place in which he has qualified himself or itself. Each one evolves by its own ability to learn, according unto its will, which is his gift, his inheritance.

The everlasting Life changes, ever on the upward way, wherein "It" goes from one dimension, or state of being, to another... ever refining, ever gathering unto its learning greater wisdom, greater refinement, greater, purer Light... purer, greater, Awareness of his Oneness with the Source.

By the Law of the 'One' mankind becomes as gods. While he is not aware of his Oneness with the All, he gives unto himself credit for being self-sufficient. He knows not that he is subject unto the Law of his present dimension. According to his every thought, act, deed, or intent, he is credited. There is no error in the accounts... the Divine System is perfect.

* * *

A GREAT AWAKENING

Sori Sori: This is the time in which ye shall give unto them the word which I have spoken unto thee. I am the Lord God which sees and knows all, for I have created the heavens and the Earth and the fullness thereof, and I know that which I say and do.

It is for the good of all that I speak out this day. So let it be known that I am speaking unto all which have a mind to hear and listen, and heed that which I say. Be ye blest this day, and go ye forward, knowing that I am with thee, that I know thy needs and thine every thought... for, I AM that I Am.

* * *

"The inauguration of the new day"

Sori Sori: Mine beloved, it is now come that ye shall give unto the ones which have held steadfast this word which I have prepared for them, that they be alerted unto that which shall go forth in the light for the good of All.

Let this be the day long foretold. It is the Will of the Father that All might be prepared to witness the great Inauguration of the New Day, when there shall go forth a great light from within the cosmos. I say at this time, it is not afar off when the greatest of events ever, which shall be as nothing ever witnessed by mankind, shall be seen... through which many shall be awakened from their inertia. This shall be the Great Ascension, when the ones which are prepared shall be gathered up with the Hosts of Light, to return NO MORE into the darkness of the Earth's atmosphere, wherein they have been in bondage unto the flesh. The Law of the flesh shall no more a bound unto these which are prepared to arise as ones prepared to ascend with me and mine host. I say the Day of Deliverance is now come!

I am as one of the light, sent that they be brought out! For this is the Day of Fulfillment of the Law... that of the change of the planets, which shall be as foretold, yet not understood. Yet, man of flesh hast wandered and wondered, watched and calculated, measured and guessed, that which he cannot comprehend.

Now I am announcing unto all and sundry, the coming of the New Day, the Day of Deliverance! So be it, I am the one sent for to initiate this, plan, which was lain in the realm of the Temple of Light, wherein All things are known.

So be it that the Source of All Light is the giver and the taker... from this are we of the Host prepared to fulfill the promise made long ago, to fulfill the Law of the ONE wherein "<u>All shall be caught up in glory, as One</u>". Who among thee have understood this "Word"?

It is written: "Mine word shall not pass away"... It Has Not!.. It Shall Not! Be ye as one to hear and heed the directions given unto thee. Be ye not deceived, for there are false voices which would mislead thee... these are from the <u>Nether World</u>, the enemy, which is the 'deceiver', the 'father of lies'.

Ask of the All Loving and Just Father that ye be prepared to partake of this glorious day. Form no opinions or preconceived ideas of the Day of which I am speaking, for it is beyond and man's imagining.

Be at peace! Ask of me, the Lord God, the One Sent! Listen!.. Hear!.. See!.. and Obey!.. and all shall be as it is so decreed, and the Law shall be fulfilled. So be it and Selah...

* * *

"A great awakening"

Sori Sori: Mine beloved, I am now speaking for the good of all. There shall be a great the awakening which shall be as nothing known by man of Earth. There shall be a great change which shall effect all mankind, and the populace shall give of its self that mankind be as One. The hatred shall be no more… all shall be as One. Let it be as the Father hast willed.

The time comes quickly... the way is now clearly seen. While first there shall come a great change in the land, and the seas shall be misplaced... there shall be no place to run, no place to hide, yet I say unto thee, there shall be provisions for the ones which shall awaken unto the call which has gone out. The provisions are ready and the plan is perfect... the day is set in the heavens!

While no "man" knows the time, it is clearly seen from the point of view which is ours in the Realm of Light. Before the hour strikes within the realm of man, there shall go forth a great "Sound", which shall reverberate around the Earth. This shall be the day long spoken of.

It is the nature of man to forget, to ignore the warnings. It is mine intent that All be spared, yet each one is responsible for his\her self... None bring another! This is afore told to the ones which have ears and a will to hear, and by their own will to come at the signal, within the moment. In order and alone shall they come!

Remember, there shall be order! None shall panic, or they perish! Ye have been warned time after time... have ye heard? Have ye given thee thought? Or *have* ye heard? Be ye alert and doubt not that which is given unto thee through this means, for it is for the good of all.

I am the one which has provided the way for thee to safety, wherein ye shall be spared the destruction. It is the will of the Father that none perish, that All hear and respond... for it hast been written that the plan is in place, and provisions made. We of the host await our signal, our orders, even as ye of thine own realm.

The action of rescue shall be instantaneous, yet orderly, without any error what so ever... for long have we of our place of operation been prepared, ready to go forth as One Unit. Indeed, we know that which shall be done, for we are well aware of the order of things to come, and our part in them. We are now speaking again that ye each learn. Listen and be as one wise, obedient, in peace and readiness. No panic, or ye perish! Each shall prepare himself according to the instructions given unto him personally.

Be not so foolish as to run to thine neighbor to ask his opinion... Ye alone shall decide for thine self! It is for thine <u>obedience</u> that ye shall know for a surety What... When... Where ye shall be when the call comes... for none shall know of, or within himself, the moment of the call.

I shall speak again for thine sake. Listen!.. heed!.. and be at peace. I am the one which shall direct this plan on the behalf of all which are prepared. So be it and Selah.

* * *

The seventh trumpet

Sori Sori: The hour strikes with a mighty sound, a mighty blast from the seventh Trumpet hast now sounded, and yet the sleepers sleep on. I say, "Awaken all ye which sleepeth, for I Am Come!" I Am Come! Behold ye me... walk ye after me. Come and be ye healed of thine blindness, thine deafness, and walk ye as I walk that ye might enter into the realm of light where I abide. Let thine hands be turned to peace... Let thine heart be turned to love... Let thine feet be swift to follow in mine footsteps, and I shall lead thee out of bondage!

Think ye that ye are free? I say, ye sleepeth the sleep of the dead! Ye have forged for thine self thine own tomb from the stones of Earth... yea from the <u>material</u> of Earth hast thou made thine own tomb. Ye have been as ones ensnared by the prince of darkness. Ye have served him while he hast woven his spell about thee, as the spider hast woven his web about the victim of his.

Now, ye shall be wise indeed to list unto me and give heed unto mine word, for I am come that ye be delivered out. While I have given unto thee in full measure, thou hast run after "man" and their works, giving of thine time and energy... of the sweat of thine brow. Ye have emptied thine pockets that your churches be built to satisfy man's vanity, and wherein I can enter. I say unto thee O man, Where is thine vanity? Where is thine humility? It abides within thee!

I see thee as a bigoted generation, puffed up with great ideas and frivolous notions of me and about me... using many learned phrases, consuming time and energy... yet, hast thou heard mine preachments this day?

I say, ye are on dangerous ground. I call, Come up higher... stand upon the Rock which I AM. I am thine shield and thine buckler... I am thine <u>Honored</u> Priest from on High, sent of mine Father that ye might not perish. While ye have turned from me, I have watched and waited thine time of ripening, when I might pluck thee out and bear thee up. So be ye one which hears mine words and gives unto me credence, and I shall touch thee and give unto thee favor.

While unto them which deny mine word, make a mockery of mine word, I shall say unto them: "Depart from me, ye have made a mockery of the word of God... I know ye not, neither do ye know me. Go unto thine place, while I go unto mine Father which hast sent me".

It is said, ye shall prepare thineself for the receive me. I have sent forth the word; have ye accepted it as it is given?... or, have ye taken it and gilded it with thine own gloss, thine own opinions, unto thine own satisfaction that it be acceptable unto thine peers? I ask of thee: Hast thou accepted me for that which I Am... or, hast thou set up thine own temple and placed thine own word upon the altar, and set <u>thineself</u> up as the priest, calling thineself wise and good?

Oh foolish ones, I ask of thee, open up thine eyes... see that which goes on about thee and know ye that the dragon stands ready to devour thee! I say, see the hand of God which is strong and mighty, wherein thine safety lies! Behold ye the light which I AM... the one sent of God the Father. I come that ye perish not!

While it is for thine own good that I come, I am come out of the light that love be manifested within man which is within (upon) the Earth, and from which hast sprung much suffering. Let it cease! Let it be no more! For I see it as done, therefore I am patient.

Yet ye are wanderers upon the periphery of the universe, and ye know not that which lies ahead of thee. I say, Watch! Walk with circumspection, for there are many pitfalls. I have pointed them out one by one, so let thine eyes be opened, thine feet planted firmly on firm ground, and ye shall not go down.

So be it I have spoken. Let it be known that I Am the Son of God, sent that ye be lifted up. So it is... so shall it be! Amen and Selah.

* * *

Sori Sori: Mine beloved, I am now speaking unto all. This is the time spoken of when there shall be great fires, great floods, greater carnage. I say, it is come, and I see that many are yet asleep. I have called many times, "Awaken!", yet many are in their places of entertainment, eating and drinking, making merry, while others perish... giving no thought of the morrow.

It is said, there shall be great and sudden changes... it is so! While they sleep, many shall go the way of flesh by the way of fire, of water, and by the hand of man and his weapons of death.

Have ye given thought of mine "word"? Have ye given unto me credit for knowing that which I say? Have ye thought me playing foolish games? I am the one which sees both ways, backward and forward. I see many caught unaware... then they shall cry, "<u>Why didn't somebody do something?</u>"

I ask one and all: Be ye up and about that "Something", which I say, is thine own preparation to meet the time prophesied... when ye might stand shorn of all that which ye have... yea, even unto thine physical vehicle! Be ye not so foolish as to mock me, for I see and know as ye do not.

For the most part mankind has not heard mine call... for this shall he be overtaken in his lethargy, his inertia, before he awakens. It is mine Will, mine intent, that All be spared... I am the one come that it be! Let it be the day of awakening! I am the one sent that ye be spared! Hear me, and be glad...

* * *

The day of decision

Sori Sori: Mine beloved, I am now speaking unto All, for the good of All. I say unto them, that it is now come when there shall be great changes which shall come suddenly... for the good of all shall they come!

The populace at large shall be in lethargy, and they shall be as asleep. For I have been calling unto them for long years... I have given unto them signs and wonders... I have set the time for the seasons. The days have been shortened, and the way hast been made obvious that a time hast been set by a power greater than mankind. Even the stars bear witness of the change. By the signs set in the heavens shall ye which sleep be awakened.

Let it be for the good of all, for it is foreseen that change is necessary, (for) the lethargy is as a bound about them. Time is now that the awakening shall take place. It shall be sudden as far as mankind calculates his time. By the time he awakens he shall wonder what has happened in his world and unto him, for it shall be as new and strange unto him, yet he shall be as one on whose shoulders rests his choice which way he goes. It is so written that this is "The Day of Decision".

These sleepers shall remember in their awakening that which they have been given in their sleep time, for their ears and eyes shall be opened unto the New Day. Many shall come forth as New Born... these shall be as ones which remember the sleep time no more, while others shall remember and wonder at their slowness. Some shall find they have betrayed themselves... these shall know great remorse, and cry out for help. Their suffering shall be great, even though it be for their own progress... slow though it be!

It is the Law of the **O** one that there be no stagnation. Forever and forever there is growth, movement forever and for all time to come... forward movement, toward the All Light, the Source of All.

The progress is not always seen by mankind, as he is bound by flesh and knows not himself to be immortal. It is now come that he hast been given the choice to arise above the darkness of his own way, which he has gone in his sleep time... for he shall become dissatisfied with his apathy, his lethargy, and seek the Light. These shall be the first to come up higher and see with greater vision. These shall be as the ones which shall be as beacon lights unto the laggards.

It is now come that many shall come to know that they are free to choose their own way... that no man is responsible for their choice or release from bondage. When they have given unto themselves credit for being their own judge and choose the way they should go, they are as ones responsible for all they do. No other shall take their responsibility.

While it is said many times that there are the beacon lights to show the way, the ones which have the will to follow that light shall see and follow there on the lighted path. There shall be one which stands ever ready to give of his love and himself in wisdom. He is the guiding and All-Knowing Light... the Truth and the Way to eternal peace and joy.

* * *

The fire of the spirit

Sori Sori: This is mine time with thee, and for this hast thou come unto this Altar. The way is clear that ye come. Thou hast prepared the way for us of the mighty host that they receive us. For this shall we touch them which are prepared to receive us.

Yet, let it be understood that there are yet many which are not prepared... these shall wait in the places prepared for them. Their waiting shall not be easy, for it is now come when the changes shall be the poor part of their waiting. They shall feel their impoverishment of spirit, their inadequacy to cope with the situations which shall face them... yet face them they shall!

It is said that the Spirit shall be poured out on all flesh... so it shall!.. and the unprepared shall feel the fire. The Spirit shall not comfort them, for they shall be as ones running to and fro as the displaced ant, knowing not the cause of their discomfort. I say, they shall be as the displaced ant, knowing not the cause of their discomfort.

Pity are they, for they have not heard that which I have said. They run as ones which have found the rainbow's end... yet it is elusive... they reach it not! For this do I say unto them: Seek ye first the Kingdom of Heaven, and all things shall be given unto thee. First I say, prepare thyself for to receive the gifts I bring unto thee.

Mine hand I extend, and hast thou accepted it? Hast thou given unto me credit for knowing that which I say?.. that which I am about?

Hast thou given unto me credit for being that which I Am?

Where hast thou given unto me the gifts of the spirit?

Hast thou been true unto thyself?

Hast thou portioned out unto me the true, the real... or, hast thou thot to deceive me in thine time of reckoning?

I say unto thee: Oh ye which hast not heard, it is time that ye hear and see, for I shall do a mighty work, and ye shall do well to see and know that I am aware of that which goes on. I shall fulfill mine mission... then I shall go as 1 come, while thou hast slept. It shall be as ye Will it!

I have said: Come ye out from amongst them and I shall lead thee, yet I see thee as ones looking for signs and wonders in thine haste and discontent. Let thine feet be swift to do mine bidding, and I shall give unto thee without stint. Therefore I have given unto thee the word... ye have but to accept it in the name of the Father, Solen Aum Solen.

Thine eyes shall be turned toward me... the Light which I AM. It is said, ye shall be as one true unto thy trust... this is thine part. For to betray one's trust is to be as the fool... the fool indeed, for there are none so foolish!

While it is said, I am the Lord God, thou hast thot to deceive me or find me sleeping. Nay, mine little ones, ye shall not find me napping. There is not one amongst thee that hast found me off guard, for I am true unto mineself... I am alert! I see and know that which goes on in thy world, for the Earth is mine, and all things which are created of me I shall claim. All that which thou hast created of confusion and in thy foolishness shall be as naught, for I have decreed the perfection of mine creation... and it is well, for i have made it Good.

There is but the Light, and it is given unto me to be one with It... I Am The Light of The World! There is but one Lord God, and none shall mock me or make of me a fool. I know the Law, there. fore I say unto thee: Be ye as ones prepared to go where I go, and I shall lead thee aright. So be it and Selah.

***

Choose ye

There went out from the country a wise man, and he knew that which he went forth to do. As he went about that which he was sent to do, some saw him and feared him, some saw him and followed him. Some followed for miracles and morsels, some followed him for the love and wisdom he did impart unto them which believed. These which believed followed in his footsteps... they heard, and acted upon his word.

Yet there came a time when they were tried... sorely tried and tested. There were ones which stood the test, and these are mine flock, the servants which I have served and sustained. These are the ones that

I have called to go forth this day to prepare the way before me. These are the ones which are mine hands and feet made manifest upon the earth this day. I've called them, "Come! Come!", and they have hastened to do mine bidding, for they know mine voice and hasten they out to give unto them mine message, mine word. Let all which hear mine voice come unto me, and I shall give unto them without stint. They shall receive of me as I have received of mine Father.

I say unto all, Come! Yet there be but few who hear that which I say. They are pre-conditioned by the voice of the deceiver. So let them choose this day which way they go... I bring none against their will. Be ye as one blest to hear and know me... I am he which is sent that ye be lifted up. So let it be as the Father wills it. Amen and Selah

* * *

Thine new place of abode

Mine beloved: Let us give unto these, to whom I have sent mine word through thee, a new lesson which shall carry with it great power and love. I say unto each of these ones, that I am come as man, clothed in flesh, even as each of them. I am that and more! I am no less for coming as mankind, for I am One with the ALL, the "Source", O, without beginning or end.

I am the Son of God, sent to find the lost, the ones which have forgotten their heritage from whence they came or whither they go. These are the ones referred to as the 'Prodigal Sons', which have long since wandered in darkness... wandering and wondering; "Who am I?.. Where came I?.. Where goest I?

Yet they see not or hear not mine call... Come!.. Come!.. Come unto me with clean hands, a contrite heart. it is for this that I have taken upon mine self human form, that (because) ye, mine beloved ones, have waited for the form like unto thine own. Yet it binds me not... I am fully aware of mine Oneness with the Source of All Life and Light. In this Source I am complete... with the power to give and to take, to bring forth or to send away. I create that which is needful for the plan given unto me of the Father which hast sent me.

The hour hast struck when humanity shall Awaken... or, be as ones removed into a place within the firmaments like unto their present environment, in which they might complete their maturity, their growth into the Light. This is the plan of unfolding Truth and Justice unto a backward and dark world, yet to be awakened. For this I have returned unto thee, the ones which have a will to come out from the traitors and the infidels which make mock of me.

I am He which has come long ago. Then I said: "I shall go to prepare a place for thee"... So I did go! I have prepared the places, each like unto thine own nature, thine own making. I have designed a place wherein ye, each, shall find that for which ye have prepared to receive. Ye shall know that which ye have created therein, and ye shall <u>own</u> that creation, to do with as ye will... for that (free will) is the only thing ye shall take with thee into thine new place of abode.

The <u>Will</u> is thine Key to the door ye have shut which ye shall now open. There shall be no mistakes, for all is according unto the Law of Love and Justice. As ye have prepared thine self, so shall ye receive...

* * *

The redeemer"

Sori Sori: Mine beloved, I am now speaking for the good of all. I give unto thee the power to use mine hand and take the privilege of using thine, for ye have given thine consent\freewill unto me to use thine hand. We are as One! I give unto thee mine hand, ye give unto me thine will, therefore we are as One in this effort to reach the ones which are crying for light.

Now let us abide by our Fathers will, for are we not brot forth for this, His will? Are we not His will made manifest in flesh? I say, we are One in the "All"... we are not excluded from our Source! It is because of, or for, the reason that He is, that we are! We, ye and I, know ourself to be... therefore we know He, the Source, which we call "Father", is that which sustains, upholds, and has a perfect plan for our eternal Being.

Let us reason: Why would the Source not know His plan for His creation... a Perfect creation! Would He forget his wayward Son... forsake him, His "prodigal Son"? I say unto all and sundry: Ne'er does He forsake one of His children! While the Son hast forgotten the Father and lost his way, it is now come when it is the time of <u>remembrance</u>! For this do I come crying, "Awaken! Hear me and be ye blest of me and by me, for I am come as One knowing mine Oneness with the Source. I have received mine inheritance in full. This is the will of our Father, that ALL be brought to remembrance, and returned unto thine rightful estate as One with me.

Can, or will, ye mine 'flock', hear me... listen unto me... be as One with me? Spurn not mine call! Give unto me thine hand in trust... no doubt, no deceit. Be not so foolish as to try to deceive thine self... for this is that which I call the 'traitor' unto thine self.

It is given unto me to know these for that which they are. None deceive me! I am the one which ye cry unto when you are in the way of the Seeker of Truth... in humility, sincerely, humbly asking for Light. When thine way seems obscure, and thine heart is crying for help, thine feet sore, I hear thine pleas for assistance.

I come in many forms. I am not limited by any form, for I am one which has all power over any form. Yet mine beloved children, I say unto thee, there is a time allotted unto each and every one, when he shall arise up and call out: "I am weary!.. I am sick! I am willing!.. I come home of mine own will! Come unto me or I perish!"

Beloved ones, I know the way unto thine eternal freedom. I come offering thee freedom, eternal freedom from bondage... yet ye have forgotten such as I now proffer thee. I am come that ye might awaken. Come with a contrite heart, clean hands, and give unto me credit for being the Son of the Father which hast sent me to lead thee, to return thee as the prodigal, home.

Be ye not so foolish as to mock me, or to turn thine face from me, for ye know not that which i have in waiting for the Son found and returned. Be ye blest to <u>know</u> as I know. So be it and Selah... I am the Redeemer...

* * *

The Impostors

Sori Sori: Be ye as the hand of me and record for them this mine word, that they might know that I am within the place wherein I am as one alert, knowing that which goes on within the world of men.

I say unto them: I see the ones which run to and fro, as ones curious, looking for signs and wonders... "making the rounds" as it were. They are as ones "prospecting", looking for the elusive gold. It is not to be found beneath the rainbow's end!

I say they seek not after me, they follow not the way I point them, they walk not in mine footsteps. They follow strange gods... they seek out places wherein there are ones which set themselves up. They have not learned the true from the false.

Yet I have given unto them the "Way of the Initiate", the "Laws", the "Portions" (Scripts) which are designed to set them aright, feet firmly plant on solid ground... yet they are found seeking out the ones which have set before them a table of poison on which to feast. It is given unto them to partake, knowing not that they shall sicken and suffer, from it and <u>because</u> of their gluttony. They are forewarned: "Partake not of <u>their</u> board", for I have set up mine Altar and I have placed upon it the Bread of Life, which ye shall eat of and be fed and nourished, and suffer not.

While it is now come that they are but the foolish, casting about in dangerous waters, they shall find they have baited their own hooks wherein they shall be caught, wherein they shall be hooked. I say, "hooked". It is well to use the word "hooked", for they understand that which I say, so let it profit them.

Now, ponder ye well these mine words, all ye which run after the ones <u>claiming</u> to be the "One Sent"... for I say, they shall find themselves caught up short. These are but impostors... IMPOSTORS I say! Mine servants put not their foot into their trap! They keep their own counsel and waste not their energy for such as that which I abhor. I say, I abhor such deceit/deception, for it is the way of the dragon to deceive them which are not learned in the way of the wise.

So let it be well with thee, O ye of little knowledge! Seek ye the Light and I shall lead thee all the way. Fear not! Flaunt not thy puny knowledge, for it is of the lesser school. Be ye as one humble and be ye as one prepared to learn of that which I give unto thee, for I see thee in thy need. I supply it, and ye shall be wise indeed to heed this mine word, for I am not so foolish as to give unto the babe mine pearls of great price, which knows not their worth.

* * *

Discernment!

Sori Sori: For this hour let us give unto thee a part which shall be for them which "claim" for themselves the part of "healer". These are as the ones which seek to display their skills, their power, their wisdom. They are living in an illusion.

The one which claims for <u>himself</u> the power to heal the body of such infirmities as that of palsy, broken bones, and the many pitiful cases of distress, is but deluding themselves, for the healing power does not lie within them! They are the ones who "claims to have the power which is not theirs. They are fraudulent, for I say unto them: Healing is a gift... the power is a gift... and the gift cometh from the Light, the Source of Light.

The ones which have the <u>True</u> gift boasts not of his powers. He struts not, for he knows that he is endowed with the gift which is the greatest gift bestowed upon man. Yet to heal him of his infirmities is not his greatest work... to heal him in his parts, whereby <u>he</u> might discern his <u>own</u> malady, and be as one clean of spirit... and within himself go as one prepared to clean out his <u>own</u> closet, and be as one clean of Spirit.

Wherein hast it been said that the ones which are as the "walking dead" take up habitation within the unclean? And then they speak of "reincarnation" as they knew themselves to be another so-and-so, until they believe themselves to be great and mighty kings and pharaohs of the Earth... while they are but hosting within their aura the impostors of the dark world of the discarnate spirits, the world of the "dead".

Death is not understood by man of flesh, for he knows not that he dies unto the flesh but once. He walks many times in flesh, yea, many times... yet he hast not fully known the magic, the so-called miracle of birth and death. The magic hast not been understood, yet the ones which practice "black magic" hast stumbled upon some of the principles, which are then used to confuse the unknowing ones.

I say, they are working their illusionary principles this day to ensnare the ones which know not. These are the ones which shall be snared in their own trap, in their own net. They shall find themselves face to face with their foolishness, for they shall be called to account for such as they have done in <u>mine name</u>… for I have not called them to do these things which they call "miracles". I say, they shall be held responsible for their own traps in which they shall be held bound. So be it and Selah. It is the law, the Just Law, that they learn.

It is said, the true soldier wears not the insignia of the enemy. I see them as one wearing the Sacred Symbols while (also) displaying the insignia of the dragon. These insignias are written within the aura which they claim to know all about. They are as the false ones!

For this I say unto thee, hear them out, see them for that which they do... they are as ones playing with their toys. While I see them as babes which have not learned the first figures of their tables, the first of their alphabet, they simply understand not that which is given so freely from the "Fount of Life". They walk in mystery and live in mystery, for they are born in mystery.

It is the way of the Mystic to seek Light, yet he claims not to know All things. He is very sure there is yet greater things that he must learn before he can truly say, "I am wise!" The truly wise do not boast or strut, claiming to do the things accredited to the Magi, for he walks quietly and gently. As for the most part he is unknown, unsung, and ofttimes he is insulted and disgraced amongst men, yet he fears naught. He hears that which they say, yet he feels only compassion for the little ones which know him not. He walks with sure foot, knowing from whence his strength, from whence his tributes, cometh.

I say he, the initiate, asks no recognition of men. He finds no consolation within their insincere compliments, their laurels. He asks not, neither does he bid for their accolades. He goes about his business quietly and as one knowingly. He wavers not before the breeze which blows his way... he is sturdy, strong in his knowing. He rushes not after signs and wonders, seeking the favors of men, recognition of his gifts, his worth.

This I would have them ponder upon! Consider well that which I have caused to be recorded for them which are of a mind to follow me where I go. I am free to go and come, for the Father hast given unto me passport. I am not denied! This is mine word unto them which would be free even as I.

Mine word I give freely... freely ye shall accept, and freely shall ye come unto me as one clean, as one prepared to enter in. So let it be as ye will it!

None bring thee against thy will... none cleanses thy house of its foulness... yet I send unto thee ones which have gone the strait and narrow way in which I have led them. These are mine servants which I have called to assist thee, that ye too might find thy way. Yet I see them which are rebellious turn from the servant, thinking themselves wise! They go out as ones knowing not the first lessons which the initiate must first learn... that of obedience and respect.

The way of the Initiate is not easy. It is the way in which I point thee, and ye shall find therein many snares... yet I have plainly pointed them out, one by one, that ye be not ensnared by the dark one. So be it I watch with diligence that the young ones (the neophytes) fall not, for I am not unmindful of them which are prone to seek Truth, the Light which fails not.

The way of the Initiate is strait! The way is exact, and turns neither to the left or the right. It is the way that leads to joy and Peace everlasting. So be it Amen and Selah.

* * *

As ye make it!

Sori Sori: Mine beloved, I shall speak for the good of all mankind. Ye shall accept this assignment of delivering it unto them which are seeking Truth, "Light", which I Am. The ones which are fortunate to find shall be as ones to give unto me credit for being that which I Am. These shall be as ones to open their eyes that they might see before them that which is going on in the 'World of Man'. They shall see and understand that these are the days foretold of olden times.

I say unto all and sundry, the time of fulfillment is now come, when ye shall see these things recorded in the annals of thine history which is now upon thee. Enumerate these prophecies if ye will, (yet) these are not of a day, nay, neither a year... these are of many generations.

The sleepers <u>shall awaken</u>! These shall be delivered out before the great and terrible day of sorrow. These shall be as ones which have the will to come out from among the ones which know not, and (which) will to stay in the dark among the 'outcasts' which have not accepted their "Inheritance". I say, it is the poison of the 'Dragon' which hast been their choice... not of the Light are these which are bringing about the fulfillment of the prophecies. These ones which have given themselves unto the 'Dragon' shall come to know wherein they have been betrayed by him from the underworld (which is now open unto the 'World of man' today, as ye know it.

The sleepers which are awakened shall learn of me, as one which has returned at this time to rescue them from "the Second Death". I come crying, "Come! Come! Come ye up! Come ye out from the traitors, the ones which refuse mine Light which I bring. For thine own sake do I come as One sent of mine Father that ye be delivered from bondage... that ye be as ones "Enlightened".

Yet I see that which I am now giving unto mankind freely for thine own deliverance, shall be as heresy in their estimate. So be it! I am come that the ones which have the will and stamina might come unto me as the 'Light Bearer", the "Wayshower"... their "Bondsman" if ye will! I say, I am called by the ones which have awakened, the"Redeemer". So be it, I am no less by any name... neither am I any greater. I AM that I Am.

I ask of no man his opinion, his praise of me and mine "word" which shall not pass away. For unto the ones who mock me, which spurn my call, 1 say: Mine 'Word' shall return to 'haunt' them when they cry for help, alone and forgotten, where they shall review their own rebellion and foolishness.

I say unto mankind: This is the "Day of Decision", the "Day of Atonement", yet, it is as ye make it! I am no respecter of persons... I come that ALL be brought out before the day of great sorrow. By thine own will shall ye be as one to choose which way ye go... I bring no one against thine will.

Hear ye that which I am saying? I am speaking loud and clear that ye with ears to hear might know that which I say! I fashion mine communiques in such a manner that the ones which seek of the Light might find. I speak in many tongues, in many ways, that the seeker, the one which cries for light might find.

For this I say unto each and every one: Remove thineself from the ways of the 'World of Darkness'. Give unto NO man a penny for thine salvation, for he is not as one empowered to deliver thee. The one which asks for the coin is in no way the enlightened one. Be ye not his pawn, his captive, for it is seen by the Lighted Ones that that which they proffer thee in exchange shall be as naught in the time of need, the Day of Reckoning.

Be ye one and all blest which accept that which I bring freely, lovingly awaiting thine call, thine answer to mine call...

I Am the Wayshower

* * *

The underworld

Sori Sori: Mine beloved, I am now speaking for the good of all, yet I am giving this 'Word' unto them through thine hand, as mine made manifest, I say, this is the time long foretold, that there shall be greater fires, greater winds, greater floods and sorrow. The ones from the pit of darkness shall come out as mad and horrible creatures... such fear mankind hast never known! These are the demons which have no mind or intent to become as changed in any manner. These are the ones which hold the "Scythe of Death"... they go forth to destroy in any fashion possible.

They 'possess' the unwary, the ones which are exposed unto these creatures of darkness, the ones which inhabit the places of darkness wherein the debaucheries are committed willingly by the ones weak of character... with no thought of the "Light of the World" which I Am... which is now come to give of mine self that they be as ones to see and know that which they are exposed to in the places wherein these beings from out the pit linger. They (these dark entities) have no sense of morality or love... they are creatures of the underworld!

I am now calling unto each and every one which has the will to be free, to learn of the way in which they shall go to protect themselves. I am now speaking unto the ones which give of themselves in the practice of sex amusement, fantasies, 'black magic' entertainment, which is so fashioned to entrap the unwary one, old and young alike!

These are ones which contaminate the very air they breathe! I say, these dark ones have no scruples, no morals, no thought of the results of their future. It is foretold in the tomes of thine literature... Know ye of these! Take heed!.. for they have been given for thine knowledge that ye be as ones on guard, not as for thine entertainment to appease thine evil intent. Be ye as ones alert! For this do I cry out unto all: Give unto thine own self credit for knowing that that which ye do brings unto thee the results of thine acts. As ye sow, so do ye reap!

I have said many times, "Come ye out from these dark ones which know not the light". Have ye heard the warnings? Have ye given thought unto these?.. unto thine tomorrow? Remember... there is no death! Life goes on!.. ye choose in what state or condition!

Be ye not deceived by the ones which have been hoodwinked, the ones which have not given unto thee the truth of conditions on the dark side, and the Light side. Which side have ye learned of? What have ye learned? What are ye doing for to enrich thineself as ye prepare for thine tomorrow? Ponder well these mine words, for ye have free will to choose!

I am come that ye might be spared. Think not that I am a traitor come to set a tap for thee or to pick thine pocket. I need no such as ye have to give. I am the wayshower unto greater heights, greater light, where there is eternal freedom from want.

Be ye as one on whose shoulders rests thine own responsibility. When ye are of a mind\intent to hear me, to answer my Call, I shall give unto one and all my hand as an Elder Brother, in love, compassion, and wisdom.., for I am sent from the Source of mine Being, even as ye. I say, Awaken! Awaken! Awaken unto thine True Being! I am come that ye be spared.

I am the wayshower... so be it and Selah.

* * *

They follow him without question!

Sori Sori: Mine word I would give unto them which seek Truth and understanding, these which seek shall find me... for I am come that they might have light, that they be delivered from their bondage. Bondage!.. I say they are bound by ignorance and the opinions of men.

I have said, they know me not, yet i stand ready to reveal mine self unto them which heed mine word and keep mine law. I've revealed unto them the law, yet they turn away... as they are ones following after the deceiver, which makes of them puppets, robots, tools within his hands, which he uses for his own selfish purposes. He, the deceiver, beguiles them with foul stench words, and they are so foolish as to heed him and ask for more. Poor foolish children!

I say, I am under no bondage unto him, the deceiver, therefore I owe him no allegiance. I am sent of mine Father that they be freed from him, from his cunning and bondage.

How comes that they prefer his cunning?

How comes that they follow him without question?

How comes that they question me which they have not tested, and which they serve not? I have asked of them: Come! Come! Follow me! Try me and ye shall not find me wanting, for I am he which hast said, "I shall return to find mine own ... that I shall gather up mine own that they might go where I go, that they might receive their eternal inheritance, even as I have.

Now it is come when the gathering is come. I tell thee of a surety, it is now come when I am come to find mine own. I am calling unto them as never before... some hear and respond, some refuse to move, others deny that which is said unto them. While some hear and respond, come and follow me; these I shall give unto as I have spoken, as I have promised, for I do not make promises I do not keep!

I am not a traitor... I am the Lord God sent of mine Father to find them which He has given into mine keeping. Yet I tell thee, I cannot bring them against their will... therefore I am not as the ass, they ride not mine back. They shall come of their own will and their reward shall be theirs. They shall earn their right to call themselves "Sons of God".

I am not of a mind to enslave them. They are free to come if they so will, or, to remain in their darkness and bondage and suffer the consequence thereof, Lo, I say the reward of following me is beyond man's imagining and his expectation, for no man, no language, can describe the fullness of mine abode... the beauty, the freedom, the joy which they shall have as their own when they have earned it. It is theirs by divine right.

Therefore I am sent that they know there is relief from their suffering and bondage, yet failure to accept that which I offer is the deceiver's first interest. He provides all the trappings that ye be turned from me, turned from the Light into the way of darkness, wherein you find the idiot's delights, wherein you dance unto the tunes he sings to delight the senses of the foolish. They dance to the pipers tunes until they find they have been deceived, then they cry loud and long, "Lord! Lord!.. have you forsaken me?" I ask of these foolish ones, "Where wast thee when I stood crying unto thee?" I ask thee, "Have ye given unto me service, or credit for being that which I am?

There _are_ ones which have heard me and answered me, which are serving me with their whole heart... and these are, for the most part, unnoticed, unheard, unseen by the foolish ones which serve the deceiver. Lest ye find thine self entrapt, I ask of thee, arise from thine dens of iniquity, thine places of gaming and the temples of idolatry... and come out from among them and see that which I do. Listen unto mine plea, and try me and mine way, and be delivered from thine torment and bondage. So may it be according to the Father's Will... Amen and Selah

* * *

First come, first serve

Sori Sori: Mine beloved, I speak unto each in the manner I see fit. I am no respecter of persons... I give unto each according to their preparation or capacity to receive me. I am not of a mine to go into the pit to find the laggards... these shall 'come out' to find me of their own free will. I have said many times, they are asleep, they are dreaming, fantasizing, which shall be a stone in their shoe when they come late.

Know ye this true-ism, "First come, first serve"? These true-isms serve a purpose in the world of darkness. The populace rushes to be "first" for to get the "best", first... yet, when I call, "*Come, I have riches unknown unto thee that never depreciate*", the laggard waits his convenience...

I say unto the laggard which first gives unto the (other) laggard his energy, that he\she is a fool indeed, for all is not well in the shadow world!

I am speaking plainly that I might make clear mine intent. I give first, unto the ones which come first, the choicest of the "vine". Be ye blest this day, for ye have answered mine call first... So be it and Selah.

* * *

Who is the "aggressor"?

Sori Sori: Be ye as the hand of me and record mine word unto them. Say unto them as I would say, that there is peace for them which <u>find</u> it. There is peace for them which have peace within them. They shall establish peace within themselves, and they shall be as ones at peace. They shall find such peace as shall benefit them, for they shall be blest as I have been blest of mine Father.

These which are prepared for the acts of war and aggression shall find that there is NO PEACE. They shall be as allies with the forces of darkness, and shall suffer by their own unknowing. Yet I say unto them, "Ye shall find no peace, for peace is not established within thee". Fear not... bear ye no arms, be ye not the aggressor. Peace I offer thee, yet ye have not accepted it, for thou hast been as one <u>with</u> the aggressor, and thou hast not needed mine word. Thou hast set thyself apart, and put thy hand into the pocket of the ones which labor for bread, that ye wage war on the aggressor? Who is the "aggressor"? Thou hast been both aggressor and oppressor, for thou hast done that which thou hast accused thine enemy of.

Hear ye me, O ye men of Earth... hear ye what I have said! 'Hear ye me, for I shall set mine hand against thee and ye shall feel the strength thereof, for I am He which is sent that there be Light. Light I bring, for I am the Light of the World, come that there be Light within the realm of man.

Now ye have gone so far that there shall be certain action taken, and it shall be as nothing before seen, and it shall be part of the great and Divine plan. Ye shall stand as one prepared to go where sent, and do that which is given unto thee to do, for it is clearly written that there shall be great and swift changes... changes which shall affect thine course, which shall bring about great and wondrous changes upon and within thy world, and all men shall be influenced thereby. Let it be for thy own sake, for it is said, "It is Well", It is good that these changes be brot about, for man hast gone headlong unto his own downfall. Yet he hast been warned to Halt! Stop! Look! Listen!.. and consider the end of his way, for he knows not that he is the cause of the end. His time is come... the end is at hand. It is said, thy days shall be shortened for thy own sake. It is So! So be it and Selah.

* * *

"Unto every ruler of every country"

Sori Sori: The Mighty Council hast decreed that there shall be an alert sounded throughout the civilized countries, and each one shall be as ones put on notice, for I say to all, that there shall be no atomic bombs or any such devices detonated. For should man take the Law into his own hands after this fiat goes forth, they shall be removed from the Earth by forces they have not reckoned with.

Now, it hast been said by the foolish (which know not that they are part of that which they shall reckon with), that we are prophets of doom. Yet <u>they</u> are the ones which have set into motion that which shall bring about their own doom.

I say unto them at this time: Halt ye! Go no further with thy nefarious sciences for destruction. I am speaking out through the voices of mine chosen servants which have worked with me for the good of all mankind, that they (mankind) be spared. I have trained them, and they have been obedient unto me, mine voice, and willing to serve in any field on which they are called for duty. I am not of a mind to stand by and see the work of the great overseers of this nation, this country, this world, this planet, go for naught... therefore, I say to every ruler of every country: Be ye up and about the business at hand. Lay aside the poisons, the lethal implements of war. Remove thineself from such as would destroy the World of mankind... be no part of it! Turn thine energies to peace and love, for the time quickly approaches when ye shall see that which has been set into motion heretofore, and ye shall be caused to remember these, mine words.

Now I say to all, everywhere... that mine voice shall be heard throughout the lands of Earth, and every word I say or have said shall be brought to memory. I say unto the ones which think themselves wise: Feign not wisdom ye fools, for ye have not reckoned with the forces of nature, or with the ones which have stood by ready for action, while ye have gone headlong into the plans which shall be unto thee thine own downfall.

Give unto me credit for knowing that which I am doing, for I say unto thee, I am the one who hast the power and authority to remove thee into a far corner, wherein ye shall be as ones far removed from the comforts and conveniences of this planet, which hast given unto thee the life and comfort ye have now planned to desecrate. My hand is upon thee, and I say unto thee: Halt ye within thine tracks! From this day forward ye shall be on trial... and pray you that ye be no part of the great power which shall be set against thee, for ye are working with forces ye know not of.

Now, I am not finished... I shall speak again and again that ye perish not! Be ye as one prepared for the results of thine actions, which shall surely and truly come back unto thee threefold. I have spoken and mine words have been recorded as spoken... so let it be!

I AM that I Am... Sananda

* * *

A rude awakening

Sori Sori: Ye shall give unto them this word and they shall remember that which I say unto thee, for it is come when mine hand shall be swift and they shall see the movement thereof. For the time is now come when they shall stand in awe of the things I shall do, and it is well.

So be it I say unto them, hasten ye to prepare thineself, for the day is upon thee when ye shall be called, and no man knoweth the hour... yet I say, "be ye as one prepared".

Fret not for the ones which listen not unto me, for I shall give unto them that which shall awaken them. Their awakening might not be unto their liking, yet they shall profit thereby. It shall be called the "Rude Awakening"!

While they refuse to give heed unto mine word or walk in mine way, they wait and sing the songs of the foolish, dance unto their pipers. While I cry from the mountain top, "Come unto me and be ye enlightened", they sit and wait... pity is their plight!

Woe unto them who follow the foolish priests who set themselves up. I say, harken unto me, the one sent that ye be enlightened and delivered out of bondage. While it is time, I ask thee again and again, "Why art thou so sluggish, ye faithless servants"? Thou hast slept while thine cities burned! Thou hast slept while thine children hast fought for their lives!.. while thine brothers and sisters have fallen prey unto the dragon!.. while the wee ones have been succored at the breast of the whore. Now ye shall see the folly of thine time!

All thine petitions have not availed thee thine deliverance. Ye have walked with thine eyes closed, looking for signs and miracles... yet what hast thou profited by thine signs and miracles? It is said, ye shall open thine eyes and see!

Hast thou understood what I have said? Hast thou seen what I have done that ye might have everlasting Life? Wherein have ye given unto me credit for being that which I Am... the one sent for thine sake?

I have come, while thou hast walked backward. While thou hast fallen into the pit, I stand by and wait until thou art strong enough to arise and stand upon thine own feet, and walk with me where I lead thee. O, ye foolish ones, have I not said I shall lead thee out of bondage? Wherein have 1 deceived thee? Come! Try me, and I shall not fail thee...

* * *

"Oneness"

Sori Sori: I am the One Sent from the Source of Being, in which all Beings have their existence. I am the one which has the Will and power to give and to take. I am the "Son of the Living God", which has given unto me the power to create, even as He.

It is seen that no man under the veil of flesh can comprehend the ALL, all power, everlasting life... ever evolving, revolving about and within the Whole of this ONE , which we (which have evolved into such a 'state' that we know ourself to be one with the Whole) call "Father".

Now it is come when all knowledge is available unto the creation known unto us as Mankind. The plan which is laid within the Heavens, within the Realms of Light, is the Law of the **O** One. Have ye heard of this Law... of this Oneness? How think ye ye are a being? By what power came ye here? By what power think ye ye leave? By whose or what power go ye from here? To where? How and why?

Know ye ye are one forever within this Whole, the Allness of Light! Never ceasing to Be!.. One within the Allness of this Life\Light!.. ever changing, evolving!.. One with "IT", symbolized by the endless **O** complete circle, unbroken circle. The nameless one we have indicated as "He"... or "It"... is simply understood as Breath. "He" Breathed upon his creation and called it good!

Earth man has now finished the old cycle... he now enters into the new one, in which he shall come to know himself to be One with this Everness, this Allness. For this I am come, that the sleepers might awaken unto their rightful inheritance... Eternal life, all knowledge, freedom from bondage... never more to descend into darkness, the limitation of flesh or the density thereof!

For this I am come... that ye, one and sundry, might prepare to enter into this new cycle\age with me. I come with a great Host of Light Beings, which are free even as I. We know ourself to be One with the Whole **O**. We are One with the divine plan for man's freedom, man's salvation!

Yea, as man is lifted, so shall the Earth be made new... the heavens too, for all the cosmos changes according unto "His" Will, His Word made manifest with perfection.

Man has long looked up and wondered, and wandered in darkness in his longing. Now that the Call hast gone forth, "Come! Come! Come!", the way is made available unto all which seek the light which I Am. As the Wayshower I reveal myself... as an Elder Brother I speak unto the ones which accept the Call "Come!". To the ones which deny the Call... they shall wait, and wait as within their own self-made present state of awareness... be it as they make it, for none are forced or coerced to come against their will.

Let it be understood... there are places prepared for each and every Being, as he hast prepared himself for. He, man of Earth, has free will, a sacred gift, which we are bound by our love and wisdom to honor. Yet, not all are aware that they have willed their condition... yet they did know, before they went into bondage.

Oh man, what a great awakening it shall be! Let it be! Let it be! Know ye that ye are part of it... accept it as thine gift divine! Arise and alert thineself! Ask of the Light in all sincerity, and ye shall be heard and answered unto thine intent!

* * *

The "light touch"

Beloved of mine being: I speak unto thee in thine own language that it be recorded as mine testimony unto them, for no man or woman can hear that which I say unto thee in mine language. I touch thee and ye know that which I say, yet mine touch is that of thought... a "Light Touch" is mine.

Ye are as one which has given of thine time in "holy communion" with me... now we shall be as 'One' to give unto others of our Light, our Joy, that they awaken... for the time is come! Count not thine minutes, for mine time is not calculated by that little instrument that man gives so much attention. I am not bound by time or space, such as ye calculate. Be ye blest. I am Sananda

* * *

"Testimony"

Sori Sori: Mine beloved, I am now speaking unto thee that they have this mine testimony... I shall give unto them that which shall be profitable unto them.

It is now come that they learn of (from) me that there is power in the "word"... that they have not been enlightened! Now that this time is come, when these Laws shall be revealed, many shall come unto me without going thru the experience of so-called "Death". This is that which I would have for all mankind, yet they are not prepared for to receive this gift of love and light. The 'sleep' is heavy and deep, yet it is mine intent to awaken them. I shall do a new thing that no man hast seen, so be it and Selah.

("Remember not the former things, nor consider the things of old... Behold, I am doing a new thing")

(Is. 43:18-19)

* * *

"As a man thinketh"

Sori Sori: Mine beloved, I am now speaking unto thee for the good of all. This mine word shall go forth as mine testimony in the time just ahead, for the time swiftly comes when there shall be quick and sudden changes in the life of Earth-mankind. These shall be as they have fortuned unto themselves... for this they shall come to know the power of the spoken word. It is said many times in ages past and present, "There is power in the spoken word"... yea too, the unspoken thought brings into manifestation its results. It is said, "As a man thinketh, so he becomes"... it is a truth little understood or practiced.

For this is it seen, the way mankind hast brought forth much destruction and great suffering. He has not reckoned with the law of manifestation. As he speaks the word it goes out into the ethers unseen, and returns unto the seen world made into its likeness... its strength and power returns 3-fold. This power\likeness is the least and last to be understood by the Earth-mankind.

The Earth and the fullness was made seen (created) by Thot... then spoken... and it became manifest in the 3rd dimension. That which goes out of the mouth of mankind (also) creates for weal or woe! He is the collective receiver of his own creation, knowing not from whence his blessings or his curses come.

I say unto "him", as the <u>collective</u> oneness of mankind "he" is both the 'sower' and the 'reaper'... his own tormentor! He hast given unto himself the bitter cup! He goes out of his mortality time after time, into the lowlands of dim/dense/heavy flesh bodies to learn his lessons for greater, lighter, higher, more joyful experiences. In this he hast not understood his part in the whole scheme of his Life existence between worlds, throughout the Cosmos!

Now it is come when man shall come to understand this law of manifestation. The Age long awaited is upon all and sundry... when "he", as a <u>collective body</u>, shall raise up and become as "One" made new, made whole. He shall be as the receiver and the sender, to transmute that which he hast defiled and debased. He shall take full responsibility for his own creation, be it Light or dark, lite or heavy. The parent shall own his son, his own creation... he shall not deny it!

While the lessons reach into the Cosmos for the refinement of man's Soul, his Everlasting Life... understand, ye of little knowledge, that <u>there is no "Death"</u>, only the illusion (of death), the change of dimension, ever onward and upward into the light. While there are many dimensions prepared for these which are loosed from the bounds of flesh, each are placed into the environment for which he has prepared for himself. Some have no Will to go forth (into other dimensions), therefore falling asleep in the only place they have remembered in their illusions (the Earth).

For this am I come to awaken them (the sleepers), to destroy their illusions that they be free to come up higher into greater light...

The "Source" of all life

Sori Sori: Mine beloved, I am now speaking unto thee for the good of all. Let thine hand be as mine, for are we not One in that which is the All, ineffable, "Source" of life, which is the beginning and the end, the Alpha and Omega **O**. For this are we One in this Oneness.

Ye have given thineself (of thine own free will) credit for being One with me... that I Am the one sent unto mankind that all might come to know that <u>I and mine Father are One</u>. I say unto all and sundry: Ye and I are One... there is no separation. Life is eternal, moving, thru the multitude of cycles... ever changing, ever upward, onward, in the All Life\Light which is (by necessity) symbolized by the unbroken circle **O**, encompassing the whole of creation. There is nothing outside, for everything or form is of this "Source", which has no beginning, no end... this being the great mystery. Mankind of flesh and bone can never fathom the Source of the All, the Everness, until he hast learned the Law of the One and become One with IT... then he becomes free from all darkness, all pain, all hatred, greed and malice, all bondage. He shall know such freedom as I know.

I know myself to be the Son of God", sent of the one mankind calls "God". O, my beloved children, I am light... I am love... I am the wayshower, the good shepherd, sent of the Source to bring thee home. For the time, the great cycle, is now come when the gates of the heavens shall swing wide to reveal its mysteries.

There are many planes, many things to learn, which ye shall learn by and thru thine own effort, thine free will, which is the precious gift given unto mankind as he went into bondage, into the World of mortality. I, the one sent, have called unto one and all, "*Come Home! Come Home!*", I have prepared a place for one and all, and each shall find it such as he is prepared to enter in. He\She shall be in his own environment... he shall be known as he is, yet again preparing for his/her next cycle, his/her greater part.

Mine time is come when I shall find the lost lambs. I know mine flock and they know mine voice. I bring no one against their will! Hear ye me! I say there is No death... life is eternal... many stages, many forms... ever lighter, brighter, and more glorious...

* * *

From the fountainhead

Sori Sori: Mine beloved, I am speaking for the good of all, that each one might be prepared for his part in the great plan which is now in operation. There are ones which have heard the word yet not understood the meaning thereof. They have (each) given themselves credit for understanding, while they do not see that which is going on about them. They see not the way of the traitors, the bigots, the hypocrites... neither do they see the ones sent of the Source, which shall overcome the darkness. I am speaking of the ones which are come to bring understanding of the work which is now being done.

When I say, "There is a time for all things, the sowing, the reaping", now is the day of reaping, the gathering in. It is not done in one of man's days or even years... yet the ones which have eyes to see shall surely learn that there are changes which are afoot. Be alert and watch with an open eye and an understanding mind, and ye shall be the one to overcome the darkness of unknowing.

To learn of the light, the "Source", is to see the light, to understand the word which I, the Lord God, give unto mortal man for his well-being. He hast but to listen and follow mine way without any preconditioned opinions. "Empty out thine cup", and ask for pure water from the fountain head, the Source, and it shall be filled... yea, to overflowing...

Other realms

Sori Sori: Mine beloved, I am now speaking unto thee for the good of all. There is a time unto all things... the harvest is now ready, The time is come when the sowing is ready for harvest, and it shall be as never seen before. The ones which have sown thistles shall reap thistles... the ones which have sown corn shall reap corn. They which refuse to accept that which is proffered them that they be nourished shall know want, for they shall be brought to account for their foolishness and rebellion.

Mine word is valid and shall stand the test of time. Be ye not troubled for their hatred, their scorn or unknowing. There shall be another day in which to prepare the soil, to till the soil and tend the crops... then comes the harvest. Be it come unto the traitors that which has been their portion, for all things shall be balanced, and that which has been made dark shall be made light. This is mine word unto all people, be they of any order they be... So shall Justice be done in all realms.

Not all realms are alike. Each one, be he male or female, brother or sister, father or mother, shall find the place befitting their nature. They shall find their own environment. Each shall prepare themselves for the next higher realm. Each shall be able to see into the lower realm for his own good, that he be prepared to see and make straight that which he\she hast made crooked. He\She shall atone for every deed in proportion, as befitting that which he finds his portion in his <u>Book of Life</u>. That he cannot deny, for each shall be in the place he hast prepared for himself. None escape, for it is the "Law of Justice".

Earth time is not eternal... 'Tis short! Each realm hast its Laws, yet the Laws are unlike that of the lower spheres... each is designed by the Source as a 'School', a 'University' (I use these words that even a child might understand). Each realm becomes lighter, more glorious.

The beings of light are free to pass through each realm, for nothing can touch these... they are ONE with the "Source". They can and do pass through fire and not be touched. They can and do go into the pits of darkness to deliver one out when one cries out "It is sufficient" (it is enough). This is the sincere cry of the Soul, which is heard by these Lighted Ones. They are known by their light... they have overcome all darkness and bounds... they are your benefactors...

* * *

False gods - false doctrines

Be ye as the hand of me and give unto them this mine word, and it shall profit them to receive it in the name of the Father which hast sent me.

I now say unto them which have ears to hear: Be ye alert that no man trip thee up... that no man be unto thee a stumbling block... that no man give unto thee the bitter cup. Let it be known that there are traitors amongst thee... that there are false gods, false doctrines. False gods there shall be, false doctrines there shall be, traitors there shall be... yet I say unto thee, follow them not! Be ye as one wise unto their schemes, their wiles and cunning ways. I say unto thee, Watch! Look! See! Know them for that which they are! See their works and be ye as one prepared for to go the last mile with me, for I shall show ye many things which are new and strange unto thee. Give ye not the bitter cup unto mine servants, for I say unto thee, there are ones which stand by which are prepared to go the last mile with them... and they (the servants) shall be as ones delivered out from the Earth as ones free from the gravity of the Earth and the attraction of the Moon. I say, they shall be freed forever. So be it I know... I Know! I Know whereof I speak!

So let it suffice that I am the Lord thy God... I am Sananda!

"Time"

Sori Sori: Mine beloved, I am now speaking unto thee for the good of all. The time is now come when each and every one shall account for him\her self... there shall be no other held responsible for another.

Now, let it be understood, that which ye count as time, "Life-times", is not as it appears in thine world. Ye are as ones in darkness concerning thine own "Being". I am speaking of the Eternal... that which knows thine Source, the Eternal Light, in which ye have thine being.

Ye have always been Life of one "Source", conditioned or fashioned within the Light, the Life of the One . Ye\We are of this One, sent forth as living creatures, given certain names\natures...

progressing!.. progressing!.. ever upward into greater understanding of our "Source".

There hast been countless changes, lessons to learn, ways fashioned for to learn them... time allotted to man * to learn, to accomplish that for which he went forth as man. He has forgotten his Divine nature... he has fallen low... and in his forgetting he has also lost his way. He knows not how to raise himself, as he hast believed himself to be a thing apart (from his Source), of short duration (one lifetime) and of little worth... lost and without understanding of his Eternality.

There is a time allotted unto each stage of manifestation for all creatures, when they (or it) shall change, move in the designated order... each being fashioned according to the divine plan. It is now come when great and sudden changes shall come about for manifested beings... meaning, that which has bodies or forms of the Earth realm, the flesh forms, that which is dense and heavy.

Now, mankind has been given certain faculties which he has used to lift himself up, or he has sunken deep into the density of the darkness of forgetfulness and despair. Time is at hand when there shall be a great and loud sound sent forth, which shall bring about an awakening among all creatures. For this am I calling, *"Come!.. Come!.. Come up higher! Awaken all ye that sleep! Hear! Hear ye me, for I shall cause ye to hear! I am not of a nature to fail! I have prepared a plan that ye be brought out... be ye prepared! For this I am speaking"*.

While ye know not that which I do or shall do, be ye not hasty to turn away. I say, "Come!" Have ye heard me or mine call?

Awaken, I say... Time is short...

* (the part of creation called 'man'... the 'man' infestation of O the One power)

* * *

Love ye one another!

Sori Sori: I, the Lord, speaks throughout the Cosmos... there are those which hear and those which turn a deaf ear. The ones which hear, listen, and act upon mine word, are mine Associates... these are the ones which work with me knowingly. The ones which work or speak to be <u>recognized</u> are not with me... they are to be seen for that which they do and say, knowing not that they are hypocrits. Give unto them credit for being that which they are, for I know that which they are. Yet the ones which give of themselves for the good of all are mine worthy servants which shall find their reward great, for they ask naught but to serve the light which I Am. Blest are mine servants, for they shall know such joy as I know.

There are ones which question mine authority... these are the antichrists. They serve false gods which shall lead them to the brink of the pit and forsake them. These are following blindly the false ones which would set <u>themselves</u> up to be seen and heard of men, to be praised of men. These are the ones which call themselves "Greatest among men" and deny mine servants which give of themselves for the good of all without thought of reward. They (the servants) serve for love, yea the love which IS.

Which of thee know my meaning when I say "Love one another even as I love thee". Wherein can ye say "Here I am Lord... I love as ye... I love everyone"? Why so then, I ask of thee, do ye say that which ye say? Why slander ye mine prophets, mine servants which I have sent unto thee? What hast thou given unto them that would lighten their burden? What hast thou given unto them that would comfort them? I ask again, "Why do yo these things to torment them"? Hast thou used them to thy own end? Hast thou put thine hand to the plow that all might be fed?

I say to mine servants, "Love ye one another... give of thyself that they be comforted! Go when I ask thee to go... come when I say come"! They, mine servants, know mine call and they haste to do mine bidding with joy. They fail not!

Be ye circumspect in thine ways and lead them to higher ground. Let them walk by the light which eminates from thine very being and ye shall be among mine chosen, for I find thee by thine Light! So be it and Selah.

* * *

There is no death...

Sori Sori: Mine beloved, I am now speaking unto thee for the good of all. Ye shall be as one to give it unto them which are within the way of the sleepers, those which are not fully awakened. These are as ones which are satisfied with that which they are... they <u>think</u> they are <u>secure</u> from all dangers which beset mankind. While I give unto them warning of things to come, (it is) not to frighten or confuse them, but to warn and prepare them! The bigot thinks he is self-sufficient unto himself... the pity of it! He has been warned, yet he has scorned the "Word" sent forth... for his benefit, his sake, is it given!

I am aware of these ones which turn a deaf ear and refuse mine counsel. I say unto all and sundry, that there shall be great and sudden changes, which concerns the ones which are prone to rebellion even as the ones which hear... while the one which hears, he\she will have the knowledge and mayhap the time to help himself to escape. For this am I speaking!

While it is seen from our point (the shape of things to come), we are prepared to give protection unto the ones which co-operate with us of the greater knowledge\light\understanding, the 'foresight'... and this is the method by which all shall be warned. It is the law that anyone be warned before being destroyed!

Now, again I say, that there is "No Death"... only the illusion! While this is true, the illusion is that which shall be <u>overcome</u> before one can be freed. While we of the over-all Council are diligently preparing for thine freedom, I have prepared for thine safety, by which ye might escape the experience which would bring upon thineself great and sad experiences. There hast been many warnings sent forth, both in word and pictures, stories and dreams. Now again, heed that which ye are shown in thine dreams. Remember them!.. and Take Note!

We of the "Host" have given warnings in many "signs and wonders" which are not understood. While they which are alert are as ones preparing for greater signs, many, (too many) are giving forth their opinions, as they are want to do. It is our desire to prepare certain places, ways, and means, for the time of certain changes... yet none can prophesy the exact date or nature of such as shall come upon the Earth and the populace thereof. Be not so foolish as to think that ye, mankind, can change the plan or that which shall come. Only <u>thine</u> <u>self</u> can ye change! For this am I come.

I bring with me a Host of lighted ones which have the power and authority to assist thee in ways unknown unto thee. Again, I say unto all and sundry... Watch! Look and See! Listen and Hear! And <u>understand</u> that which ye hear! For this we are prepared to assist thee as ye are prepared to receive. For this do we say, "Prepare thine self to receive us".

While there are many voices from the Nether World, the lower Astral, crying out for attention in their <u>own will</u>, with no light... depending upon wherefrom they speak and that which they bring. I say unto these of the pits of darkness and (unto) the ones which give forth the words of the unlearned of the "Word", such as confuse and deter their progress: "*Be ye as ones finished, for ye shall be justly and lawfully dealt with!.. for the time is come which no man knows!*"

It is written, that the Earth shall be as one made new... purified! It is now going through its birth pangs. <u>Take Note!</u> I shall speak again and again. Weary not of thine preparation... be ye alert and hear, see, and be diligent! Make no mock of me or mine mission. I am come that all be prepared to return unto their rightful estate, and receive their inheritance willed unto them of their "Source of Being". I am the one sent that it be... So let it be as the Father Wills.

* * *

Know the true from the false

Sori Sori: This day is the day for which they have waited, the day of salvation, the day of "The Coming", the day of deliverance. I say, wait no longer for the Coming, for I AM COME! I am come with the host, mighty and strong, prepared to go forth as mine ministering assistants, as mine hand made manifest unto them which slumber.

Now they (the sleepers) shall stir, and be as ones quickened... then I shall touch them and speak with them, counsel them, lead them in the way they should go. These shall hear mine voice and obey it. They shall arise at mine touch and do mine bidding. They shall know the true from the false, for the false shall mimic me that he deceive them which have not been touched. They (the sleepers) shall be as ones deceived and they shall follow the deceiver, declaring falsely that they have known me as their savior, as their Master, as their servant.

Yet know ye this: I am not the deceiver. I make no promises that I am not prepared to fulfill. I say unto thee, try me, give unto me credit for being that which I Am, and I shall do mine part. Look not for signs and miracles, for I make no show to satisfy thy curiosity. I say unto thee, try me... obey the law... walk ye as one sober. Give unto me thy hand and I shall lead thee in paths of righteousness and I shall counsel thee.

Ask of me and be ye as one blest. Heed that which I say... do thy part and I shall do mine. Rest thine head on mine bosom, and ye shall find peace therein. Let peace be within thee.

Let thine hand be mine and ye shall do that which I do. Ye shall walk with me, go with me where I go, know that which I know, rejoice with me, so be it and Selah. Ye shall have no need for soothsayers, no need for charlatans, no need for the "gadgets" which are designed to enlighten or emancipate thee, for I have said I shall touch thee and ye shall know. Ye shall be blest as I have been blest.

While it is said, "Ye shall know as I know", let it be understood that ye grow in wisdom... ye shall grow to maturity as the child grows. The man-child shall grow to maturity, unto the strength wherein he shall bear the responsibility of the adulthood, the manhood, the Adeptship, the initiate. He shall be as one prepared to walk with me, to go with me where I go. So be it that I have said, "Come unto me and I shall give unto thee as thou art prepared to receive". So be it and Selah.

This I would have thee know: Provide thineself with the proper credentials and I shall give unto thee passport into mine place of abode, wherein ye shall abide with me and rejoice with me, and wherein no harm shall come unto thee. So let it be as ye have prepared thyself. So be it and Selah.

* * *

The two paths

Sori Sori: Let this be mine word unto thee this day: Let it profit them to accept it in mine name, for they shall come to know the true from the false. They shall find that the enemy is the enemy, that he is the deceiver. He lies in wait to ensnare them. He is merciless and filled with deceit... he is cunning. He is not of a mind to let them go... he finds means in which he can hold them bound. He hast the blood of generations upon his hands, the blood of the innocent, the unborn. He whispers the promises of his deceitful plan... he finds ways in which to distract them. He gives unto them that which flatters them... they accept it because of their own ego, their desires... they have not yet learned the way of the wise, the way of the Initiate.

They seek the way in which they go for the glitter, flattery, ease, and the praise of others. They have not found mine way attractive, for it is said, "It is not the popular way, it is not the easy way". Wherein have I said they shall choose, they shall be as the one to choose which way they go? None bring them against their will, so let it profit them to choose wisely the path I have pointed unto them. Let them walk therein and be blest.

Let them find their way... let them wait. Be ye not downcast, for they are as the green nut. They shall find their time cometh swiftly when the winds shall shake the tree, and the ripe nuts shall fall unto the harvest and be gathered in... the green ones shall be left (for another day). So be it and Selah.

* * *

The seventh day

Sori Sori: This is mine word unto them which have followed me unto this point: There is a time and a place, a season for all things. It is now the time/season for this mine word to become manifest in the world of man. Man hast had his day... this is mine, wherein I shall do that which I have said I shall do. There are ones which have covenanted with me, and these have kept their covenant. Unto these shall I make known mine works, and unto them shall I manifest. So be it and Selah.

I have waited this hour when I shall do these things which I have said I shall do. This is the time for such as I shall do, for man is now in his "Seventh day", and the time is at hand when he shall come into his own. He shall be as one responsible for his own part, and for his inheritance which he hast forfeited so long ago. Now he shall see and know that which he hast forfeited.

The way is now made clear before him.., for this am I come, that he might follow where I lead him. I shall not fail him. He shall lift up his feet and follow me where I lead him... and he shall walk upright and stumble not, nor shall he fail in his mission. The way of the Lord is strait and narrow, yet it is sure and safe. So be it and Selah.

Forget not that I am He which is sent that ye return unto the Father's House in this thy time, for thy time hast come when the door stands unbarred. Ye have but to turn the Key and enter in, all ye which are prepared. I stand at the door and I say, "*Pass ye in, all which are prepared*". None else shall find the door, for they shall not see that which is hidden from the unprepared, the ones which have thot themselves "wise".

So be it that I am come that ALL be prepared, yet they have not been true unto themselves, unto their trust. They have played their merry tune and danced in the time of destruction. Destruction is now upon them and they are yet paying for their own folly. While i stand before them crying "Come!", they sing their songs of sorrow. They beat their drums of war and mourn their dead, and they are bowed down with their burdens... yet they give unto me no credit for being that which I am.

I say, I am come that they be lifted up, yet they are wont to give unto me credit. They serve the enemy with diligence... they provide him with their energy and strength... they are devoted unto his will. They put their hand in his and he leads them down to destruction, I say he is their enemy, and they know not that they are serving him in their unknowing. This is the pity of it... they know not!

This is the day of awakening when they shall <u>KNOW</u>. For this am I come. I say, Awaken ye! Awaken all ye Nations. Sleep no more, for the hour is come when ye shall know the Truth, and it shall be thy freedom. Walk ye with me and I shall direct thee in all thy ways, and ye shall be delivered out of bondage. So let it be as the Father hast Willed. Amen and Selah.

* * *

The healing of the nations

Sori Sori: Let this be the time for this word, this mine word which shall go forward to bless and to heal the wounds of the Nations, the Nations sore and bloody from the hatred and darkness of men. Let this healing go forth as a power of Light, which it is, for it cometh at a time expedient unto men of understanding.

The man in darkness shall not see or know the expediency of such as this mine word, for they shall not have the understanding which brings such help as they are in need of. I say, they stand in need of such help as I bring.

I am the host of a mighty Army... an Army which far out-numbers the host of Earth. The entirety of Earth's population could not equal one part of the great Army which I bring this day that man of Earth might be brot out of his bondage, for men of all ages cometh as ones prepared to assist me in this mine work. Wherein is it said, "I am not finished"? I am NOT finished! I shall do that which I have said I shall do. So be it mine Father's will, Amen and Selah.

However, I shall not put mine foot upon the threshold of them which defile the Word of God, nor the door shall I open unto them which set foot against me or mine servants. I shall bless mine servants with mine word. I shall give unto them mine assistance, for they ASK of me, making no mockery of the Word of God. They devote themselves unto the work which I do, that which is allotted unto them. They ask not for signs and wonders, neither seek rewards. They ask no favors of men, and for this do they ask of me only Truth and Light. They stand ready to do mine bidding, go where I go, do that which I do... the Father's Will.

Blest art these, for they have heard me and answered me. They have gone the long way to serve me and with me, that all be blest. So be it and Selah.

* * *

The open door

(between the Realms)

Sori Sori: Be ye as one blest to receive me, for I come in the name of the Lord God, sent forth as the one prepared to show the way. So be it that I am come that we might do his will. Let it be Amen.

While it is now come, it is as the door is open unto us. It shall open both ways; ye shall pass thru, I shall pass thru, and we shall commune one with the other. That shall be as the Father wills, for it is now come when much Light shall be shed upon the planes which have been obscured from the sight of these in which thou hast thy flesh bodies.

These planes hast been obscured by the curtain of fog, hazy substance, created by man's mind and thinking, his rebellion for long centuries. Few have penetrated these dense fog curtains to pass within the places wherein they find greater knowledge and Light. Even as the ones within the realms below his (the Lord God's) have raised toward his, the progress is upward toward his Realm. Even tho there are ones who reach earth-ward to assist the ones which reach upward, those who bend low to assist are greatly blest, for they are given greater strength and assistance.

These which have turned to lend a hand unto them which cry for assistance are as the ones which have gone before thee. They have known the sorrows, the longings of the lonely heart, the shadows of despair. Their reward is the word, the selfless service, the love which sustains them in his love... and he is the Radiant One, sent that we be lifted to loftier heights. This is the way in which we serve with love and patience as he. We follow in his footsteps, for he leads us far afield that we might learn the meaning of the word "SELFLESS SERVICE". When we see the one below cry for help, we are glad to assist when possible.

It is not always lawful that we do that which they ask, as if in prayer or pleadings. We go not on such foolish missions, for it is given unto us to know that which is lawful. We transgress not, for that would be to error, and we have learned (about) the great price paid for such errors.

Let it be said here: To error is to fall, when we have entered into this estate wherein he, the Lord God has so graciously brot us. Therefore to serve diligently and wisely is our reward, for this is the joy of the Lord, the joy of Being. For this do we go forth gladly giving of ourself, our love and wisdom, that his will be done. So be it and Selah.

It is said: There are none so joyful as him which serves... It is so! Amen and Amen.

* * *

I SHALL BREAK THESE BARRIERS

Sori Sori: Mine beloved, I am now speaking unto thee for the good of all. There comes unto thee these ones which know but little of mine way, mine "method of operation". I am now speaking as one of their kind that there be no barriers between us.

It is now come when I shall break these barriers which hast long existed between us. This has been the way of the priesthood, to hold in bondage the populace, that they hold sway or power over the ones asking for light. These of many minds, many ideas, opinions and intent, have taken mine <u>words</u>, mine work of the Age past, yea Ages, and used it to build great and impressive Cathedrals, Temples, Synagogues, and places wherein they prey unto their unknown "gods"... not knowing me or remembering that which I have given unto thee in the light of mine Father which hast sent me unto these, which have lost their way among the many various methods they have encountered in their many cycles of going in and out of mortal form.

Through the denseness of the many planes of the higher world they have come and gone, remembering little or nothing of their everlasting Being, or their Eternal Being, or their Oneness willing to arise and learn of his inheritance, his with the Source of Being, which makes of all men brothers. These are the ones bound... Bound I say? Hoodwinked are they!

I am now come this day with the intent, the Will and the Authority, to bring light unto them for to break loose the ties that bind them to the fog-mist wherein they have labored, wondered, and wandered long in darkness. Now I come in the time of great and sudden changes, crying AWAKEN! Come!.. Come!.. Come up higher!

Unto them was it given in the time of going into mortal bondage as mankind, the gift of "<u>Free Will</u>". This is a Law which We of the Host of the Lighted Ones honor and obey. Yet we are bound by the Law of the One **O** *(which is Love of All... of our Source in which we live and have our being)* to give of our love and assistance and wisdom as ones which know the Law of the One... as we see the over-all, the whole of the way, of the eternal journey thru the Cosmos. While it is not given unto mortality to understand the plan fashioned for his return into the light from which he descended into mortal denseness, he hast fallen asleep in his forgetfulness. For this I am come, crying, Awaken! Awaken!

It is mine intent that all might hear and respond unto the call. Yet as ye, man, count time, there is no time for to wait or loose. The time of great and sudden changes is upon thee, the populace. Have ye seen or heard? Have ye slept? The time is upon all flesh to be as changed! These changes shall come about in the twinkling of an eye, according unto that which each one hast fashioned unto self. It is written that no man is responsible unto another, yet this is not understood by the laggard, the sleeper.

The whole totality is within the Law of the One **O**. Each one is but part of the One Source, from which he, as self, cannot be separated... while he can, if he wills, go to sleep. While he is eternally bound to return unto his Source, understand that this is (only) as one is prepared and willing to arise and learn of his inheritance, his Source! None are brought by force!

While we of the great army of light are presenting ourself "as One", of one mind and intent... that of showing unto all of mankind the way he shall go forward into the light of the New Day... We, as One (which I am leader, so to speak), come unto the ones which have the will to follow me. I am the wayshower... I lead, I do not push! I give the Law, I show the way, and say "Come, I know the way." I forget not that I have called thee! I wait not for the laggard, for I know the difference between him and the one with the will to come up higher where I lead. So be it, I leave not mine flock to the wolves... for I am a watchful shepherd...

* * *

"I shall pass this way no more!"

Beloved of Mine Being: I am come this day to give unto thee this word, that all men might profit thereby. It is for this that I say, "Pay ye heed unto that which I say, for it shall profit thee".

Let it be given unto them as I give it unto thee, for it is now come when great things shall be made known... and for this have I given unto thee mine mantle, mine name. And I am the one which hast first revealed unto thee (Sister Thedra) the name Sananda, and first I proclaimed it unto thee, that they might come to know me.

So be it I am he which is known by many names, yet they which are mine flock shall come to know me as thou knowest me. And for this shall I touch them, even as I have touched thee... then they shall know and they shall no more turn their face from me. It is said, as they are prepared so shall they receive... so let it be! While it is said, I have greater things for them, they shall be as ones prepared to receive them.

Now it is come when many shall proclaim the name, yet they shall not be as ones prepared to receive that which I have kept for them. I say, to proclaim mine name is not sufficient... they shall (also) be as ones prepared to enter into the place of mine abode. They shall wait upon me, the Lord God. They shall not deny mine handmaiden... they shall accept the word and they shall be as mine servants, and they shall earn their passport into the place of mine abode.

They shall bear their own burdens and walk humbly before men. They shall be as brothers of one Father-Mother, and no hatred or bigotry shall be in them. They shall have the part of servant, for service shall be their part. And no man shall judge which (one) is qualified to serve me. for I shall raise up a tool to do the work of a man... and he shall be as one qualified, for he shall know from whence cometh his learning and his wisdom. I shall set him up and place before him the Table of The Lord and he shall not want, for I, the Lord God, am responsible for that which I do and say, and I have promised that I shall do these things.

And I say unto thee, Look! See the Hand of God move. I shall perform mine wonders while they sleep... and the scorners shall be as the "sleepers" and they shall sleep on, knowing not that I am come to do that which I have said I shall do. I have said, I shall come as a thief in the night, and it is so... for I AM COME and finding them sleeping. I speak out that they awaken... yet they but stir themselves and then return unto their dreaming.

So let them which will, stir themselves, and arise and follow me, for I pass this way no more. I shall move on and return unto them NO MORE, for another shall come after me, and they shall wait, and their waiting shall be long and hard.

So be it that it is now come when one shall go forward as the voice of me, and he shall proclaim the word and it shall be as the Clarion Call. And he shall pass from city unto city as the "voice". And he shall wait upon me, and he shall give unto me credit for being the One Sent. And he Shall walk gently and humbly before men... and he shall bear the Authority and the Number which I shall give unto him, and it shall be recorded within these records. And he shall have that number written within the palm of his hand, and no man shall know that number.

But woe unto anyone who-so-ever which takes it upon himself to falsify a number which he shall put within his own hand, for I say unto him, he shall be as the fool which knows not the power of the Law. I say, it shall destroy him! I say, he shall destroy himself by the Law, for it is a power which he knows not! Poor in Spirit is he which pilfers the Spirit, which plunders the secrets of the Most High... they which use the Sacred Symbols, knowing not the power thereof. I say, they have not the knowledge of the power which they (these symbols) represent.

Let it be that this be given unto them which seek the Light. Let them see that which thou hast heard, and let thine name be written that they might know for a surety that I have given it unto thee. And fear no man, for I say unto thee mine beloved, that I am thine Shield and thine Buckler... I am Sananda... The Lord thy God.

* * *

The following was given to Sister Thedra several years ago by Sananda concerning various subjects.

On food

Beat the pores (the physical bodies) and cast no portion unto the food, for I have given no thought for what I eat. Give the best of thy fortune not to food, and not to the poor part of thee.

That which I eat I fret not for... I am a portion unto myself, and not unto the food. I eat not that which hast been killed, and I eat not that which hast been forgotten and let to rot, for I am a particular person. And not any place can I find a funnier one than I, for I am not particular, and yet I am... and when I have said I eat of nothing which has been killed, I eat of the fresh garden which has been plucked and killed, yet it has not the former pain to remember.

And I have given no thought to my food, yet I give the utmost care for it and the preparation of it, yet it burdens me not. And I have been no part of my food, yet it becomes a part of me. And as I am master, food bothers me not...

On pain

Pain is the portion that the pores (physical bodies) have portioned for themselves. The positive knows no pain... the positive knows only peace. And forget the pores and the spores and their pain... I say unto you, the peace I bring knows no pain, and my peace is upon thee. Beleis

On peace:

Peace is my part of thee, and no place can I see the pores who have my peace. Fortunes have I put at their command, but they squander it on the poor part of themselves... and the peace which I would give them they sell for the potters (undertakers) fee.

And wherein have I said unto thee that there shall be no peace among them? Fortunes (money) have they of their own inheritance, and fortunes have I... but they know not my Father and receive not any portion of my inheritance, therefore their fortunes know no part of my peace, which is a princely inheritance.

Be ye aware of them, but partake not of their fortunes (of wealth), for it availeth them naught but misery and want. Foolish Beings (are) they, for there is no fool so great as one who has given away his birthright. Beleis.

On friendship

Because of friendships has the poor red star Earth been a better place. And because of friendships has there been a fraternity of brotherhood which could not have existed without friendship.

Friends are the foundation for the unity of mankind, which begets brotherhood, such as the Brotherhood of which I am a member. And as I have told you, I am not a poor member.... I give of my friendship unto all who seek it.

Be unto me and my brothers a fellow member and forget not thy pledge. And swear allegiance to no pore (no one in the flesh) for I am the Porter and I am the Portal. Beleis.

On disappointments

Be a person who can say there is no disappointments... for I have told thee that there is no future, only the eternal now, so why should there be any plans for the future? Bless the NOW and live it to the full and to the highest and noblest of thy stature, and fret not about thy future. As each day becomes the NOW wherein is there a future? Forever and ever is NOW!

And wherein have I said there is a "time"?.. for the only "time" is NOW! Foresee thy future as NOW, and bless this moment and our communion, and be it such that profiteth thee. Beleis.

On imagination

Begin thy imaging with a drop of dew... and enlarge it unto an ocean. And begin the ocean with the Cosmos... and there is an organism within that ocean of Cosmic energy, and that is man in the red star (of Earth). And his imaging has begot him his pores and spores, his torments, his pleasures and his pain. His imaginings have destroyed or saved him.

Be a person who can image to perfection and peace, and unto the Creator of the things which are eternal, that pass not away or rust within the junkyards. Be aware of thy imaging and image the things which you desire to have manifest unto the seen world, for they do you know. Beleis.

On loyalty:

This is no small part of friendship, for I am the part of loyalty which has been taught me by my Father and Mother. They have been unto me no poor part of loyalty, and wherein have I said they have been loyal.

There is no method to improve upon loyalty! It is of the essence, and that essence is <u>Unto thy own self be true and to no man you can be false</u>. I am unto you the teacher of such sobrieties and my loyalty exceeds my patience... and that is another lesson. Beleis.

Note: At one point in the scripts Sananda remarks, "Many times ye shall try my patience... yet so be it my Love far exceeds my patience".

On sin

Sin, my darling, is a poor part of knowledge, and a place within thy beam where knowledge is not... and without thy knowing there is distortion of facts. Blame not the sinner, and forgive him his distortion... forgive him his lack of facts. Be unto him a lamp, yet cast no shadow before it. Be unto him a beacon, yet porter not his pores, for he has his own port to porter. Beleis.

On duty

Duty is the portion that one establishes unto himself... and this follows loyalty, as they follow unto the place which has been established by thy own Source, and from which thou has been sent out. It is a connecting link with thy Source.

There is no sense of loyalty unto any other, other than thy own Source and being. From this time forward it is the Oneness, with no beginning and no end... and to this Oneness of Being be loyal. No place is there a division, no place are there many or few... just the eternal Oneness of thy Being. Beleis.

On hope

Hope is but a poor part of reality. And nowhere did I say that I would teach you of hope, for that is not my mission, to teach you of hope. I come to teach you of "knowing", and that availeth you the fortune of which I have been speaking... and that is your inheritance from the Father. Brag not of thy fortune, but be thou a fortune unto my teaching and know wherein thy treasure lies. Beleis.

On understanding:

Understanding bringeth much wealth, and the place wherein I am is peopled with those who understand thy weakness. And thy porters are not among them, for they have gone to thy port and no place can they be found. They are in the ports of those who have no understanding of the Laws of which I teach, and they put forth their will and their might for a cause they think to be the right one... yet the other puts his Will forth and there is a clash of ideologies, and a fortune is lost, and no man understands the reason.

Be a person who can see the reason and not the results of the misunderstandings and the frailties of the poor in spirit. Be about the business of understanding the cause of misunderstanding, which is the negative. And the positive is understanding, and that is from another standpoint or point of reference and no part of the unconscious part of the great forces which are at work to beset the peace of the Earth. Beleis.

On secrets:

Secrets have I, but secrets you have none. My secrets are not to be plundered by thy time... I shall be unto you a revealer on mine secrets in the time which is allotted to such things. I shall give of my treasure trove and be unto you a porter.

And wherein have I said I have not told you secrets... but my secrets are no longer secret after I have revealed them to thee, so be ye wise as the serpent and silent as a sphinx. Beleis.

On revelation:

Revelation is the portion which I have prepared for thee, for I have, since the beginning, portioned out thy lot... and as thou hast squandered it or valued it have you coined thy tonnage. And what has thy tonnage been? A portion have I given unto thee of much value, yet my pearls I give not to babes. I have revealed my prospectus to thee... this is revelation. Beleis.

On judgment

Judgment is the part which belongs to no part of thee and no part of me, for judgment is for each man to be his own (judge). And as he stands before himself as a naked boarder in his own house, he shall see himself as he is. By his own deeds he shall judge himself, and for himself he cannot become the personality he is not (pretend to be something he is not). There is but one judge... that is the Law, and the Law must be balanced. Beleis.

On balance

Balance is a Law, and that Law must be served. And the Father is the author of that Law, and no man is exempt from the Law of Balance... thus is it (the Law) ever striving to become balanced. There is no inequality in nature, only an imbalance... and as the scales are balanced there is harmony.

Unhappiness is a striving for balance, and sick- ness is an imbalance in the Law... harmony being that of balance, Laughter and tears are the Laws of Balance. Beleis.

On innocence

Ponder my words: "There are none innocent, and none pure upon the Earth... for were they (pure or innocent) they would not be there. There is a laboratory, and that laboratory is the Earth, wherein are many experimenters who are returning by the hard route. And by their labors are they known to the few who have become the initiated... and by their fortunes have they paid the price for their admittance into another laboratory, which is my portion of their inheritance. And no place have they saved for me, but they have set up idols unto the scientists... and they have belittled the powers which they have plundered. And when they have been stripped of their gadgets they are at a loss to know which is which... and when I fail to look unto their "gadgets" for the part they have given unto me they call me unjust! And these are the innocent who have said that I am unjust?

Beleis.

On the inner circle:

The inner circle are those who are the ones who have been tried and have been found worth the processing... and worth the admitting unto the whole for the benefit of the whole, and not a single unit for the sake of a few. And when these have been found worthy there stands a princely crowd to assist with the ones who do qualify for admittance...

and none who qualify are sent away. There are none who have come without sanction by the whole of the inner circle... and by their own passport are they known, yet they carry no passport or portfolio. Beleis.

On man and woman

Bless them, and be it such that they marry and divorce and try to find happiness... for this the pores are better pores, but in no wise are they happier. The experiences are but the parts through which they learn that there is no place wherein they can find happiness in the negative but to be positive... and to be a positive to the negative is to be whole. And no negative is without a positive, but the negative is in the seen (world) and the positive is in the unseen... and the positive is the keeper of the negative.

And my place is in the positive, for I am unto the negative the positive. But the negatives are not the masters, for they are not whole. As my negative you (Thedra) write... and as you write the written words are the negative and the spoken words are the positive. The person who speaks is the positive to the spoken word... yet man is the negative to the positive which he does not see. So the woman is the positive to the male, and the male is the positive to the pore... and thus is the balance established. Beleis.

On wisdom

Wisdom is the better part of knowing... and whereupon thy knowing has failed thee thy wisdom has served thee. And no wisdom is so great that there is not more light to be gleaned from that which you call experience,

That which "you" call wisdom is but the idiot's delight compared to the Father's words, which shall be revealed in all their purpose. Forget not that this is but the 'beginning' of thy learning and no part of wisdom... it has been forced upon thee by me.

No wise man has the wisdom of the Father. From the beginning have you sought 'wise men', but they are but the ones who seek to be as wise as thyself. Wherein have I said, 'There are none wise save through the Father". Be sought by the Father and receive thy inheritance. Beleis.

* * *

"The records"

Sori Sori: Mine beloved, I am now speaking unto thee that there be understanding of that which ye shall be given to do. It is for the good of all that I speak thusly unto thee.

This is mine time in which I shall release the revelations long withheld, for the time was not come. The New Day is now come, therefore it is propitious that the 'Word' of the Lord God be made available unto all which are prepared to receive it. This shall be as the prophecies of yester-year shall be fulfilled, the promises fulfilled.

This shall be the first of the opening of many a record of old, which shall be verified and understood by the ones which have the will to learn. These records shall be brought forth by the Masters of the ancient days which have kept them for this time in which to release them.

Be ye as one to be prepared to do thine part. It is so written and revealed that ye shall bring forth such work as has been held for the 'Day of Revelation', which is now come. By mine own hand shall I set mine seal upon these most precious records.

These shall be released in such a manner that no man woman or organization shall be able to pilfer or plagiaries, for mine hand shall be heavy upon these ancient revelations. And they shall be released as befitting unto the time, and into the care of the one which hast been prepared for such a responsibility, which is a heavy one. While I have given unto this one the responsibility, I have watched and waited for this day when I might open the record as a living, true, and accurate record for the good of all mankind... which shall open up great doors, and revelation which shall be great light unto all that are prepared to share such as is held within the great vaults of the Ethers, where no unworthy hand hast touched or defiled.

Be ye as one alert, for there are many a one which are awaiting this coming event. Be ye as one tried and found true trustworthy. I am at mine Fathers business and He hast given unto me the authority and the responsibility of this assignment, and I know well mine part. Be ye as one I have called and prepared for this part... I am with thee unto the end. I am known as the wayshower... Sananda by name.

The recall

Sori Sori: Mine beloved, I am now speaking unto thee for the good of all. Let it be known that I am now prepared to bring thee in... to recall thee in from the field. So be it that ye shall go out with me as One with me... no more to wait and watch in longing.

I have shown thee many things which ye knew not their magnitude, for it was not yet time that ye could bear the light or glory of it. It is now come when ye shall see as I see and know as I know... for this is it written in the heavens. And it is not given unto any "man" to deny mine word, for I have spoken and it is everlasting, written within the Book of Life, which no being of mortal flesh is prepared to read.

Be ye joyful that thine time is come... Peace.

* * *

The lamp

The time alas has come. Let all ye who know the Light go forth, and let the light be seen... for the lamp is lighted, the time is now, and the working order is "Light ye other lamps".

Go ye forth my carriers... Go out amongst the multitudes, and let not your flame be hidden. And those who have spent their time wisely, and who have laid up their lamps with oil, will say unto you, "*Give unto me the light, that through myself I may cast out the darkness, and be as a beacon unto others*". And lo, the light shall be given unto them, and they shall become. But, unto those who have foolishly wasted their time, in deeds to satisfy and benefit themselves... who shall say unto you, "*Give unto us the light, that we too may see the Lord*"... you shall pass on by, as the wheatmen pass the thistles. And when they cry out after you, saying, "*Lo, why has the Lord forsaken us, that we are his children*"... ye shall turn unto them and say, "*Nay! Nay! The Lord has not left, but been driven out... for it is ye that hath forsaken he. And even the bud of the blossoming rose, though it captures the whole of the minds eye, knows that it cannot stand apart from the bush upon which it grows. For were it to sever itself from its source, it would surely bring the wrath of death upon itself... and lay the blame thusly...*"

SISTER THEDRA

May 6, 1900 - June 13, 1992

In our desire to make available messages of encouragement and instruction from those of greater understanding, we know very well that to progress one must be always ready to move forward into greater fields of learning.

As many of you know, Sister Thedra's 92 years on this Earth have not been easy ones. Having worked with her, and often being around her 24 hours a day, for over 20 years, I was always aware that she was never free from the physical pain. The past six months have been extremely trying days, and often I would hear her quietly crying as the pain only increased... however, never once did she ever fail to get up at 1, 2, or 3:00 a.m. every morning to receive those wonderful messages which have inspired and guided us all so much... and never, never, did she ever complain,

On Saturday, June 13, 1992, at exactly 10:00 p.m., Sister Thedra made her final transition in the comfort of her own bed here at A.S.S.K., with two of her friends present. When the time arrived she simply took one small breath and then slipped quietly away, without pomp or fanfare. She left just as she had lived... as a humble servant for the greater good.

She always said, that she was simply a messenger... the importance being in the messages. This being acknowledged, we would also like to acknowledge our mutual feelings, one and all... that this is one messenger who will be deeply, deeply, missed.

During her time of preparation for her departure, both Sister Thedra and Sananda left specific instructions as to the nature of the work of A.S.S.K. after her departure. Please know that this event does not end the work carried on by Sister Thedra, nor that of A.S.S.K.... to the contrary, this event signals the beginning of the greater work for both. You might say that thus far she has simply laid the foundation... and the cornerstone is solid.

The messages that follow are compiled to try to give you some idea of the significance of her passing, and of the expansion of the work... as she is now free to work unencumbered by the physical limitations and the pain which have so encumbered her in the past, and also from a place of "Knowing", with greater vision and first-hand knowledge. She has worked here on the Earth plane for the last 50 years because that's where the work was needed... rest assured that her work now in the higher realms will simply be an extension of that work.

For those of you with a subscription to A Call To Arms newsletter, we would like you to know that we do not know at present when the next issue will be sent out, as we do not know when the information will be given. However, be assured that there will be a next issue... and we would expect that it will be well worth the wait... no matter how long!

Sister Thedra's desires were that her body be cremated and the ashes be scattered, without any services or fanfare. The ashes will be divided into three portions...

One portion will be scattered here in Sedona, Arizona...

One portion will be scattered at Mt. Shasta, California, where she first established the "Gatehouse", and where she carried on the work for over 25 years...

The final portion will be scattered in the high Andes Mts. of Peru, South America, where she underwent her initial training and initiation into the Order of the Emerald Cross, and the Brotherhood of the Seven Rays...

In honoring her desire, this will be done without services or fanfare.

Sister Thedra once told me about part of the 5 years she spent living in the high Andes Mts with the Indians of the area. She was living as they did, literally on pennies a day, surrounded by incredible poverty and hunger. At Christmas time she received a bundle of mail from the United States which contained several Christmas cards which had obviously cost a dollar or more, plus the cost of the postage from the U.S. to Peru. She told me how she wept at the thought of those cards, and how that little bit of money could have done so much greater good had she been able to use it to feed those around her who were going hungry on Christmas day.

In light of that, for those of you who might be inclined to send flowers, cards, etc, we might suggest that you simply send it in the form of a small donation to keep her work going during her absence. We are sure she would approve.

* * *

Sori Sori: Mine beloved, I am now speaking unto thee for the good of all. It is time that ye prepare thine self to depart this place wherein ye are. This shall be as a great sorrow unto some, while it shall be much joy unto others.

I say unto thee, it is now come that ye come into the place wherein I abide, wherein ye shall write mine story, the earth-walk (as Jesus), which hast been so messed up and changed to suit their opinions. I have said there shall be great changes... so be it! It is so great that men shall bow down in humble contrition before the light which I Am. It shall be well!

Let every knee bend... every tongue confess their weakness and be made strong. Be ye made glad, for I have spoken the word and it shall be as it is spoken. Let it be! For mine work is valid... made manifest. So be it and Selah.

* * *

March 20, 1992

Sori Sori: Mine beloved, I am now speaking unto thee for the good of all. It is now come when ye shall see the wisdom of thine pain as well as thine dreams. Let it be remembered that thy dreams are the extension of thine self... thine teacher,

Be ye quiet and at peace and poise. Bless this day... I am with thee.

Sananda

* * *

April 2, 1992

Sori Sori: Mine beloved, I am now speaking unto thee for the good of all. Thine harvest is come... ye shall be gathered and the harvest shall be bountiful. The way is made clear... ye shall be as One with me and ye shall know such joy. For there is much to be accomplished for the good of all. By ye joyful... rest in peace, for I am with thee unto the end.

I am Sananda

* * *

April 29, 1992

Sori Sori: Mine beloved, I am now speaking unto thee for the good of all. Ye shall be as one made new and there shall be great rejoicing. I am come to fetch thee, for there are many which await thee. There is great work to be done e'er the great awakening of the sleeping populace. Listen for thine name to be called! Remember how to answer me... for I shall speak loud and clearly.

I am the good shepherd

* * *

Note: This was the last message that Sister Thedra was able to write down... and a copy of the original message is reprinted below. Following this she became too weak to even hold the pen.

May 3, 1992

Sori Sori: Mine beloved, I am speaking unto thee for the good of all. It is now come the time that ye come out from the place wherein ye are. Ye shall shout for joy! Let it be, for many shall greet thee with glad shouts! So be it, no more pain...Amen... Sananda

The recall

Sori Sori: Mine beloved, I am now speaking unto thee for the good of all. Let it be known that I am now prepared to bring thee in... to recall thee in from the field. So be it that ye shall go out with me as One with me... no more to wait and watch in longing.

I have shown thee many things which ye knew not their magnitude, for it was not yet time that ye could bear the light or glory of it. It is now come when ye shall see as I see and know as I know... for this is it written in the heavens. And it is not given unto any "man" to deny mine word, for I have spoken and it is everlasting, written within the Book of Life, which no being of mortal flesh is prepared to read.

Be ye joyful that thine time is come... Peace.

* * *

"The records"

Sori Sori: Mine beloved, I am now speaking unto thee that there be understanding of that which ye shall be given to do. It is for the good of all that I speak thusly unto thee.

This is mine time in which I shall release the revelations long withheld, for the time was not come. The "New Day" is now come, therefore it is propitious that the 'Word' of the Lord God be made available unto all which are prepared to receive it. This shall be as the prophecies of yester-year shall be fulfilled, the promises fulfilled.

This shall be the first of the opening of many a record of old, which shall be verified and understood by the ones which have the will to learn. These records shall be brought forth by the Masters of the ancient days which have kept them for this time in which to release the.

Be ye as one to be prepared to do thine part. It is so written and revealed that ye (Thedra) shall bring forth such work as has been held for the 'Day of Revelation', which is now come. By mine own hand shall I set mine seal upon these most precious records. These shall be released in such a manner that no man woman or organization shall be able to pilfer or plagiaries, for mine hand shall be heavy upon these ancient revelations. And they shall be released as befitting unto the time, and into the care of the one which hast been prepared for such a responsibility, which is a heavy one. While I have given unto this one the responsibility, I have watched and waited for this day when I might open the record as a living, true, and accurate record for the good of all mankind... which shall open up great doors, and revelation which shall be great light unto all that are prepared to share such as is held within the great vaults of the Ethers, where no unworthy hand hast touched or defiled. Be ye as one alert, for there are many a one which are awaiting this coming event.

Be ye as one (which has been) tried and found true trustworthy. I am at mine Fathers business and He hast given unto me the Authority and the responsibility of this assignment, and I know well mine part. Be ye as one I have called and prepared for this part... I am with thee unto the end. I am known as the wayshower... Sananda by name.

* * *

The Story of Jesus

Sori Sori: Mine beloved, I am speaking unto thee at this hour that ye be as one prepared to come with me into mine place of abode. This is the place prepared for thee, wherein ye shall do greater things. Ye shall be as one to write the story, as it was in reality, at the time of mine existence in the Earth. Long have I waited that this be done as ye shall do it. It is so seen, and the plan is perfected. The time is at hand when this part of the story shall be made straight. It has been changed many times by many people for to please their wishes or limited understanding.

This is the New Day. This part of mine plan shall be a part of the great awakening. For this ye shall be as one on whose shoulders shall be placed the part of bringing forth the true record of the one called by the name which I was given by my Father, also the one I was known by in the Temple of man as it existed at that time, and that which I did and taught. Be ye blest to be the one given this privilege... it is so given unto thee for thine steadfast loyalty and honor.

This is that which ye have not remembered in the fullness of it, thine time with me (in Galilee). Yet ye shall be as one with me, without any doubts, for ye shall know as I know. There shall be a clarity, and it shall be as presented unto the populace as a book of books, which the world of man shall understand in their own tongue... for this shall it be the first of the kind to be known in the Day of Awakening.

This shall be as the book long promised, while it was not yet time for the fulfilment. It is now come when mankind is crying out for Light\Truth. It is now come when there shall be great changes, when man of all nations shall gather themselves about their council tables and agree upon the plan I shall set before them... for their hearts shall be cleft, their eyes made to see, their ears made to hear. They shall walk in the way I have planned before them, which hast been desecrated!.. made unholy!

Now it shall be changed, when man, woman, and child, shall live in peace and safety. So be it, it is come when each head of state shall bow down in holy contrition and see the way which he shall lead these ones, by the light of his wisdom and love which he shall live by, as it is given unto him as his calling within the light. There shall be no more tyranny, no war... every man shall be as brother to brother, one and all!

This is that which I foresee. The plan is in place and the awakening now in motion. Be ye as one to see, hear, and act accordingly. By mine own hand I shall lead thee... be it so, so be it and Selah...

I am the overseer

"Beauantu speaking"

ℰℰℰ : With this signature ye shall know me as one of the host... For this am I come, that ye be as one prepared to receive me. Long ago I came, yet I have not been far from thine presence. I am he which holds thee fast in the dark hours of despair. Now, once again, I speak as one of the Light that ye be learned of that which has mystified thee.

It is said: "All things shall be known", and it is so! For this, we of the host stand by... we are as ones prepared to receive thee into the place wherein we are. While I use such terms as ye are comfortable with, we are not unaware of thine being... every action, every word, we see and know the intent well.

Now ye shall begin a new part, which shall be as the beginning of a book, which shall be finished within this place wherein I am. This is but the foretaste of that which shall be thine new assignment... for this there shall be a great change and it shall be well, for it shall be as ye have not envisioned.

Now ye shall begin thine assignment at this time, and it shall be well to begin this day. Let it be as the Father wills...

Beauantu (bo-an-to)

Note: At this point Sister Thedra began to receive the first part of this book (which is separate from the book about the life of Jesus, which Sananda spoke of). The first part of this book was given and is now in waiting for her to complete it from her new place of abode.

* * *

Excerpt from the opening pages of this partially completed manuscript...

Beauantu speaks:

⟐ This shall suffice for this part which is now being prepared for thee to bring forth, which shall be but the beginning of a new book. From the "Source" of all Light does it come.

While this is but a minuscule part of the <u>Greater Book</u> to be written by and through this one which is called Thedra, which hast been qualified through her loyalty, dedication, and labor, to do this assignment, which is no small task... I say unto mankind, they shall profit to learn of this material so planned by the one which is known in the Realms of Light as "Sananda", the Son of the Living God, which we call Father.

Now it is come when many shall come forth from their deep sleep, and be as ones prepared to go the 'Royal Road", even as he, Sananda, our Brother and Lord of Light, which hast shown the way in which all are asked to go... Be it their choice however. By his grace he hast made straight the way for all which will follow in his footsteps.

Now it is come that we of the Mighty Council, of which he (Sananda) is Head, are as his hands made manifest so to speak, even as ye. While we have greater knowledge of our part, ye have forgotten thine relationship with us of this plane. While we are free of all bondage, unbound by mortal flesh, ye are as ones yet within the world of illusion, which ye refer to as the "dream world"... and is it not?

The purpose/intent which is ours is to awaken mankind to their inheritance, which is eternal life, abundantly, with freedom, wisdom, and love! Blest are they which awaken. These shall be as ones come alive... they shall remember their "Source" and rejoice that the day of deliverance is come.

The time is come when there shall be much joy, for this is the time of fulfilling, when man shall be brought out of bondage... (that is) those which have given of themselves unto their preparation. There hast gone forth from this source, the explanation of "Prepare". The Law is plainly written, it hast been explained by words in many languages. We desire that all know the Law, that none shall say, "I haven't heard... I haven't been appraised of such". It is our intent that every living being might come to know.

Now, it is given unto many to think themselves wise, yet it is said, these are the greatest of fools! Let it be known that there are many which go about the land crying: *"I am come to bring thee into mine camp... I have been initiated into the White Brotherhood... I have seen a light in the sky... I have seen an unknown object in the sky... they are coming to get me, or to save us"*.

Now let me say unto thee, be ye not so foolish as to leave thine house, thine field, etc, to follow him which has this as his banner. These are the ones perhaps, who strut themselves in the street and public places in their robes, soliciting alms, mayhap with their crystals about their neck, seeking thy favor as their trap is carefully laid for thine foot.

I now say unto thee which seek thy freedom: "Be ye as one wise... give unto them nothing! For thine enlightenment comes not from these which solicit favors of man, neither "claim" to be the one come on the so-called 'saucers'.

Let it be known that the ones sent need not ask alms, neither do they boast or betray themselves. The Lighted/Awakened ones are of humble nature, and quietly do they move among the populace. While they speak softly and gently, as brother to brother, they are ofttimes not noticed, yet they sow their seeds of wisdom and leave a lasting impression which is of gentility and wisdom... then the seed ripens within the consciousness when the ground (mind) becomes fertile. This is the awakening! The Awakening comes not from opinions, neither preconceived ideas... these shall be of no account what-so-ever in the time of accounting.

There are ones which have gone before thee to prepare the way that ye be as one prepared to enter into the inner temple, where ye shall know as they know. For this hast the Host come nigh unto thine dwelling place, the Earth, which hast been thine "Mother" Earth. She hast fed and clothed thee, and given of herself that ye be comforted. Have ye noticed? Have ye bowed thine head unto her and counted thine blessings? From whence think ye thine substance came? or comes?

Let us consider for one moment... think ye could live without food and water, or a place to lay thine head? Hast ye remembered when ye were thirsty for the taste of pure water? Do ye remember the day ye hungered and ye plucked a morsel of fresh greenery which stayed thine hunger? Possibly, ye came to the bare cupboard to find naught? What did ye say? Do ye remember thine words? I ask thee, ponder these mine words, for they have been fashioned on thine behalf, that ye become aware of that which is about thee.

Now let us consider the day when ye had no place in thine society... ye were enslaved by those of high cast. What didst thou do to free thine self and thine 'Brother'? Or did ye do anything at all? These which struggle, giving their all, their heart, perhaps their physical vehicle, are the one to which ye owe allegiance, even unto thine self... for it is not robbery to take that which is thine by right.

While the humble boast not of their victory which hast been won by the effort and devotion of thy fellow man, too, I would remind thee at this hour, that one wise does not waste his time speaking of the past, which is past, gone, when the eternal time/day is "now".

"Now" is the new day! Why walk ye backwards, counting and recounting the past, (be it sorrowful or victorious) when ye might be as one looking up, seeking greater Light, new ways to better thy fellow beings which are a hunger... with no place to lay their head... no bread for their belly... no hope for tomorrow? What of the little child which knows not where he came from or who his father/mother is? Yea, what of these? Who are they? Do they or their parents know that which they are? <u>Who amongst thee cares</u>? I give unto thee a parable upon which ye shall ponder.

Do ye care enough to ask "How can I help"? When your answer is a positive one, a sincere trust, "YEA"... I promise thee, ye shall be given information truly worthy of thine sincere effort for the good of all... even the yet unborn generations. For there are none which turn their back on such as these (the homeless - the abandoned children)... be they whoever they be they (which turn their back) are as the traitor unto the whole of society, the ones which "take" without thought of the ones which have prepared for them the comforts of this present day generation.

What of the pioneers which had a vision of this day? Have ye a vision that al might be free, fed, clothed, comforted? Have ye visited the sick and dying? Where of have ye given comfort to the lonely and forsaken, alone and forgotten, crying for a human touch, a comforting word?

Whereof have ye dinned sumptuously on the choice of viands, drunk the choice of wine from the vine, without thought of where from it came, this great privilege? I say, be ye blest by the ones which have given of themselves that it be as ye partake... even unto the source, Mother Earth. What hast thou done to bless her, even as she has blest thee?

On thoughtless uncaring children of the Earth... I remind thee again, the time of accounting is nigh upon thee, when ye shall be reminded of thine thoughtlessness. So be it as ye prepare thine self.

End Excerpt...

* * *

Greater knowledge - greater vision

Sori Sori: Upon the precepts of the light of the Great Creator of all beginnings are our works and plans formulated. This is that which we of the Christ Council would have thee understand, for it is now seen that the time is come for thee to be further learned in the things, ways, of the progression of "man". For man, such as ye, is sleeping within flesh. He hast little knowledge of his Being, his reality, his eternal reality.

Now, it is known amongst us which make up this Mighty Council of Light, that it is now time that ye (Thedra) awaken unto thine true identity. For this it is necessary that ye be brought into the place wherein is a place for thee, that ye might go all the way into the Light that never fails. This hast been given unto thee in any ways which ye have not comprehended. While it is so planed, so shall it be!

Now that it is most expedient that ye be prepared for the greater part, there are many to assist thee in that which ye shall be allotted to do, for there is a place wherein ye shall see and hear, and know that which ye see. Then ye shall return unto them fully prepared, capable of conveying unto them that which is truth... for there are few which have the full knowledge of that which they proclaim/expound as truth.

It is foreseen that these with whom ye have knowledge of, these which have asked for truth, shall be as ones blest of thee that ye shall return unto them in the manner which is given unto thee... as ye shall return unto them as new and they shall be as ones to bear witness of these mine words. I have said, blest are they which holds fast unto me, for they find me a friend and benefactor. I forsake not that one which I call forth as mine chosen, yet the one I call shall answer me and follow mine precepts. He shall be blest to know mine voice, mine touch, and I shall walk and talk with him until the time is appropriate to bring him in.

Let this be known, (this mine word unto thee at this hour), at the time of thine departure, not before, for it would be misunderstood. This is not 'our' intent to mystify them, for there is no mystery except thine unknowing. While it is a time of sitting and sorting, there is timing in this... all things are timed by events. Is it not said many times; "As Ye Are Prepared So Shall Ye Receive". So it is... So it is... So shall it be.

Be ye as one now prepared to enter into this place prepared to receive thee, and ye shall not fear or be alone, for there shall be many to receive thee and ye shall know such joy as ye have never known.

Such things which have mystified thee shall be made clear unto thee, then ye shall go forth as one qualified to give unto them as ye have learned... that is, unto the ones which are prepared to receive such learning. I say "<u>learning</u>", for learning is quite different from <u>information</u>. We are not simply informers, we are at the place wherein we are that man of Earth learn of his heritage and accept it as his precious gift of the Father, which ye call God... thine Source of Being.

This is the day ye have long awaited as thine awakening, when thine eyes shall be opened unto the glory of the Heavens. There shall be nothing hidden... all shall be revealed in Truth/Light. Blest are they which are prepared to enter into the place which is now ready to receive thee. So be it and Selah.

* * *

Sananda

Sori Sori: Mine beloved, I am now speaking unto thee for the good of all. Ye shall be as one prepared for thine flight with me, for it is I that be thine deliverer from bondage. Ye shall depart the place wherein ye are as One with me... it is so written and it is so. So be it as the Father wills.

There shall be a great host to accompany thee, and ye shall be as one to know as I know. Ye shall go as I go, where I go, for ye shall be as l. There shall be no pain, no more sorrow, for I say, ye shall be as one made new... never more to be bound in flesh, never more to be born of woman, for ye shall be as one of light substance.

There shall be freedom... ye shall go as I go, come as I come, yet ye shall be free as I am free. Ye shall know as I know, do as I do, for there shall be no limitation.

Ye shall give of thineself that all be blest. There shall be great joy, and much shall be known by the populace of thine new birth, which shall be the "Inauguration of the New Day", when many shall awaken unto their rightful estate. For the Father hast sent me that there shall be a great light, which shall be as the herald of the New Age, the end of the dream-time. Let them which sleep arise and throw off the old and put on the new.

As it is written so shall it be, for it is willed of the Source' of all Light. It is so written in the Heavens... So shall it be! For this am I come!

I am come that the Fathers will be done... so be it, Amen and Amen... Selah.

I AM that I Am

* * *

Concerning the symbols

The information which began in newsletter #66, of which this newsletter is a continuation, concerns the various spiritual "Orders" within the "Order of Man". These various Orders are represented by symbols signifying their position according to their spiritual development and attainment. Below are the symbols which designate these Orders and an approximation (from what we have been thus far given) of the nature of these various Orders.

ℰℰℰ This is the first and highest of the Orders, often referred to as the "Elders" which make up the Mighty Council. Although these are within the "Order of Man" just as we are, these underwent their spiritual evolution and development in a much earlier cycle than this present cycle, possible even before the earth existed. These are of the higher dimensions of life and are not bound within forms of flesh.

ƤƤƤ This is the second of the Orders, often referred to as the "Guardians" or the "Shepherds". These were the first of the "species of man" upon the earth which begin to awaken to their true nature as spiritual beings. They function now as "guardians" or "shepherds" to the Orders which are still struggling to awaken to their true spiritual nature. Some within this Order are currently embodied upon the earth.

ᒍᒍᒍ This is the third Order, often referred to as the "sleepers". Despite the unceasing efforts of the above Orders to awaken them through greater light and a greater understanding, these have slept on within the illusion of flesh through countless cycles here upon the earth. Many within this Order are currently embodied upon the earth.

ᖇᖇᖇ This is the last and lowest Order, usually referred to as the "Laggards". Through cycle after cycle these have repeatedly rejected any light or help which has been offered them for their spiritual awakening during their long sojourn here upon the earth.

* * *

A brief note

Since Sister Thedra's passing in June of 1992, we have put out only two newsletters... the first in June of 92, in which we announced her passing and printed her final messages, and the second in December in which we printed some of the information which she had received in the months before her passing. Since her passing we have had no direct communication with her apart from a brief message shortly after her passing in which she simply conveyed that she had completed her transition and was presently re-adjusting to her new found freedom and beginning her preparation for the work which was to come. Having known her and worked with her over a period of almost 25 years this silence does not surprise me in the least. Her approach to the work has always been very disciplined, and she simply did what was necessary at the moment without ever looking back.

Since the last issue was printed in December we have heard from so many people who have expressed their feeling that they truly missed receiving the A.S.S.K, newsletters and the messages of inspiration and encouragement they contained. Many have asked if we would continue publishing the newsletter with information which perhaps had not been released as yet. So, in order to keep this connection of inspiration and encouragement going, we have decided to again resume the publication of "A Call To Arms" newsletter.

As many of you know, Sister Thedra began receiving information for a new book in July of 1990. However, the first thing she was told was that she would begin this book here at but that she would not complete it until after she had made her transition. Since the completed portion of this book was never released we have decided to begin releasing this information in these newsletters. This will begin with this issue and will continue until the portion which was recorded before her passing is released in full. When the unfinished portion of this book is given we will then publish it in book form in its entirety. Perhaps this first portion of that work will give us some idea where the new work might be heading. May it be of profit to us all...

Before beginning this newsletter with the communications, we thought we would like to share with you a short story which was previously given by Sananda. We had intended to print it at the end of this newsletter, however since the communications which follow seem at times to mirror this story we thought it might be of greater benefit to print it first...

* * *

A short story

In 1989, Sister Thedra and I were visiting with a man in St. Louis who had been receiving instructions from Sananda for several years. While visiting with him he told us of a vision which Sananda had shown him concerning the many distractions associated with the spiritual awakening process now happening here upon the earth. Since then I have related this story to many people which have stopped by at A.S.S.K., many of whom have expressed a desire that we print it in the newsletter. Since it might possibly be of benefit to some of you I will relate it here, in short. I also realize that some people may be offended by it, but it is not meant to offend or to discredit in any way. Simply give it some thought...

The Great Speaking

As the silent awakening call was being sent out upon the earth, those seekers after 'Truth' and those with an inner ear attuned to the greater spiritual reality began to be drawn from around the world. They were gathering outside of the entrance doors to a beautiful building, awaiting the "Great Speaking", or the Great Teaching, which was soon to take place within. Inside of these entrance doors was a great long hallway which led from the entrance to an immense stadium where the "Great Speaking" was to take place. Inside of this great stadium a seat had been reserved for each and every one who had responded.

As the ever-increasing crowd waited outside of these doors several "ushers" emerged from out of this great stadium and walked the length of this great hallway to the entrance doors at the opposite end. As they opened these doors the anxiously awaiting crowds began to file in, and in mass began to make their way down this great hallway to the stadium.

However, before long, some within the crowd began to stop along the sides of this hallway and set up booths. This went on until the sides of this hallway were filled with ramshackle booths advertising such things as... "crystals", "pyramid energy", "sacred trinkets" "psychic readings", "past life readings", "tarot card readings", "astrology readings", "UFO information", "Sacred mandalas" "natural concoctions & potions", "sacred mantras", "spiritual healings", "dolphin energy", etc, etc, etc...

Soon, many within the crowd began to become entranced by the claims being made, and many began milling around these booths looking for some spiritual formula or magic "thing" which would help open their consciousness to the greater spiritual realities. Most soon found that in spite of what they were being told these counselings or "things" did not fulfill their desires and their attention was quickly drawn to some other booth where they soon became entranced again by the words of another seller.

Now, some of the people who had filed through the entrance doors simply ignored these booths. They kept their focus and attention upon the real reason they had come and proceeded directly down the length of this great hallway and entered the great stadium where they took their seats. Some of the people who had at first become so entranced by the wares offered in these many booths soon tired of the distractions and joined those entering the great stadium where they also took their seats.

Finally, when the last of the crowd waiting outside the building had passed through the entrance doors and into the great hallway the "ushers" closed these outer doors and began to walk the length of this great long hallway. When they reached the end of the hallway they grasped the doors leading to the Great Stadium, turned and simply announced to everyone still milling along the hallway: "Last call".

When the last of the people which had reached the end of the hallway had entered this Great Stadium the "ushers" simply closed and locked the doors, and this Great Stadium then began to raise in vibration until the vibration reached that of the fourth dimension, where the minds and senses of those within this stadium were heightened and where the Great Speaking and the Great Teaching finally took place.

Now, back within the great hallway there were still countless people who had been spiritually drawn to this place by the silent call to "Awaken to the greater spiritual realities", but who had somehow become entranced within a web of psychic manifestations and things which they believed was somehow necessary for their awakening process.

They had become entranced in a search for some "thing" which they hoped would unlock the door into greater realities and expand their understanding of God. Like climbers, who, in milling about the base of the mountain to discuss their many methods, had lost sight of the summit...

* * *

Ending note

A lesson we might consider: If all life springs forth from one "Source"... and if we are a part of that "life" and seek a greater understanding of that "Source"... then the spiritual awakening process is a "living" process within our own consciousness which forms a direct link between our own consciousness and the "Source of all life. We so often become distracted by the many "side trips" which we then come to believe are essential to our awakening process... when the real process is simply the awakening of that link between our own consciousness and the "Source" of life...

Instructions

ƤƤƤ With this signature ye shall know me as one of the host... for this am I come, that ye be as one prepared to receive me. Long ago I came, yet I have not been far from thine presence. I am he which holds thee fast in the dark hours of despair.

Now, once again, I speak as one of the light that ye be learned of that which has mystified thee. It is said: "All things shall be known", and it is so. For this we of the host stand by. We are as ones prepared to receive thee (Thedra) into the place wherein we are. While I use such terms as ye are comfortable with, we are not unaware of thine being. Every action, every word, we see and know the intent well.

Now ye shall begin a new part, which shall be as the beginning of a book, which shall be finished within this place wherein I am. This is but the foretaste of that which shall be thine new assignment. For this there shall be a great change, and it shall be well, for it shall be as ye have not envisioned.

Now ye shall begin thine assignment at this time, and it shall be well to begin this day. Let it be as the Father wills...

Beauantu (bo-an-to)

* * *

BEGIN BOOK

July 12, 1990

Note: *This first message was originally printed in newsletter 64 which announced Sister Thedra's passing. However since this is the message which begins the book we have decided to reprint it again here for the purpose of continuity of the messages which follow.*

Beauantu speaks

⬨ This shall suffice for this part which is now being prepared for thee to bring forth, which shall be but the beginning of a new book. From the Source of all light does it come. While this is but a minuscule part of the <u>Greater Book</u> to be written by and through this one which is called Thedra, which hast been qualified through her loyalty, dedication, and labor to do this assignment, which is no small task... I say unto mankind, they shall profit to learn of this material so planned by the one which is known in the realms of light as "Sananda", the Son of the Living God which we call Father.

Now it is come when many shall come forth from their deep sleep, and be as ones prepared to go the 'Royal Road", even as he, Sananda, our brother and Lord of light which hast shown the way in which all are asked to go. Be it their choice, however, by his grace he hast made straight the way for all which will follow in his footsteps.

Now it is come that we of the Mighty Council, of which he (Sananda) is head, are as his hands made manifest so to speak, even as ye. While we have greater knowledge of our part, ye have forgotten thine relationship with us of this plane. While we are free of all bondage, unbound by mortal flesh, ye are as ones yet within the world of illusion, which ye refer to as the "dream world"... and is it not?

The purpose/intent which is ours is to awaken mankind to their inheritance, which is eternal life, abundantly, with freedom, wisdom, and love! Blest are they which awaken. These shall be as ones come alive... they shall remember their "Source" and rejoice that the day of deliverance is come.

The time is come when there shall be much joy, for this is the time of fulfilling when man shall be brought out of bondage... (that is) those which have given of themselves unto their preparation. There hast gone forth from this source the explanation of "<u>Prepare</u>". The Law is plainly written, it hast been explained by words in many languages. We desire that all know the Law, that none shall say, "I haven't heard... I haven't been appraised of such". It is our intent that every living being might come to know.

Now, it is given unto many to "think" themselves wise, yet it is said, these are the greatest of fools. Let it be known that there are many which go about the land crying: "*I am come to bring thee into mine camp... I have been initiated into the White Brotherhood... I have seen a light in the sky... I have seen an unknown object in the sky... they are coming to get me, or to save us*".

Now let me say unto thee, be ye not so foolish as to leave thine house, thine field, etc, to follow him which has this as his banner. These are the ones perhaps, who strut themselves in the street and public places in their robes, soliciting alms, mayhap with their crystals about their neck, seeking thy favor as their trap is carefully laid for thine foot. I now say unto thee which seek thy freedom: "Be ye as one <u>wise</u>... give unto them nothing! For thine enlightenment comes not from these which solicit favors of man, neither claim to be the one come on the so-called 'saucers'.

Let it be known that the ones sent need not ask alms, neither do they boast or betray themselves. The Lighted/Awakened ones are of humble nature, and quietly do they move among the populace. While they speak softly and gently, as brother to brother, they are ofttimes not noticed, yet they sow their seeds of wisdom and leave a lasting impression which is of gentility and wisdom... then the seed ripens within the consciousness when the ground (mind) becomes fertile. This is the awakening! The Awakening comes not from opinions, neither preconceived ideas... these shall be of no account what-so-ever in the time of accounting.

There are ones which have gone before thee to prepare the way that ye be as one prepared to enter into the inner temple where ye shall know as they know. For this hast the Host come nigh unto thine dwelling place, the earth, which hast been thine M<u>other</u> Earth. She hast fed and clothed thee, given of herself that ye be comforted. Have ye noticed? Have ye bowed thine head unto her and counted thine blessings? From whence think ye thine substance came, or comes?

Let us consider for one moment: Think ye could live without food and water, a place to lay thine head? Hast ye remembered when ye were thirsty for the taste of pure water? Do ye remember the day ye hungered and ye plucked a morsel of fresh greenery which stayed thine hunger? Possibly, ye came to the bare cupboard to find naught. What did ye say... do ye remember thine words? I ask thee, ponder these mine words, for they have been fashioned on thine behalf that ye become aware of that which is about thee.

Now let us consider the day when ye had no place in thine society... ye were enslaved by those of high cast. What didst thou do to free thine self and thine 'brother? Or did ye do anything at all? These which struggle, giving their all, their heart, perhaps their physical vehicle, are the ones to which ye owe allegiance, even unto thine self... for it is not robbery to take that which is thine by right.

While the humble boast not of their victory which hast been won by the effort and devotion of thy fellow man, too, I would remind thee at this hour, that one wise does not waste his time speaking of the past, which is past, gone, when the eternal time/day is <u>Now</u>. "Now" is the new day! Why walk ye backwards? counting and recounting the past, (be it sorrowful or victorious) when ye might be as one looking up, seeking greater light, new ways to better thy fellow beings which are a hunger... no place to lay their head... no bread for their belly... no hope for tomorrow? What of the little child which knows not where he came from, or who his father/mother is? Yea, what of these? Who are they?

Do they or their parents know that which they are... Who (amongst thee) cares?

I give unto thee a parable upon which ye shall ponder. Do ye care enough to ask "How can I help"? When your answer is a positive one, a sincere trust, "YEA", I promise thee, ye shall be given information, truly and worthy of thine sincere effort for the good of all, even the yet unborn generations. For there are none which turn their back on such as these... be they whoever they be they are as the traitor unto the whole of society, the ones which take without thought of the ones which have prepared for them the comforts of this present day generation.

What of the pioneers which had a vision of this day? Have ye a vision that all might be free, fed, clothed, comforted? Have ye visited the sick and dying? Whereof have ye given comfort to the lonely and forsaken, alone and forgotten, crying for a human touch, a comforting word? Whereof have <u>ye</u> dined sumptuously on the choice of viands, drunk the choice of wine from the vine, without thought of where from it came, this great privilege? I say, be ye blest by the ones which have given of themselves that it be as ye partake... even unto the source, mother earth. What hast thou done to bless her, even as she has blest thee?

Oh thoughtless uncaring children of the Earth... I remind thee again, the time of accounting is nigh upon thee, when ye shall be reminded of thine thoughtlessness. So be it as ye prepare thine self.

* * *

Wherein is it written that as ye prepare thineself so shall ye receive? So let it be, for none become Master without effort and dedication. This is as it is... the Law. Ye cannot come into this place wherein we, the host, abides until ye have prepared thine self by obedience unto the Law, that which we are now revealing unto thee. It is clearly written in many and sundry places. It is spoken in every language that ye might know.de

We, the host, which come at this time, hast waited long for this privilege. It is for our love that we come unto thee that ye be prepared to return unto thine rightful estate... the place of thine going out.

* * *

It is now come when great shall be the revelations which shall go forth from thine (Thedra's) hand... for this have ye been called out from the populace. Ye have within thine hand the gift which ye have earned by thine dedication and obedience. It shall be for the good of all mankind that ye take upon thineself this assignment. We of the mighty host of light shall be unto thee thine assistants, thine strength and Sibors. This is that which ye have earned in the time of thine waiting.

Now ye shall bring forth that which hast been hidden from mankind lo, the many seasons. Many shall awaken from their slumber and cry for joy that this day is come... others so steeped in their lethargy or dead on their feet shall not be touched/moved, for they have chosen their own way, therefore we dare not interfere with their choice.

Let this be, as it is given unto thee aforetime to learn the law of free will. This shall not be trespassed on in the world of mortal man, for he hast gone forth as an individual soul with the gift of free will, the greatest possible gift man could ever have. All others are the lesser. This is that which brings about the many diverse opinions and preconceived ideas of their origin, their nature and their heritage. Yea, and that which hast been imposed upon them by the ones which have thought themselves wise, which hast made laws and punishment to suit themselves.

It is now come when the Law of being shall be brought forth for their freedom. It is for our knowledge and wisdom, our love of all life and the will of the Father that we are sent to alert these which have the will to awaken and return unto the "Source" of all life. This we know as the day of awakening, for the long day of darkness is at an end. The dawning of the light is now come. The generations to come shall know this day which is now dawning upon the eastern horizon as the "New Day", the coming of light. They shall have understanding of "light" and how to use it for the good of all. None shall perish at the hands of their fellow being, for they shall know themselves to be brothers all, "One" with all life, and no life shall be destroyed or misused. For these ones, which are yet to be prepared to come into thine world shall bring a new order... they shall know the law of life and respect it! Too, they shall be appraised, see, and know this age which is ending as the 'Dark Night' of man and his works. They shall see and know aforehand that which man hast brought forth as his own, his 'ego', and for that his destruction.

While there hast been pioneers come from afar to teach and guide, bearing gifts of light to reveal the law of love and brotherhood... for that matter many of these benefactors hast been martyred, slain in anger and hatred because of their (man's) opinions and preconceived ideas.

Your generations for ages past hast bowed down unto their so-called 'gods'. They have sold their freedom unto them which hast sent them into bondage. Man hast sold his soul for a poor potage. He starves for a crust of bread, he knows not where to find peace, neither where to turn for surcease. While few know that by which he is bound, he fights for justice for all. He raises his hand in defense of his fellow man, and he, too often, is stricken down.

I say unto all men: Freedom is thine inheritance. I too say, it is that which we of the host of light are bringing unto the ones which have a will to accept it. So be it our intent that all be made aware of their heritage.

* * *

While it is now the time of accounting for all of mankind, each hast accrued his share at this time, when each shall answer for his own wanton ways. His own sowing he shall reap, for harvest time is now come for all and sundry. I say, each one shall reap as he has sown... then he shall be accountable for that which he shall do with the reaping. He shall either learn from it or build upon it, the harvest.

Pray that it be as profitable unto thee, O man of bondage. Give unto thine self credit for being thine own porter, for ye bring thine own self from out the darkness wherein ye might be found... or ye may languish in lethargy and wait (in vain) for a brother to carry thee on his back.

We of the host of light say unto thee: Tarry ye no longer in the pits of ignorance/bondage. Arise and come forth as one prepared to partake of the manna which we bring, which shall be unto thee life abundantly, everlasting.

While we call unto one and all, "Come forth and accept that which we offer unto thee", ye shall come of thine own will. It hast been clearly stated that none bring thee out of bondage unless ye will it so. Yet, as ye will it, ye shall be as one to arise, shake off thine lethargy, cleanse thine self, and extend unto us thine hand that we, thine brothers of light, might take it in love... for we are thine benefactors.

* * *

The time approaches earth man when he shall stand shorn of all his laurels, and every man shall be equal. I say, equal, for there shall be no rich or poor. Every man shall be as his own porter. He shall be as one responsible for his part in the whole of mankind's environment, for it shall be one for all, all for one.

I say, all shall be as "One"... one mind, one intent. There shall be no war, no hunger, for man shall learn that which is now proffered unto him is for to bring him into the state of the brotherhood of man in the Fatherhood of all created beings. Man shall then learn of his heritage, his "Source", which makes of all brothers in the one Source, which we of the host know as Solen Aum Solen. Ye shall come to understand that which has been hidden up from thee for the age which is now dawning upon the eastern horizon.

O, what a New Day when all mankind shall come to know himself to be as brothers in the Fatherhood of God. By the will of the Father Mother God it shall come to pass, even as it is written.

* * *

Beauntau Speaking: This I would have all mankind know: That I speak for the good of all. I come from the Inner Temple of Light wherein all things are known... wherein there are no mysteries, no secrets. For this I am qualified to speak unto mankind with authority and wisdom. For this shall I speak as I see fit, in any fashion I choose for the good of all mankind, that they might be able to understand mine messages. For the time of "Awakening" is come. Too long hast the man of earth labored in darkness, wrestled with the mysteries of his 'being', knowing not the meaning of his existence upon this little beautiful planet.

Now it is come when we of the Mighty Council hast come nigh unto the earth which gives thee footing that ye be enlightened of thine own being which is eternal. I bring unto each that which shall be unto thee that for which ye have looked... "Answers". I say, thine questions shall be answered when ye put forth thine energy\effort to learn of these things which comprise all the questions ye could ask However, there are none, none prepared to receive all the answers at once, for there are none strong and powerful of spirit to comprehend it all, all of their history of existence, which entails many, many master cycles of existence throughout the cosmos. Many forms hast ye used for a time. Again and again hast thou come into this orb which ye now exist upon as man.

Be ye not so sure of thineself, for ye are not so wise as to deny that which I am bringing unto thee that ye be as one prepared to come learn of thine history, thine existence, that all thine questions be satisfied. Yet be not so foolish as to imagine that all thine curiosity be satisfied in one day, or week... nay, not a year. While ye have groped long in darkness to this point, ye are yet not enlightened unto thine Source of being... Know ye that!

As it is now time that we of the host are come for the purpose of delivering thee out of darkness, it is expedient that ye, the children of earth, give us credence for being thine "benefactors, that which we are. Ye may call us the Elder Brothers, come that ye be prepared to return unto thine rightful estate/inheritance. By thine humility, obedience, and loyalty unto the law of love, ye shall be as one prepared to go all the way with the ones sent to appraise thee of the law and thine deportment, that ye be as one capable of our effort to assist thee in thine search, or schooling ye may call it, for that it is!

* * *

The school

For this day let us speak of the school. This school is for the sober sincere one which has the mind, the character, the will to follow the benefactor where he leads, with the knowledge that he (the benefactor) is that which he is, of the 'Lighted Ones' to bring him out of the pit of darkness. For this is he accepted as a neophyte, as one prepared to enter into this place so prepared for him which has cleansed himself of all his wanton ways... his hypocrisy, deceit, hatred, selfishness, bigotry. For this he humbles himself that he might learn of his lighted Elders.

Then he is accepted as one qualified to enter into the outer school, wherein he prepares himself to enter into the next place, wherein he learns of the greater laws of existence and the fullness of that which he hast not known. Thus he progresses at his own capacity, or within his own capacity, as he hast applied himself.

Let me say that there are no laggards within this school. It is brought forth in wisdom, and great the purpose and intent which hast been told aforehand (in two previous books). Forget not that which hast been said unto thee, as thy qualification includes attention unto thine benefactors mandates or instructions.

* * *

This I would have thee understand: "As ye prepare thine self, so shall ye become". Now we offer thee that which no mortal man of earth is prepared to give.

While there are many this day which are "claiming" great power and wisdom, many are their willing "students" shall I say. These ones pick thine pockets and leave thee no comfort. Be ye, one and all, alert unto these charlatans, for they have two tongues and wear painted masks to deceive thee. Many deceive themselves... The pity of it!

To be aware and heed not the warning is the greatest of folly. Be ye circumspect in all thine dealing, and listen unto thine inner being. Practice listening unto thine heart.

* * *

Sananda

Sori Sori: Let this be mine word unto all mankind: There shall be a great coming of lighted Ones. They shall go out amongst the populace wherein they shall, by their very presence, do a mighty work. They shall project rays of light into the consciousness of man. They shall be as ones modest and of humble form... humble, with no crown upon their head, no token of their intent or wisdom. They shall sit in thy halls of justice. They shall sit with the lowly, the meek, and silently shall they pass by the unknowing ones and touch them which hast the mind to feel or hear that which is silently sent forth with the sound which is only felt by the open mind and heart.

Therefore, I say unto all: Keep thine eye open... Take thine fingers out of thine ears... Purify thine heart. Rid thine self of all thine carnal ways such as lust, lust for self-satisfaction, be it what so ever... sex for self-entertainment... power over others... the many pit-falls which have tripped the wanderer which knows not that his time is limited upon this little orb of earth.

I say it is now come when we have come in concert from lands afar, that ye, one and all, shall be awakened unto thine responsibility which is thine to take, and come forth to meet the great new world which is in the creating\making at this hour. Be ye not so foolish as to turn a deaf ear unto our speech or touch. However, I would adjure thee, be not so foolish to think that all which shall mimic me is the one that ye should follow... for it is not given unto me to leave thee uninformed. Yet it is said and truly so, "To be informed is not knowledge/knowing".

O, man listen, listen, listen for truth-light which is of thy Source. Be not so hasty to go wherein they sit in silence, in secret and mystery, clothed in their robes of mystical origin. Seek not of man thy freedom. I say unto thee, feign not wisdom, for ye shall not by any other means become wise than by the grace of the living God, which is thine "Source" of being. Prey not before idols for thine deliverance, for there is no pardon with these. These are not thine benefactors. They (the idols) have no power within them, save within thine own imaging, which is thine own fancy, which is like unto a counterfeit coin. Know ye that which I say unto thee?

Bear ye in mind, I am come as the manifestation of mine Father which hast sent me as his hand made manifest that ye be delivered up, out of the pit of ignorance and darkness of despair. I abide in Him, for He and I are "One". I <u>know</u> mine self to Be, for I have received from Him mine inheritance in full. Therefore, I am prepared to speak as He, and to do that which He does, for we are One, even as ye and I are One. However, I know mine self to be One with the "All", which includes the child of many forms, many places.

* * *

ccc While there are many which are dedicated to bringing forth such work as ours at this point in time, there shall be no interference with any other method or choice on thine part. Neither shall there be any criticism of each others work, for it is not thine to choose our method of communication or our fashion in which we choose to employ it.

I am speaking now unto each and every one which has a part in these communications from the higher realm of light, for we see and know as none upon thine plane do see. There is purpose in our ways, the many ways in which we endeavor to bring thee out of the unknowing state, which we refer to as ignorance of that which hast been given unto thee in wisdom and love.

* * *

ℱℱℱ Justice is the law which makes of all men brothers, that which is of perfect love. This is mine word unto thee, for we shall speak much of love: That which we know as love, mankind knows but little, as he hast forgotten his "Source", which is love. I say love *is* the Source... do ye comprehend this? I say not... not so! All manifestation comes through this power, for love and life are synonymous... little understood by mankind.

Have ye heard it said, "For the love of life"? It is the "Source" of all life which man hast not understood as yet. For this have we made our being known unto the world of man. In the next few years of your calendar time, ye shall remember these words, for it is the greatest thing that ye could learn, to come to know... that is the power of love as we know it to be.

For this shall ye, man, come to know justice, justice for all mankind... then they shall love each other as brothers. There shall be no inequality, no war, no hatred. Then there shall be a "New Earth and a New Heaven", even as it is written. And man shall be as "One" with the All, which is destined to bring this about. For both heaven and earth shall be One, for earth shall be as purified and lifted up into a new orbit, wherein she shall be free from all pain and suffering.

* * *

♂♂♂ The hour hast struck which heralds our time of communication (3:45am), this be the time most appropriate...

By the grace of the Living God, our Father, we are prepared to bring forth this portion for the good of all mankind. The time is now when the populace of the earth shall come to know that they populace of the earth shall come to know that they are not alone upon this very small and beautiful planet, which hast been a place prepared for their benefit, that they\it (the whole of the populace) might come into the fullness of their estate. This be our part, to assist them as a whole to come into the reality of their inheritance as Sons of God, which hast sent them forth, even as we have come.

Long age, aeons ago, we of the mighty host wast called forth that we be prepared for this our present mission unto thee of this present day. For this day of fulfillment of our waiting period we have come unto thee, a generation of confused and sorrowful beings, lost unto their heritage, knowing not their Source.

Now it is come when they, as One, brothers all, from the same Source, shall be as one awaken, as 'One' alive, and come forth knowing that which they are in Truth and in Reality... brothers... for this is our mission unto the earth man. By the full-ness of his inheritance he shall be lifted into his new place of abode where he shall be as a new man. He shall be as the whole of man... one mind, one intent... even as we of the host, which are as one body, which makes up the host of the Lighted/Illumined Ones which shall reveal itself unto the world of man. For this have we (as one body) come at this crucial time. There shall be a light which goes forth as man hast not ever seen. He shall be drawn unto it as he hast been told aforehand in so many ways, which he hast not comprehended.

Now, the word hast gone forth unto all lands of the earth: Awaken! Awaken! So shall it be as the Father wills... For this are we come...

"The prophecy"

It wast written unto the Jews of old: "I shall remove from you mine gift unto you, and give it to the Gentile".

Thedra speaking: With the word "Come", the power for the pen was withdrawn, 'mercifully' I thought. By holding the furniture I reached my bed with great physical pain and effort.

I felt the (unseen) loving hands help lay my body on the bed on my back. That great overwhelming love consumed the pain...

At last, relaxation...

Into my vision came a large, long, heavy sewing needle. "What of this", I asked... "surely not the hospital," I thought...

"No", came the gentle voice of love... "You are the needle... I am the thread which shall sew all this together. Now it is come when another shall come, and the change shall come to pass as it is written. By mine own hand shall we continue that which hast been foreseen and recorded... So be it and Selah".

* * *

ℯℯℯ By the power and the light of the Living God shall you and I be as "One" in this assignment, for it is so written within the heavens. Therein is the plan, the Great Plan, revealed unto mankind. This is for his release from bondage.

It is foretold that it is mankind's heritage to be free to go and come at will throughout the universe... to be free from sickness and so-called death, destruction, for his freedom is his heritage, the gift of the Source. We of the host of light have now come to be as the deliverer. For this we are "One" with the father God which hast sent us forth.

It is so planned from the beginning of man's sojourn upon earth that when this cycle or time came that his awakening should be at its beginning as ne'er before. However, it hast been long, yea many aeons, that we have prepared for this, the day of awakening. This hast been recorded in thine book in many languages, and many ways or languages of every tongue hast it been given unto mankind, yet ye hast waited this day. While he hast wandered thru the lands of earth as strangers, without the knowledge of his Source of being, he hast been as ones lost within the fog-mist of unknowing or forgetfulness. Many stories, times upon untold numbers, have been recorded in the time of darkness when little was given unto him. For this he waited and cried out for surcease from pain, pain of unknowing and forgetfulness. His longing hast been great. Yet, this day we find within these which we call mankind, that there are many which know not that we, the host of light, are come, is come, as one body, that they be delivered out of the sad state of forgetfulness. We come offering them their freedom. We give of ourself as of one mind, one body, one intent, that of bringing them out that their memory might be restored, that they might see and know that which is their inheritance willed unto them in the beginning. Their beginning shall be made known in toto (total). There shall be no more mystery, for they shall know that which they are in reality. All their illusions shall be as naught. They shall be as brothers, returned unto their rightful estate willed unto them of the Source of all light. For this shall they awaken this day.

This is that which hast been referred to within some of thine 'holy' works called the 'Bible'. Many other records hast been left for man, which he hast not fully understood the meaning thereof. This great day of deliverance hast been called the 'resurrection day'. By many means it is referred to in graphic pictorials left for man's deciphering as record of his long existence, as they comprehend it to be, or knew it at that time.

Man hast wandered far from his place of origin. He has not given unto himself credit for his heritage, for his beginning of mortal existence. Now he shall come to know and understand where he came from and his destiny. By the time he hast learned this he shall be mature as mankind, and he shall become as God. For this are we calling unto him now, that he awaken unto that which he shall become.

Our intent is to bring him home that all his longings be satisfied. For this have we entered into thine world of ❡❡❡ of flesh, which hast had its day. Mankind shall become that which he wast meant to be before he went into bondage. He shall know the true story of his origin, of his inheritance. He shall be as 'One' with all life, in truth, principal, and in reality. No more shall he grovel in the darkness, in the forgetfulness of his true origin. No longer shall he war with his species, in hatred, fear and jealousy. No longer shall he fear.

Some fear to learn of himself, of his origin, his purpose on the planet. Others cry out in their dream like confusion, seeking truth of the self... such desires send them into foreign lands seeking signs of their beginning upon the earth. They make records and interpret them with that which they have at hand, that which they have accrued in their time as man. Yet, he hast not, as yet, had the knowledge which is now available unto him this day when he is on the brink of his awakening, or, as ye would put it, a breakthrough.

Let it be recorded herein, that this is our purpose... to awaken him unto the fullness of his being... of thine being. I say unto one and all, that it is now come when there shall be great changes which shall come swiftly. Whereas mankind hast had many, so many, aeons of developing himself for this point in time, it is written that "Time shall be shortened"... it is so, yet not fully understood.

* * *

Mans' evolution

While mankind hast groped in darkness, in forgetfulness, we of the lighted Ones, which are his guardians and benefactors, hast watched and guarded his progress. It is now come when he hast come into the time, or cycle, of his ability to comprehend greater learning, which we now propose to give unto him as his heritage... this being the opening/beginning of the new cycle/day of enlightenment.

It behooves us, which have the power and knowledge of his (man's) beginning, to come unto him in concert, that he might be prepared to come into the fullness of his being. We are his brothers (which were before him) known as the "Elders". We place before him the way he should go as man. While we watched and cared for him as the Elder Brothers, they (man) became estranged from us and brought upon themselves as divided entities, and wandered far, forgetting their own kind or Order. For this they took upon themselves strange images, upon which they "became" their imagings, which were fanciful indeed. They experimented.

They tasted of many a strange morsel which was forbidden. For this we waited and watched their progress, as they multiplied into various forms and species. When they became capable of understanding that which was now prepared for their progress, we sent entities unto them that they might learn to walk upright. We gave unto them the power of speech, such as they, at that time, were capable of. At this time when they were upright and with speech, then, with another change and with another cycle came other brothers from the lighted realms. These gave unto these ones the power to think, to plan, to create that which they could image... this became their part to use as they chose.

We watched for millennium upon millennium to see what they would do as separate entities with their own creations... for this we felt great responsibility. Then we came unto them as the Elders to train and guide them thru the next phase of their development... then, for a time, we, the Elders, returned to watch from the heights... for long we waited.

They, the first of the species, rose up as man which walked and babbled in his own language. For a period he was left alone again, in which he created many forms, abominable, unknowing, and forbidden. They brought forth that which was not their kind.

For this, we, the guardians, have given of ourself that these children of earth might come to know of their beginning as man. While this form which he hast this day is but the result of many, yea many, cycles of preparation for this day which is now "dawning". For this do we now call unto all of mankind to arise up and soar like the Eagle... no longer to grovel in the pit of darkness. Behold the new day and come forth as one pure of all thine own willfulness, which hast been unto thee thine bondage.

We come unto thee that ye be unbound, and know as we know. Great shall be thine joy and power. This is the day of awakening unto thine rightful place, and that which ye really are. So be it a Great Day.

* * *

The origin of man

ℰℰℰ This is the day when all things which hast been hidden up shall be revealed. There shall be no more mystery about thine origin into the world of flesh. Let all mankind arise and come forth as one body of Lighted Ones, for this is the day of revelation.

* * *

𝒞𝒞𝒞 shall be the ones which have come to bring thee out. These, known by this seal, shall be as the higher order of mankind. These 𝒞𝒞𝒞 shall abide with mortal man (even as with their earlier 𝒥𝒥𝒥) as creators of the species as it began to manifest as a thinking being... at which time they (𝒞𝒞𝒞) gave of themselves that these ones which was of the earlier specie might become as they.

These shall again give of themselves, yet in another fashion, or method shall I say... for the earlier specie has reached the 𝒞𝒞𝒞 state, in which they can understand the greater things which pertain unto their creation and development into the present state and form.

This shall be as strange and unacceptable unto many. While they shall come to understand, it shall not come to pass within one decade. Nay, it shall be another age when it is come that the specie hast been removed into another place within the cosmos. Each shall be in his place for which he hast prepared himself. Therein he shall progress at his own pace, for this is the time of sifting and sorting.

For the sifting and sorting have we of the host called unto mankind, "*Come, Come, Come ye out*". Unto the ones which come as ones prepared shall be given the 𝓟𝓟𝓟 part of the next higher specie of mankind. - These shall be known as brothers which shall be the mentors of the ones which are not capable (at present) of coming up through the next Order of Man. These shall be known unto the 𝓟𝓟𝓟 as the neophytes of the new Order, over which the 𝓟𝓟𝓟 shall preside, even as the 𝒞𝒞𝒞 the Elders preside over them.

It is the law that ye learn, then teach... for that hast 𝒥𝒥𝒥 been brought forth unto this day. From this day forward progress shall be swift and sure.

* * *

𝒞𝒞𝒞 This Order is the over-all highest Order, which hast been the brothers overall the lesser Orders. They are that which ye know or refer to as the "Mighty Council". From this comes all power, all wisdom and love. The lesser Orders take from them their sustenance, their strength and wisdom, as they are prepared.

So be it that the whole of mankind is lifted up through and by this Order, which is the over-all Greater Council. By the love and wisdom of this Order all are lifted-up. ♪♪♪ is the Order under which his Master gives unto him freedom from the past, which enables him to pass into the next higher.

When I use the word as singular "I", it refers unto the whole of this Order with the greater responsibility, for they are of one mind, one intent... they are the ones which have the greater knowledge. All power is theirs for they know themselves to be "One" with the All, even the lesser groups.

Now I use the word "lesser" that ye, the reader of this portion of these papers, might distinguish one group from the other. All are "One" in our mind, and each is given as they are prepared... yet we give of ourself all that is lawful at each period of their development.

When it is come that they (♪♪♪), as a group, are come to the fullness of their capacity to learn that which we offer them... (that they be given yet another time/place in which they might raise to greater heights, greater knowledge of their Source of being, as humankind), we again come at the time of fulfillment of time allotted, that there be a sifting and sorting.

ᵖᵖᵖ is the Order that hast come time after time unto the ႖႖႖ which are, or is, referred to as the laggards. These are the ones which have slept on their feet, making little progress. Thus the ᵖᵖᵖ is the one which gives of itself that they learn or progress. (We speak of these groups as "One", for that do we speak in terms of the singular)

When the ᵖᵖᵖ group is sufficiently prepared to enter into the higher state, they are placed in the proper place prepared for them, which shall separate them as a specie. Then the next higher Order takes upon itself to lift up the ᵖᵖᵖ. Again, these are responsible for the lesser Order... this is the order in which we are concerned at this period of time.

We of the Order of the ℰℰℰ, the ones referred to as the Mighty Council, has the greater responsibility. It is ours.

This is the word I give unto thee at this time.

* * *

৭৭৭ With this signature ye shall know that which is given unto thee comes through and of the Order of Man, of the first or lowest Order which hast awakened... which is the exception, where one becomes progressed to such an extent that he is al- lowed such a privilege. Yet it is given unto us to extend our hand that he be as one lifted. When that one gives of himself to such an extent, we give him all the assistance necessary for his progress and the direction he shall take for his development into the next phase of his being. Not always does he take the path we would have him, yet it is the law that he has his free will, which we dare not trespass upon, even if we see him turning from the way of light.

Many there be which are in so many stages of development. Each one is given the amount of assistance necessary for his development, and in like kind necessary. It is the Soul of which we are concerned... the form of man is of secondary interest. The Soul being that which is the light which was given unto him as he drew the breath of Life, the spark given from or within the "Source", which was/is implanted within the seed of man at the beginning of the specie. The seed which carries the power and light which man hast come to call "genes", which is convenient.

The creation of a new generation

When the ℙℙℙ father, or parent male seed, is implanted within the mother at the time of bringing forth a 'new generation', he (the offspring) which is endowed with the power of creating a new specie comes forth with a plan... he therefore is encoded with a symbol, a number, and a color, as well as a musical note. Now it is by this combination that he, the Soul within the new generation, is known and followed throughout his sojourn. We follow his progress with great caution/care. When he has followed the pattern set for him and his new generation, he becomes the 'parent' of a lesser source, another breed, as man refers to this process of lesser manifestation.

There are no limits as to what the Source of all manifestation can accomplish, yet when it is seen that the 'parent specie' has taken it upon self to go from the pattern set up in the beginning, there springs forth many malformations, which are abominations, which have also multiplied as abominations, parasites upon the planet earth. These are without "Soul", or that which is the Eternal Spark. When that spark is not within the form he is not given the power to re-enter into his line of existence that he continue his designed course. He is cut off, with no power to again create in his own image... for this shall be the ending of many an one in this new age, when the mother earth shall reject the old and take upon herself a new garment, a new place of light. And a new course shall she take with Order and Power to take upon herself greater beings, and greater shall be her light.

* * *

In newsletter #65 we ran an excerpt from a book by William Dudley Pelley, which was entitled "Star Guests". The response which we received to that excerpt was overwhelming, and many of you have since written to us asking about additional books by this same author.

Because of this we have decided to print a few short excerpts from another of his many books, entitled "Seven Minutes In Eternity". This is the remarkable story of how it all began for William Pelley, which was first printed in The American Magazine in March of 1929, and which attracted such incredible world wide attention. He tells of an experience one night in which he makes the transition from the earth plane into a higher dimension of life, where he is greeted by others whom he had known before their own death. Fully believing that he himself has died, he begins to adjust to this new reality and is very shocked when this experience fades and he is again pulled back into his physical body. After this shock had subsided, he is again "guided" to let go of the physical body, and he again returns to these higher dimensions of life, where he undergoes a dramatic transformation of both mind and spirit before willingly returning 3 hours later. This is one of the clearest and most fascinating accounts of someone who has made this transition into the higher dimensions and then returned again to the earth plane. The following are excerpts from that account. Excerpts From:

* * *

Seven minutes in eternity

by William Dudley Pelley

Around two o'clock in the morning - the time later verified - a ghastly inner shriek seemed to tear through my somnolent consciousness. In despairing horror I wailed to myself: "*I'm dying! I'm dying!*"

What told me, I don't know. Some uncanny instinct had been unleashed in slumber to awaken and appraise me. Certainly something was happening to me - something that had never happened down all my days - a physical sensation which I can best describe as a combination of heart attack and apoplexy.

Mind you, I say physical sensation. This was not a dream... I was fully awake, and yet I was not. I knew that something had happened to my heart or head – or both – and that my conscious identity was at the play of forces over which it had no control.

I was awake mind you, and whereas I had been on a bed in the dark of a California bungalow one moment when the phenomenon had started, the next I was plunging along a mystic depth of cool blue space, with a feeling not unlike the bottomless sinking sensation that attends the taking of ether. Queer noises were singing in my ears. Over and over in a curiously tumbling brain, the thought was preeminent: "*So this is death!*"

* * *

Next, I was whirling madly. Someone reached out and caught me, stopped me. A calm, clear, friendly voice said close to my ear: "*Take it easy, old man. Don't open your eyes just yet. You're all right. We've got you and are here to help you*"

Someone had hold of me, I said - two persons in fact - one with a hand under the back of my shoulders, supporting me, the other with arms slipped under my knees. I was physically flaccid from my "plunge" and lay inert in a queer opal light that suffused the place into which I had come.

When I finally managed it, I became conscious that I had been borne to a beautiful white marble pallet and lay nude upon it by two strong-bodied kindly-faced young men in white uniforms, not unlike those worn by interns in hospitals, who were secretly amused at my stupefaction and chagrin.

"*Feeling better*" the taller of the two asked presently, as physical strength to sit up unaided came to me and I took note of my surroundings.

But I took note of more. I took note of the speaker. I knew him, unmistakably. He was Bert Boyden, former Managing Editor of The American Magazine, who had been killed in France in July of 1918. The other man, slightly bald, was a stranger.

"Bert!" I gasped

They exchanged good-humored glances. "*Don't try to see everything in the first seven minutes!*"

"*Bert, am I dead?*"

They did not need to answer my question... it was superfluous. I knew what had happened. I had left my earthly body on a bungalow bed in the California mountains. *I had gone through all the sensation of dying*, and whether this was the Hereafter or an intermediate station, most emphatically I had reached a place and a state which had never been duplicated in all my experience. I say this because of the inexpressible ecstasy I felt in my new state, both mental and physical. For I had carried some sort of body into that new environment with me. I knew that it was nude. It had been capable of feeling the cool, steadying pressure of my friends' hands before my eyes opened. And now I was reawakened without the slightest distress or harm, and I was conscious of a beauty and loveliness of environment that surpasses chronicling on this printed paper.

* * *

Again I found my voice. Looking beyond them and around me, my gaze came to the bench beneath me. I thumped it with my palms. My next words were: "*Great Scott! Its real!*" "Of course its real," my friend returned, still smiling.

I got up from my marble bench and moved dazedly about the portico till I came and stood at the edge of a pool. "Bathe in it," the instructions came. "You'll find you'll enjoy it!"

I went down the steps into the most delightful water. And here came one of the strangest incidents of the whole adventure. *When I came up from the bath I was no longer conscious that I was nude... and the sensation of nudity did not occur to me again throughout my visitation.* On the other hand, neither was I conscious of having donned cloths. The bath did something to me in the way of clothing me. What, I don't know. But immediately I came up garbed, somehow, by the magic contact of that water.

It did not occur to me to feel either wonder or awe that I had left my physical body and penetrated to this delightful place. It all seemed as natural as it seems to me at this present moment to be sitting in a fleshy body again, putting these words on a sheet of paper. Thus it had no more occurred to me to discuss the fact that to all intent and purposes I was "dead" than it occurs to me to go about this life discussing the fact that I am alive... there seems to be only one continuity of life and consciousness, and we feel as comfortably at home in one vehicle or environment as in another.

While I had been bathing, the second man who had received me went somewhere outside the portico and I never saw him again. But my first friend stayed with me. Clothed, I sat down again on the pallet and we entered into converse. I did not ask *why* I had come there. I was not particularly concerned about those I had "left behind" in the earthly state. But the great pertinent fact that I learned that night, and which has since altered my entire conception of life in the world, came out subsequently in one hour's conversation.

The friend who had received me had been in earthly life the Managing Editor of The American Magazine when I had first come down from Vermont in 1917 to join its writing staff. Yet, so sublimated in appearance was he, so ruddy and stalwart over what he had been in earth-life, that at first I scarcely knew him. It took me some moments to get oriented to him again.

Quizzically he asked me: "Don't you remember being here before?" "When have I ever been here before?" I asked him. "Countless times," he assured me, smiling more indulgently. "You left this plane or condition to go down into earth-life and function as the person you (presently) know yourself to be. Don't you remember *that?*"

"You mean I lived as someone else before being born as William Dudley Pelley?".

"Everyone has lived before - hundreds of times before. People still in earth-life will live hundreds of times again - as they have need of the mortal experiences. Its the very basis for all human relationships."

* * *

I cannot make anyone understand how natural it all seemed that I should be there. After that first presentment of dying - which experience had ended in the most kindly ministration - all terror and strangeness left me and I never felt more alive. It never occurred to me on either occasion that I was in "heaven," or, if it did it caused me no more astonishment than that at some time in my adolescent consciousness it had occurred to me that I was on "earth". After all, do we know much more about one that the other?

... End Excerpts ...

As many of you know, Sister Thedra began receiving information for a new book in July of 1990, concerning "The History Of Man". The first thing she was told was that although she would begin receiving this book here at A.S.S.K, she would not complete it until after she had made her own transition into the higher dimensions of life. Prior to her passing in June of 1992, she completed the recording of approx 100 pages of this new book. In this interim of her absence we have decided to begin releasing this information.

SISTER THEDRA

The assignment

Sori Sori: This is that which I would have thee do at this time. I am come at this time that ye be as one prepared to be brought in, into the place wherein I am. For it is now come that it is necessary that this work of thine portion be as brought forth. There are other parts/portions to be added unto that which hast been started. This is but a start.

While it, the whole of this thine assignment, shall demand thine full attention and much more information, there shall be no errors, no doubts, for ye shall know without a doubt that which ye do. Ye shall have the advantage of our facility here, which shall be as visual records, therefore ye shall work from this vantage point. Ye shall know for a surety that which ye see and record it, that this true record of "man's origin" be given unto him as the verities of his being, his development from the first of his earth walk. This shall be the first of its kind brought forth for his enlightenment. So be it that ye shall find that ye, as man, as mankind, have not one iota of thine history recorded for thine enlightenment this day.

By the grace of the Father which hast sent me. I shall now send thee (Thedra) as mine emissary. By the authority and power invested within me, I shall give unto thee this assignment, which shall be carried out to the fullness of this most precious documentation mankind hast ever inherited.

It is now necessary that this work shall be done with greater ease. Great shall be the cooperation of the ones herein, for each shall add their strength and expertise. Mankind shall be as the recipient of this record coming through this source and from 'The Source". No longer shall it be necessary for him to grope (for artifacts) within the ruins left in his past travels upon the face of the earth as unknowing entities.

Be ye (Thedra) as one called forth, for this assignment hast now begun, and it shall be completed with perfection. This I would give unto thee, mine word... as the variety of mine I shall show unto thee that which no man of earth hast ever seen. This is the "Day of Awakening", for this is this method/plan so designed for man's upliftment. Blest shall ye be.

So be it I have spoken and ye shall respond unto me. I Am Sananda, the Son of the Living Father, the "Source" of all life upon the planet earth... That which man hast called God.

* * *

𐐖𐐖𐐖 - "Ra-na" speaking: I am come unto thee at this hour that ye might know me. I speak as one which hast given of mine self that mine own specie might come to know their inheritance. It is long since we (Man) as a specie hast lived in the shadows of our benefactors, knowing not of their existence. It is now the time of awakening. They, as a whole, knew not that for which they were destined to become.

This day the 𐤐𐤐𐤐 are the inheritors of that which the 𐤂𐤂𐤂 founded, as the 𐤐𐤐𐤐 built upon the foundation they laid. Their time was shorter, they learned quicker in their period of preparation for their fulfillment than the previous (original) 𐐖𐐖𐐖 which took many ages.

Now the 𐤐𐤐𐤐 have progressed in a shorter time, or cycle of time, unto the present day, in which they (as a group hast become as gods that worship their handiwork, call themselves wise/great, mimicking the forerunners, knowing but little of them and the inheritance they left for to build upon.

Now, there are but few which are prepared to receive that which we, as the ᶜᶜᶜ, bring unto them this day. For these which are prepared we give of ourself that which is expedient for their ongoing progress, which shall be swift and sure. These we have provided for. A plan hast been devised in the realms of light that shall be as nothing before... the reason being, none hast been as prepared for such knowledge aforehand.

* * *

The warriors and the destroyers

ᵟᵟᵟ hast given unto themselves great torment, as they have been so deep in sleep they have been rebellious and slothful. They have divided themself, tormented each other, slaughtered and eaten their fellow man... yet they have come into mortal flesh time after time, making little progress if any what-so-ever. Now we find these which have taken this upon themselves shall be as ones brought to account for their wanton ways, for they have brought upon the earth planet much destruction and darkness.

For this we have brought about a plan for them, pertaining to their development as man, as was the intent in his beginning. This is beyond the present day concept of either the ᴾᴾᴾ or the ᵟᵟᵟ. These two Orders shall never again mix or cohabitate, for they shall be sifted and sorted... then they shall know that which they have created is their individual responsibility.

While the ᴾᴾᴾ Order shall be as one Order, one body of greater knowledge and development, they, for the most part, are prepared to take their place as provided them at the sifting and sorting. For this we of the ᶜᶜᶜ have come into the near earth, the place wherein we shall be the ones which have to be the brothers unto the ᴾᴾᴾ, which shall come to learn of all the mysteries of being as "Man".

It is now come that this place (the school) is prepared for to receive the 𝑃𝑃𝑃, which shall become the shepherds of/to the ones yet to be prepared for to receive their passport. Just as they which have gone before them, so shall they be shepherds unto their brothers... shall we refer unto them here, for the sake of clarity, as the "late sleepers".

Wast it not said that as ye learn ye shall teach? Yet, we find a great number of these "late sleepers" are simply poll-parroting that which they have pilfered from others of their specie, knowing not that which they do... even adding unto or taking away from the meaning or substance thereof. This is the cause of much confusion and unrest among the ones which are reaching forth a hand unto the lighted ones, which are the &&&.

* * *

𝑃𝑃𝑃 - This is the Order in which we of the 𝓔𝓔𝓔 are directing this communication to at this time, for it, the 𝑃𝑃𝑃, is now prepared to arise into the place prepared, as they, for the most part, have given greater service unto the unfoldment of the lesser Order (𝔍𝔍𝔍), that it, as a whole, might progress.

This Order of the 𝔍𝔍𝔍 hast now progressed to the point that they might take their rightful place on the scale of evolution, yet they are not, on the whole, prepared to receive the fullness of their inheritance. These of the 𝔍𝔍𝔍 are the ones which shall preside over the ∞ as the next in line up the scale. This is to be the Order in which they are to be known, and their placing within these records recorded. It shall be as a clear record, for there is much to be added unto these words within the days ahead. So be it that all other records of mans' findings and recordings shall be as naught, for the so-called literate and "learned men of science" hast added to and overlooked the truth of these beings which hast been their forerunners.

These 𝔍𝔍𝔍, in a fashion, hast been the teachers of the 𝑃𝑃𝑃. These so-called primitive pioneers hast left their records which the 𝑃𝑃𝑃 have deciphered, in part. While they have not come to know as we of the 𝓔𝓔𝓔 know, as we have known each Order as they sprang forth over the aeons of time and space, at their own pace as they progress, each contributing his part unto the whole of creation as mankind.

These early creatures have come from the efforts of the ℭℭℭ Order to begin the order next the ∞∞∞, which crept upon their belly. Then the call went out unto these: "*Arise, walk ye upright... use the mind which is given unto thee. Bear ye offspring, and love thine offspring*". And this Order progressed thru many ages unto their potential at that time of change in the experience which we of the lighted ones were making when we came into the planet, that man might be the inheritors, that man might come forth as a specie prepared to bring forth progeny of a higher Order, of greater intelligence. The ℭℭℭ gave of its self as the seed of this project of great proportions, which took many an age.

Now, as we came at various times/ages to assist, we found that few were of greater mentality, of greater will to understanding, or more fit to carry the "genes" of the first of the specie through unto the next title wave of light upon the planet, in which we of the lighted ones came unto them (the first Order) which at this time had learned to walk upright, bear offspring in love and with great caring and understanding. This was their greater gift which was endowed unto the first Order of man. For this he had given great promise of his capability of growing into a higher specie.

It was at this point of their progress that we, their guardians and progenitors, came unto them to bring out from this Order the most intelligent of the specie. We gave unto these of our energy, our insight and desire, and that which would enable them, as individuals, to progress into a higher mental and physical Order.

Now, know ye that these were primitive beings, as ye hast learned through thy own record left to witness of these beings. Ye know not of the time in which we watched and cared for these as they grew into greater capacity, greater understanding and dexterity. Unto ye it was unknown ages. Many seasons came and went while the growth/development took place. Then we again sifted and sorted until we found the ones most likely to be the carrier of the seed for the new 'generation', the new Order, which would follow upon a greater, more

- intelligent scale. Then again we gave of our wisdom and that which they could comprehend, that in line over they might grow and prosper as man.

At this point of time, again, a sifting and sorting... taking the most promising of the specie and giving unto them that which would be for their greater benefit, that they might arise as the ones of - greater knowledge of self and their relationship to the whole of creation. These are now unto the age of understanding and greater accomplishment! While not all have the mind or will to arise unto the potential of their being, as man... again, this day, we of the ℭℭℭ are come for the sifting and the sorting.

We have labored long in the vineyards of mans' making. While he hast sown his seed, some hast brought much sorrow and torment, while there are ones which have accepted that which we bring unto him this day. For these ones we have provided in great measure for his progress, that for which he hast prepared himself. We have nurtured these which now make up the 𝒫𝒫𝒫 Order... which are next in line unto the ℭℭℭ. It is clearly written, that each finds his own place prepared for him... as he is prepared, so he becomes. Alas, some shall find that he hast a very poor place wherein he shall abide for a season... until he wills to arise.

This is the Law of Creation.

Man's freedom

𝒥𝒥𝒥 man hast come of age. It is now come when he shall be as he wast designed or destined to become. His time is come when he shall come into the fullness of his estate, wherein he shall be free from all bondage. He shall be free to go into all the Realms of Light as one on wings of light... no need for any form of conveyance as is known in the world of illusion. By his inheritance from the Source of all light, this shall be his last and most profitable sojourn upon planet earth. It is foretold within the firmaments of the cosmos.

* * *

Cycle after cycle

𐌔𐌔𐌔 - With this I come unto thee as man. I am as man, yet I am unbound. I can, and do, move freely among mankind as one with the specie. I speak for myself as one with the whole thereof. I give of myself as man, for I know that which is necessary unto their greater knowledge and the part that each shall play within the whole.

For this is it said, "*come ye forth and accept that which we bring unto thee this day*". For this is the day of deliverance, the day of fulfillment of thine understanding and maturity as 𐌔𐌔𐌔, wherein ye become one in, with, or of, the Order of ℭℭℭ. Wherein ye of the ℙℙℙ shall likewise be lifted unto the ℭℭℭ, as ye have served thine time as the 𐌔𐌔𐌔 and the ℙℙℙ... each hast come up through the time allotted unto each for the maturing.

It is now come that a new Order shall come forth which shall create even as the Father God of all. For this shall the Mother Earth be prepared to foster them/it, this new Order. It shall be known as the Fathers right hand made manifest. In his nature they, as individual beings, shall be as He... without any limitation of any sort. They shall be 'God'... and as such, each shall be unto himself as such. Yet, each shall know himself to be "One" with the whole, the entirety of all of creation. Each shall know his origin in the beginning, even as he was meant to be in the beginning when he was first given the Spark of Life, as the first of the specie called and known as "Man".

For this have we of the Order of the 𐌔𐌔𐌔 walked as man thru many a cycle, unto the day of our maturing, wherein we, as a whole, are prepared to merge into, and become one with, the ℭℭℭ ... wherein we are known as they/it, as a whole. There is no distinction, as all are of one calling, one gift. One and all share as one body, the same gifts, the same knowledge, without thought of "his or mine", as is the want of the immature being.

Thus, all mankind shall come to their full maturity and arise as of one body, called the "Source", or the Universal Mind, which ye, man of earth, hast called "God".

While this is sufficient unto this day, and of what he is able to understand of himself, he shall be as one with the power and authority of the "Source" when he hast merged with the Source of all life. This is man's destiny, his calling, his heritage as Sons of the Living O, the everlasting light, which is the over-all creator from which all things come into being.

Each in order, in which he develops unto his full potential in his allotted cycle. Then the next in order, he goes out as another form. He takes upon himself that for which he hast prepared himself, or itself, according unto his signature, which hast not, as yet, been designated in this report or papers, as this would be too tedious to mention at this time. For this day our concern (as this report is begun) is 'Man - Mankind' and his maturing.

The history of man

ℂℂℂ : Mine hand shall be made visible unto thee as ye write these records, which are available unto thee for the good of mankind. Therefore there shall be the Oneness of spirit, and the ᔑᔑᔑ the ℙℙℙ, and the ℂℂℂ shall be as One in the writing of these documents. They shall add their portion one at a time, and then they shall be placed side by side to make the whole of this book, The Story of Mans' History, as it shall be given through this means/plan. When it is complete it shall be released as perfect, complete in its content, as one document of light. There shall be no doubt of its origin and the Truth of its content.

By the means which we are privy unto, ye (Thedra) shall bring forth such as hast never been available unto man of earth. This is now made possible, for the time is at hand that the old shall be made new and the new shall put on immortality. While the old shall be as Man still, he/it shall wait another cycle in which it (mankind which hast not progressed to maturing) shall await their day of maturing, which shall be far off for these which have, of their own self, chosen to wait. The waiting shall be long and hard, yet necessary for the fullness, the maturing, which shall be within another place within the firmament of the heavens. Unto these shall be given the law of their being, and the law shall be for their progress. They shall be even as the ✣✣✣ before... they shall once more be freed from their bondage.

It is the law that each shall grow unto such a stature, a designed pattern, which shall free the requirements of promotion unto, or into, the next Order of progression. By the time a new cycle comes, within a certain measure of time, each and every entity shall move up the scale according unto his ability, as he hast prepared himself. There are no favorites, no praise for accomplishments, no injustice within the plan which hast come forth through and by the "Source". It is the law of the 'One' which governs all phases of life, in whatever place he finds himself, or whatever specie.

Now the time of sifting and sorting, the harvest, is on. The field is prepared for the reaping. So be it the reapers shall gather in that which they have sown, be it heavy or light... no judgment, no less, no greater than that which each one hast portioned into himself as a living entity, given free will to choose that which he wills to do. The choice is given in the time of going out from the Source.

When he chooses the straight way, he is given full knowledge of his heritage. When he chooses to experience of himself, on his own volition, as elf, he is given a plan by which he may be able to find his way insufficient, hard, and unfulfilling. He is then given another choice that he might be brought into the greater light.

So be it as a greater plan in this his new place, and a greater understanding of his own responsibility unto the 'oneness' of the whole of his specie. He then may begin his upward journey, as he shall choose his way again. He shall be able to stay in any part of his journey or move up into greater heights. At his own speed he shall go, for none are given more than he can bear. There is an economy of service rendered unto each and every entity, on whatever plane or place they be found.

* * *

The new cycle

ƐƐƐ : As for the coming of the end of the age, it is now come when the old age, called the "Picean" by Man earth dwellers, is ended. I say unto one and all, the new Order of man is come now. There is a new day in which mankind shall change as nothing like that which he shall become in a shorter period of time.

The plan is new, as none before in his (man's) early times, or cycles of developing. The ones which have not been prepared to arise (as was the purpose of his being upon the earth in the beginning) shall be removed into 'yon place' for his final development. He shall begin at the point of his development where he is when he is removed from the earth. Should he be of such nature that he is incapable of any progression, he shall be as one left off, as of nothing... no existence.

It is the law that mankind progress even through the many cycles and forms of manifestation... however, each cycle should be into greater heights, greater light. Yet there is a great provision made for the laggards. At the coming of this present new age, new day, there is a method we have referred to as the "sifting and sorting", for never more shall 'the sheep and the goats' lay side by side. The laggards shall not labor side by side with the ones which are prepared for the next place within the light, the temples of light, as this higher realm hast been referred to... it is also referred to as the "heavenly realms". Be that sufficient for the present, for it is of no use to give unto the ones, which have no knowledge of the way the plan we have for this sifting and sorting.

Some are of the mind/opinion which is part of great fallacy... that when they die they shall receive the same measure of their inheritance that shall their so-called Jesus their Savior has... that he paid the price of admission into their heaven wherein the Angels shall entertain them with great anthems of praise to welcome them.

O, man of the dark age, awaken ye, arise and learn of thine Source that which is the law of thine being. Nothing concerning thine Source of being is haphazard! The plan provided for thine progress is just and perfect, for it was given unto man as a divine experience. Learn and be as one alert. Learn of thine environment and his relationship unto each one being responsible for his own part in the whole. This was his earliest teaching which he was able to comprehend... that he was part of the whole of mankind and responsible for his part.

Some of the specie called man have found their way hard, yet they have given of themselves that others too have a mind, a soul, with the same feelings, and struggle to better their society that others might be prepared to climb the upward way unto greater heights. While others care not for their fellow man, giving unto him no care, no thought of his struggle... leaving for the brother of his specie his (the laggards) offal to clean away or transmute that others might have a cleaner, freer existence. These are the laggards. These are the ones which have despoiled the earth unto its fill. While they but make mock of love and caring for another, they make liars of themselves. They speak falsely, for they are the wolves in sheeps' clothing. "Money, more money" is their watch word. They coin their own money worth naught that they might enslave their fellow men. They drink of his blood and wash their hands of his sweat. This is as we see him which hast no mercy, neither love for these which fills the 'traitors' pockets.

Let it be said here in these documents, that his time is at hand when he shall make straight that which he hast "made crooked". In other words, he the 'Tyrant - Traitor shall clean out his privy with his own hand... that which he hast despoiled he shall make clean. For it goes to say, he hast been a wastrel and of no value unto his kith or kin, therefore he shall be weighed in the balance. He shall atone for every last drop of sweat which he hast rung from his slaves! I say he cannot escape the law!

I say unto the traitor which hast been his own worst enemy, "*Take ye heed, for the day of reckoning is come!*" I am not the judge... Thou art thine own judge, and paymaster!!

* * *

Sananda

Sori Sori: With mine own hand I shall bless thee this day, and ye shall give unto us thine hand and we shall give forth a part unto the ones which have a will to awaken. These then shall arise from their sleep state and listen, hear, and obey that which I shall say unto them, for their own sake they shall learn of me the law of their Order. They shall learn that they are responsible for that which they do with that which I bring unto them this day, this "New Day". These which listen and follow mine precepts, mine mandates, shall be as ones wise, for they shall be brought out before the day of great stress.

I have called... I have given signs and wonders... I have spoken unto them in their dreams that they - remember that which I have said or caused to be done. I have given unto them a new law, a new order wherein they might come forth as one free, one clean and whole. It is now come that there shall be great provisions made for every living being within the earth to come into the realm of light as ones made new.

They shall, for the new dispensation, arise and sluff off their lethargy, cleans themselves of all their hypocrisy, hatred, prejudice, their lust in any manner, such as pride, bigotry, deceit. They shall stand as one alone before the judgement bar, and they shall be their <u>own judge</u>. None other shall judge him, for he, each entity, be he male or female, shall be weighed upon the scale of justice. He shall read and know that which he bast done or sowed... what his worth might be. When he hast sowed unto the wind, he shall find the chaff to be his harvest.

He shall be his own judge of his own harvest. The responsibility is his... his alone! For this is the price he paid for the great and only gift that he wast given in the beginning which he could call his own, for it was a <u>free will</u> gift of/from the Source... and his sole responsibility.

Now the day of reaping, sifting and sorting, is come, when great is the light being shed upon mankind that he be freed from the bounds of earth. With this freedom he shall arise as one on wings. So great shall be his power, his light, that he shall be as free from the attraction of the moon, and he shall know himself to be free to go and come as a free being, as one come into his heritage and full possession of his heritage. He shall then see as I see. As I, he shall know his Source and be as one which is filled with love... <u>Love</u>, which shall be his complete and only nature.

I speak unto all mankind, for this is the new day in which each and every living man or woman, every "Soul", shall be called for an accounting, for it is said, and rightly so, it is the time of sifting and sorting.

I ask of thee, 'children of earth', Awaken! Listen unto that which I say unto thee for thine own wellbeing, for this is mine mission unto the planet earth at this time. Form ye no false images of me, neither make ye a false idol of me, for I come as one free of all bonds, as one sent of mine Father. Yet, I come of mine own free will. For the love I bear for thee as mine brothers all, I come. I bring with me a host of lighted beings which are free, even as I. We come as one body, of/with one mind, one intent... that of giving unto thee, man of earth, that which is rightfully thine by inheritance, willed unto thee in thine beginning as His sons. The free will is thine passport.

Art thou aware of thine divine inheritance? Dost thou calculate that gift as one no man can take from thee? How hast thou used this precious gift? I ask of thee an answer, <u>"How hast ye used this gift of free will"</u>? What shall thy answer be when ye stand before the great mirror where ye shall see thine self as ye really are, as ones bound in flesh?

Make ye no false opinions, for I tell thee, ye shall see thine self as ye have created thine own 'self, yet that self ye have created in thine sojourn in the shadow world shall be changed in the twinkling of an eye. Either for light or dark, as ye have created so shall it be. It is the law!

Yet it is now come when the Host of light hast come to awaken thee. We are offering thee that which is rightly thine <u>for the will to receive it</u>. The conditions in which this shall be done hast been clearly stated, clearly written. Every living creature shall be considered and weighed, and receive his reward as he hast laid up. As his harvest, he shall reap the reward of his sowing.

Yet, provision is now made for thine immunity. This new dispensation hast shortened the time of thine sojourn within the earth. While there is preparation for the sifting and sorting, each one, be he of his own specie, shall be put into the place in which he is prepared to go. Be it as he has prepared for himself, for he, each one, is solely responsible for himself... none other! There is no such law that another can bring thee out of bondage against thine own will.

Be ye alert! Ask! Prepared to receive, and heed that which is said unto thee in a multitude of ways. For this have I given unto mine prophets and prophetesses the power to bring the word unto thee in many and sundry ways.

* * *

Mans total freedom

ℭℭℭ : When it is given unto man to be prepared, he shall be as one with the whole of the lighted Order. He shall have the privilege of going and coming between worlds. As one of these, he shall be without limitation of any sort. He shall have knowledge of all creation, as we of the ℭℭℭ.

He shall be as the Father created him for to be. This is his "inheritance". This is that which is meant by "*Be ye free, even as I*".

Let thine time be spent profitably, for the call hast gone forth, "*Come! Come! Come ye out*". What think ye is meant by this call? It means, now is the day of awareness. Time is short... give heed unto the call and hasten to prepare for thine departure from the Mother Earth, for she no longer shall carry thee upon her back.

She is now prepared for her new berth within the firmaments. Her time is come that she bring forth a son which shall foster another generation (*see: Mine Intercom Messages from the Realms of Light*), while she, the Mother Earth, shall be free of her own spores and whores which have tormented her. She shall be free, even as man which is so prepared to arise into the light as spirit, free from pain and sorrow... So shall it be as the Father wills. No longer shall the sons of man linger in darkness and unknowing... ignorance of his inheritance, his origin.

Behold ye, Oh man, the signs of the time. The day is come when ye shall move. Ye shall be as one come alive and come out from under the 'black hood' which hast blinded thine sight. Ye have been <u>hoodwinked</u>! Ye have followed the dark one down the primrose path! Ye have been tantalized by his bewitching speeches, his fetching ways, his <u>glamor</u> and all his false promises.

I say unto thee that hast followed him to the brink of destruction: "*It is now time that ye heed the instruction which is coming forth from the Source of thine existence*". Be ye not concerned through which, or by what means we of the lighted messengers choose to give thee instructions or protection. We use any means available unto us, be it human or innate matter. We even use the elements! Know ye that we have all power and intention to use it for the good of all!

Yea, this 'All' indicates other realms of light also, for earth is not alone in the family of the many planets and stars of the universe... Yea, universes. All are as 'One', one power, one whole, composed of many Orders of creation/life. Life is continuous throughout all space. All is kin, and bound by the "Love of Life", which is eternal.

Man, as he is at this time of his earthly existence, is but the shadow, the shell (shall I call it) of himself, the eternal being, like unto the "Source" of his being. At present, the age in which he finds himself as flesh made manifest is but the age of awakening from his long sleep wherein he forgot his "Source". Long his weary wanderings... Sad his plight! Now we of the Cosmos have come nigh unto the earth in concert... as light we come that man be made aware that he is not alone, doomed to darkness and destruction...

***

Orderliness

𝟪𝟪𝟪 is the seal of mine Order, of which I am able to do that which I am given to do at this special time. I be known by the symbol 888, for it betokens mine stationary position. The double seal 𝟪𝟪𝟪 - ℙℙℙ is another part, which betokens another part... this is the greater part. This is but that which is done within the ℙℙℙ Order in which we come together for a great service. Our work is that of bringing certain records forth for to be presented unto the ℂℂℂ. This is the reason in which the double seal is used... it denotes/depicts this special assignment... otherwise, we use the 𝟪𝟪𝟪 singular to denote our station.

By this signature it becomes apparent that we are with consent of the ℂℂℂ to enter into such activities as the ℙℙℙ ... in other words, it betokens the alliance with the PPP in good standing. This is not to insinuate that the ℂℂℂ does not know, yet it is like thine so-called protocol... It is for good order and records.

Yea, we keep record even as the Council, however they are more orderly, not quite so complicated. For by this orderliness is it known at any moment that which is being done within any certain time. However, this orderliness shall become understood by the ones now holding forth within thine halls of justice, wherein they have lost sight of their reason for being. We know the wisdom of orderliness and decisive records.

Now it is nigh time that some of thine own kind or Order, (not to be designated in this paper by seal or name), shall be brought into this place to learn of our system of justice as we know it, as we practice... therefore, there shall be a great change within the system of the entire so-called civilized world of earth.

The time is at hand when we of the higher civilization Orders shall take action in the affairs of man of earth. We shall be as justified in the method employed to bring this change about. We shall go about this movement as brothers of light, with love and power endowed unto us of the Source. There shall be no bloodshed in our course of action, simple in its operation, it shall be that mankind come to know that it is far easier and wiser that they follow our plan. Even though they be slow to learn, it shall come to pass within the next decade...

* * *

✠ By this signature ye shall know me and mine mission. I come as one of great compassion I am one of a great number which hast been called forth at this present time that the populace of earth might come of the age, wherein they come to know themselves as brothers that there be understanding among them.

This be mine mission as I pass among them of the dreary and dismal places wherein they have no peace, neither knowledge of their heritage. For this am I come that they come to feel their One- ness with the whole of life and its manifestations Give unto me credit for being that which I am and we shall be as one of purpose and intent... that of bringing peace and understanding unto the ones which have forgotten their place within the whole of creation.

This is our purpose and intent, that of bringing the consciousness of these so-called sleepers into the light of their being, that which they truly are. This is part of the great awakening which is brought about through the love and wisdom of the Elder ☾☾☾ which hast called us of this ✠ Order to go forth among the populace of earth that they be prepared for greater learning.

So be it we have responded unto the summons, for this we are prepared to take our place among the many benefactors of the whole of mankind. I shall make mineself known unto thee and we shall be as one of mind, purpose, and intent... that of bringing understanding and love to a sad and darkened place, that the darkness and ignorance be gone forever more. So be it... Let it be!

Let it be as the Source wills...

* * *

The guardians

ɞɞɞ : By this signature I come for the purpose of bringing thee into the place wherein I am. For this is it given unto me to know the hour in which this shall be done. No man knows the hour. While I say unto thee, the time is "now", who among thee knows how we calculate the time in our realm? We consider the signs of the heavens as well as the conditions that man has created, and are creating.

We of the host are prepared for that which is necessary in any situation. We have the knowledge of man's nature, his passions and intentions, however, we watch with caution. We have called ourself, and rightfully so, "The Guardians", and that we are! We have the power and permission to take any action necessary to prevent the destruction which is at the 'door' through the rebellious and wayward lot.

We of the Grand Council have the means by which to do that which man has not yet imaged, for he hast been as ones in deep sleep with his fearful nightmares, his paranoia and hatred. Yea, we are prepared to go all the way for the good of all. It is written that the earth shall not be destroyed... "only the intent", as man is in the humor to do that which would destroy the way of life on the planet earth.

This is our part, to uphold Justice Supreme. We say to thee, mankind: "*Be sure of thine footing... consider well that which ye fear and the results of thine feverish actions, for we are a mighty Host of Power ye have not reckoned with. We are sent of the mighty Source that justice be done*". Ye have been warned that ye shall not transgress the Law which is the law by which ye shall survive, yet nation after nation hast raised its hand against nation. Transgression means destruction. Ye have been as a pack of mad dogs, giving forth great signs of the madness which shall consume thee. I say ye shall be as ones consumed. By thine own hatred and greed shall ye go forth in thine tremors of madness.

Be ye reconciled. Study well thine ways. Listen unto the words which have been given that ye go not so far that ye are the victims of thine own device. It is said: "*Ye shall drink of the cup ye prepared for thine fellow man, thine brother"*. Be sure of that cups' content mine unknowing ones which now clamor for superiority, supremacy among the nations! Give ye heed and listen ye intently, for ye are dealing with a power beyond thine wildest imagination. Ye have not conceived anything of so great a magnitude. Be ye blest to heed, and turn thine hand to the way of peace and peaceful coexistence.

I am a voice from out the cosmos, speaking for the purpose of bringing forth great knowledge that ye be spared a fate worse than death. Ye have but to cooperate with us of the light. We are offering our service in sincerity, with Love and Wisdom.

* * *

Note: The following messages was given just as Iraq was invading Kuwait. It was given at this point within the record. Although the Gulf war is long since passed it is being left in its sequence that it might broaden our view in retrospect.

August 5, 1990

The great tribunal

ඊඊඊ While there are ones which have rebelled against the word given forth from the Great and Mighty Council, we have given the word of Power which shall bring them to the awareness that there are ones which have the greater knowledge and power. This power which belongs unto man is subservient unto the ones of light. Man hast not as yet learned that he is not the highest or most powerful.

While he hast gone headlong in his unknowing, in his lust for power, he has brought forth that condition which is now necessary for us of the light forces to set in action a reasonable and just measure to set things in order. I tell thee, man of little knowledge, of the light forces which is now prepared for to give assistance unto the ones of peace and justice. Be ye appraised of that which hast been said here-to-fore.

The time is upon thee when ye shall be as ones caught within thine own trap which ye have foolishly set for thine brother. It is clearly seen and noted that each one which hast the mind to give unto his brother the "bitter cup", shall drink of it. That which he hast prepared for his brother, he shall drink! It is the Law!

Now is the time for reconciliation, before there is a great and mighty catastrophe which should be the end of all the hate and greed. For they which have set up the conditions which now exist within the land where they are at the business of taking from each other that which indeed belongs to NO MAN, for the man of earth owns nothing that he can rightly claim exclusive right to. I tell thee, no man is justified to bring disaster upon the whole of the earth's manifestation in his rush for power and the gifts of Mother Earth. No man shall be justified to destroy his brother!

I here, this day, say unto one and all, be he whom-so-ever sets himself up as a supreme authority with the intent to destroy his brother, be it for oil, land, or any other of earth's gifts unto man, which he was given to share as one family of 'man'... he hast become as foolish fiendish animals, with the power which he hast created with evil in tent, that of being the supreme power over another of his specie. While one rages and cries against the other without any agreement or understanding of the higher law of justice, of love for one another, they set themselves up for self-destruction.

Now, it is seen that the time is upon us of the Greater Tribunal, that we shall be justified thru and by the greater law of Justice for all, that we of the Greater Tribunal shall take action to prevent the greater destruction. While we cannot (by the Law of which we are speaking) bring unto the ones of such evil intent any assistance what so ever... as ye, O man of evil intent which set thineself up as a great power to rule over thy weaker brother, shall be as the looser in your game. I say in simple language, ye have set the fuse for thine own destruction... while we are helpless to assist thee in your plan which ye have been so intent on, that of being the "Super Power".

Oh, pity art thou oh fools of little understanding of the greater Law which ye have overlooked in thine mad rush for "supremacy. Be ye here forewarned of that which is our intention in this diabolical dispute, so foolishly purposefully perpetuated and engaged in by the ones of no knowledge of the Higher Laws which all manifestation comes under. We are aware of thine action and intent. We are prepared to do that which is in our jurisdiction and power, with "justice for all", to bring forth and set straight that which thou hast made crooked.

We, as the ones of greater knowledge and power, herein this day "do solemnly swear unto thee, oh man of evil intent, that ye shall not go farther in thine evil intent without self-destruction". Let it be understood before it comes to pass. Let thine mind and intention be turned unto peaceful and wise solutions.

I am the voice from out the light, which sees and knows the results of man's ways, be they for weal or woe. Justice is mine name and nature.

Recorders note: So powerful was the atmosphere charged wherein I was given this assignment that I felt overwhelmed with the intent to bring these to whom this proclamation is given, into line. The earnestness and determination so great...

Sister Thedra

* * *

The day of preparation

ℰℰℰ This is the day of preparation for greater patience, more understanding and love for thine fellow beings. Give unto thine preparation for greater changes. Stand ye tall and give no man the bitter cup. Consider thine self-responsibility for thine actions... blame none other for thine weakness. Be ye accountable in all thine dealings with thine brother. Do unto him as ye would have him do unto thee.

This is the part I would have all men consider before he lays to rest his head at the days end. Ask thine self, "*Have I been a comfort unto mine brother this day? Have I given unto him that which I would receive of him? Have I kept the Law of love this day? Be this mine portion which I have portioned out for mine self... I thank thee, for this is mine portion and I accept it with gratitude and understanding of the Law. "As ye sow, so do ye reap"*.

This newsletter is the third in a series in which we began to release the information which was given to Sister Thedra prior to her passing. When she began these transcripts she was told that it would eventually become a complete book concerning the true history, origins, and the development, of the Order of Man. She was also told that, although she would begin these transcripts here, that she would not complete this work until she had made her own transition into the higher dimensions of life. There she would have access to the true records of the long forgotten past, and where she would complete this manuscript through her own first-hand knowledge and experience. The information within this newsletter is a part of that manuscript which was completed before her passing...

The symbols used were given to designate the different Orders within the *Order of Man*. The ℭℭℭ, while still part of the Order of Man, went through their development and maturing in a much earlier cycle, prior to that here upon the earth. These are now referred to as the Elder Brothers, and as the elder brothers they now over-see the spiritual development of both the ᛞᛞᛞ and the ℙℙℙ here within this present cycle. As this present cycle now draws to a close they seek to guide us through the sifting and the sorting process which is now going on, that all of those who are ready and willing might now go forward into higher dimensions of life, with a greater understanding of our own life, and of our relation to the "Source" of all life...

* * *

For this am i now come

Sori Sori: Mine time is come when I shall come as man, and be as man, for the purpose of allowing man to know that he has the same heritage and Source as I. It is written that all the mystery about me shall be made clear as for mine parentage and existence as man of Earth.

Long, long ago, man walked and talked with me as one of their kind. It was given unto me to be as he... the difficulty was that he know not of his Source. While I was one of his kind he did not know of our Oneness... this I taught them, that we were One, of one Father, one "Source", which had sent me as the Elder Brother..

Then there sprung forth much fallacy which wast taken to be truth by the priesthood, for their fallacy gave them such power and ambitions that it swallowed them up. They grew in power sufficiently to bind them (the masses) which were willing to follow them blindly, making of them (the masses) servants which bowed before these priests which knew not of their Source. These which bowed unto these unknowing ones became as they, perpetrators of lies, which they pass on generation upon generation, until little truth of mine teachings now exists.

For this am I now come, that I might straighten that which hast been made crooked. I shall bring forth for the sake of all mankind the Truth, as I taught it unto man so long ago. By the means of mine existence into flesh shall I bring them into the light of their true being, even as I.

It is not mine intent to make mystery or gather unto mine self-worshipers. I shall gather together the ones which hast the will to learn of the verities of mine precepts, and the knowledge of their own gifts bestowed upon them from their beginning of their going out into the world of flesh creatures, made man by design of the Source of all life, the Cause of their being. I shall bring these willing and lighted ones forth as ones prepared to go forth with me into greater realms of light, greater heights, wherein they shall know themselves to be One with me. And these shall know as I know... no more shall they bow down unto the ones which call themselves "Father" or "Master" over the ones in ignorance of their Source.

I shall give unto the source of all knowledge and Truth credit for that which I Am. I shall reveal unto these which have the will to learn that which shall free them from all bondage. I shall give unto the "Source" the credit for the power and knowledge of our being, that they be as ones free from all bondage such as they have been subservient to lo the many aeons.

It is now come that many shall be brought out as free born, renewed of spirit and flesh. These shall be the ones delivered up as ones "made new" by the authority and power invested in me as the Son of God, the Father of us all. I come in his name, his nature. By his will I come unto man of Earth this day!

I come that he, mankind, be as One with me, for it is written as of old, 'The Father and I are One". So it is as it is written! Thus, these which are willing to go all the way with me shall find that they have chosen the greater part, that which is, and shall be, their freedom.

This is the word I give unto thee, mine devoted and beloved handmaiden, at this hour in the Day of the Lord. By mine own hand I shall bless thee as I have been blest of mine Father which hast sent me.

**

Note: Just prior to her passing Sister Thedra was told by Sananda that after her transition she would have access to the actual records which no man had seen, and that eventually she would bring forth the true story of his time as Jesus of Nazareth.

The chain of evolution

ℓℓℓ - ♪♪♪ This is the first of our communication such as this. There is necessity for this part at this time.

We of both Orders are as one intent, one mind in this great mission unto mankind, for it is now come when both Orders shall be ♪♪♪ O

And the ✝✝✝ shall be as the last to be given their assignment, for this ✠ is the order which shall be the ✝✝✝ ... these two shall become one.

This is the beginning of a new Order which shall come forth as ☪☪☪. The blending of these two shall bring forth a new temple of light, wherein a new concept shall be taught, learned, and practiced. For this shall the ✝✝✝ give of its self, (from the highest of its gifts, unto the lesser of its place or newer of its company) that it be given a new part, a new place wherein there shall be brought forth a new specie. This one shall be as nothing yet seen by the ✝✝✝, for it shall be another day or time that this, the maturing, be accomplished.

This is the plan in/on which there shall be brought forth the new generations which shall glorify the 'Creator' which shall be unto it (the new specie) as the Father God is unto the ☪☪☪. While it is, and shall be, of one "Source", yet the coming together or blending of these two Orders shall be as of the one source, the overall "Source" of all life.

This begins the new cycle which is now come. There shall appear within the firmaments a new 'Star (*see "The White Star of The East"*) which shall be as a sign unto the future generations, such as hast never been seen by man as the manifestation upon the earth. This shall be as such as no man can image in his present manifestation in flesh, as flesh. The firmaments shall take on new meaning for the ✝✝✝, and it (the ✝✝✝) shall be as the ☪☪☪. This blending of light energy shall be as of both the new earth and the whole of the Cosmos, therefore there shall be freedom from all the fear, all the lower vibrations which might come from out the lesser & orders, which hast never been brought into form or made flesh. This is that which shall come forth from out the primordial substance, known unto the science of Earth as the black hole", which hast been a mystery unto them.

Now within the time which is come as this new cycle, ye, as of the blending of these orders, shall come to know the science of the plan, and the beginning of the greatest of knowledge which shall be as the ultimate that these orders shall reach for untold ages or cycles. The ✝✝✝ shall be as the one Order to be enlightened in this day for to herald or to shepherd the laggards in their ongoing time of maturing...

* * *

Sori Sori For this hour let us speak of the first few of mankind to reach maturity. These are the ones which ye shall know as the 𝒅𝒅𝒅. This group, which hast come of age, have given of themselves that their specie which fell by the way might be as ones lifted up. This group hast had a fearsome beginning, yet it hast been that which hast been unto them great strength. They have profited by their struggles and extreme suffering. They have now come forth as one specie which hast been victor overall trials and hardship.

While there are some which hast not come through the purification, have not given of themselves that they be as ones lifted up, these are what is called the laggards. While each group have some laggards, 𝒫𝒫𝒫 has its share. Now the 𝒅𝒅𝒅 which have risen to the state of maturity has the part of benefactor unto the order of the 𝒫𝒫𝒫. By this I am saying, that the few which have not come forth as potential beings of light hast become the whores and spores. These shall no longer be given a place upon the planet earth that they bring forth their kind, for they, the laggardly beings, hast been an abomination unto the 𝒅𝒅𝒅 which hast moved forward through the aeons to their maturity.

It is now come that this group hast fulfilled all requirements that is required to join with the order of 𝒫𝒫𝒫. While the group which has come up through the 𝒅𝒅𝒅 have such great strength, endurance and loyalty unto the specie, these are the ones which have such gifts as the 𝒫𝒫𝒫 shall benefit by. Therefore it, the 𝒅𝒅𝒅 group, becomes the benefactors of the 𝒫𝒫𝒫. For this the two have the unity and mind that bring forth great strength and light unto the whole of both species.

It is by this union that they become one of great light and wisdom, by which they have held fast, willingly following the directions of the 𝒞𝒞𝒞. For this shall the ones of the three Orders bring forth a new specie upon the new earth. This specie shall not be as man of the earth, for he shall not inherit any of the tendencies of either 𝒅𝒅𝒅 or 𝒫𝒫𝒫 ... for this shall be as no other specie yet produced by natural means, such as man hast come from or portioned out for himself. This shall be as the beings which shall be as one of a kind within the universe. They shall not inherit any of Earth man's tendencies, neither his 'genes', neither his physical appearance. This new order need no physical dense body. It shall be as none other known unto the present orders, which have come up through countless changes into his present time when he has reached his present state of development.

Now it is come when the three groups shall be as one, each being of one mind, one intent... that of bringing light unto the lesser beings of their kin. Each shall take his assignment within the whole of the ℰℰℰ . Each shall work as One, in harmony, that they might come forth again as one body of light. While there be no lesser, no greater, each shall be as 'One'... no higher, no lower in rank, shall I say for thine understanding. Each shall have its place, its part portioned out unto it for the good of all... all created beings.

* * *

While it is come that there is so much conflict and bitterness within the nations of the East, there shall be given unto the ones which are the peacemakers the part of passing among thee, as one with thee, as man. These shall be of the light, of the Source. These shall know the ones which have reached the point of their ♂♂♂ maturing. These of the ♂♂♂ and the ℙℙℙ shall be as One, as brothers in mind, spirit, and intent. These, as a body, shall take the position which shall be as the ℰℰℰ in a manner so designated. This shall be the beginning of a new day when the two Orders shall work with the ℰℰℰ.

There shall be great power and light which shall be used to bring forth a new generation upon the new earth... while the young moon (*see Mine Intercom Messages*) shall be the footing of the laggardly ones left from the Mother Earth. It is written: "*She shall no longer give unto the laggards footing*", 'tis so, for these shall be as the traitors which have betrayed themselves. Their lot shall be to inhabit the young moon and begin anew. These shall have no memory of their former or past bodies in which they inhabited the earth, in which they were tutored and examined as to their progress. Upon seeing, noticing, and acting upon their findings, their monitors gave unto them in proportion unto their ability to go forth as the manifestation of the Lighted Ones, which are/were their progenitors.

There are ones within the laggardly group which closed themselves off from their Source, thus bringing forth a great abomination upon the entire planet. These ones shall be separated from all others, as the 'chaff from the wheat. No more shall these be part of the former species which have come full cycle, wherein they shall be as ones unbound, free to move into the light as ones enlightened, illumined, to be as "Sons of God"... to more to go into bondage.

These Ilumined Ones shall be forever free from the bonds of flesh. Yet they shall have all the knowledge and freedom which shall enable them to go into any place in the universe, or take any form which would be favorable unto that which they would be given to do. I say "given" to do, for it holds that one and all of these lighted groups are active in the on-going evolution of whatever specie they be given to monitor and assist... in the case of the laggards for instance.

These lighted beings hast also their councils, under the Source. Be not confused, for I speak in a manner that ye might understand that which I have in mind. When I say *'under'* it is to say 'within the Law of the One', which is symbolized by the single **O** For all things, be it beings of light, or yet unmanifested energy... All is within the one "Source", the one and only "Source" of all life and love. From this Oneness all things come into being, be it flying, creeping, or leaping... All things have their/its cycle in which to mature or to return unto its designated place, be it the "black hole", or the "High Holy Mountain".

* * *

Sori Sori: This day there shall be ones which shall awaken unto the Greater Power which they have, as yet, not tapped... this shall be for the good of all manifested beings. I say this awakening shall be for the good of all beings, whatever form he may be.

Let it be understood that there is a power which is supreme, over which no man presides. The first and last... this the Supreme Power which no man can pilfer or mock. This is the "Source" of which we speak. Let no man deny it or make mock, for this Source is that which no man knows. No man can fathom the power of the all-encompassing Light Power... that which is and ever shall be the Source of all life, in which every living thing exists.

When one comes into flesh, made manifest as man, it is by the will of the   , the One, which is by its own nature the 'Source'... there is no beginning, no end. While there is neither light nor dark within the All as the manifestation of man, this All is the substance of will, thought, and action.

There is stillness such as no man hast known. There is the Word, there is the movement, and sound follows the action movement). This is that which brings forth manifestation **O** form as dense matter hast been created by this means. I am using such expression for the sake of the reader of this paper, for none can say, "I understand", for it is not possible to express "Creation" in language of earth. Therein is no word, in any language, to convey life, the formless substance which hast no beginning, no end... endless. How could the fragments understand the ALL of life/love.

Ye, oh man, have vainly tried, yet ye are without answers! I say unto thee, out of the Cosmos comes one within this All Power, the Source, which shall be as the one sent that ye, one and all, learn of greater Light, of thine Source, of thine inheritance.

* * *

Freedom is earned

Sori Sori: By the time there is another moon (*see Mine Intercom Messages*), there shall be a change in the affairs of man. Unto him I say: "Ye, O man, shall take off the old and put on the new... there shall be a new Earth and a new Moon".

Be ye as ones which hast the will to go into the higher, greater, light and understanding of thine self, that which ye really are, and thine inheritance... for this is thine inheritance. Long hast thou waited this day. Be ye not deceived, for there is no other to bring thee out of bondage or give unto thee a refuge wherein ye may be as one of the 'little angels' within a 'glory land', than the one ye call by the name of 'God'. No man can give unto thee passport into the kingdom of light. The Kingdom of Heaven is thine freedom from bondage.

Freedom is earned, mine children. I say, "<u>freedom from bondage is earned</u>". We of the Lighted Council, the Great and Mighty Council, are helpless to deliver thee up before ye have purged or cleansed thine self of all hatred, all self-glory, greed, and malice. There shall be the will to learn of thy Source, which is "light", that which is the All-Power, signified by O... a single unit, a signature of/for the single Oneness of all created creatures. By this signature ye shall learn of thine Source, of thine inheritance... and unto this O ye belong, and shall return.

Let no man give unto thee the 'form of some mystical book and the orders set forth to hold thee bound. I tell thee of a surety, there is no need for thee to bow down before the altars made of man, and the bloody images he hast designed to hold thee fast that ye be beholden unto the false god. I say unto thee, oh children of one Source, FEAR NO MAN.... ASK OF NO MAN THINE FREEDOM... it is assured thee as thine divine inheritance when ye have given unto thine self-credit for being one with O, the One "Source". For within the 'Allness' ye live and breathe and have eternal life. No man can add to or take away one iota of thine divine inheritance!

By the nature of thine being One with this All Light in which ye live eternally, as One within the whole, ye are One with and equal unto all other beings. Let this be as thine nature. Love thine self as thine Source lovest thee. Love all creatures as ye love thine self, for all creatures, great and small, come into manifestation through and by this undivided Source.

It is now come when ye, mine brothers of little knowledge of thine origin and thine being as Eternal Sons of this, this Oneness, shall come to know that we of the Council of Greater Knowledge and Power, is/are the custodians of all the history, of thine heritage, thine time of going into the depths of flesh made manifest as man. The experience and the results accrued by and through the long dark night in the dream state of illusion. Now, after the aeons of so-called time, ye have learned to walk upright, ye have learned to bring forth offspring in thine own image and love and care for it. Ye have learned to feed and clothe thine self. Ye have learned to say "help". Ye hast looked up and asked, What is there? Where did I come from? This was thine first step as man... the first word spoken as man... What? Where? and Why? This was his nature, to learn, to explore. For this he was designed to learn that which was his potential. For this was he, as primitive man, placed upon the Earth, to explore, to expand his talents encoded within his being, to learn his way.

We are the Guardians of these beings which are our responsibility, for they are of our own creation as far as their specie goes. We were the progenitors of such, as far as their form and learning process is concerned. These Spirits of the Source O were willing servants for such as was brought forth at that period as an experiment for populating the planet earth.

***

Man's progress

By the time man had come of age, he had become self- responsible. He gathered information from faraway places... he made comparements. He builded for himself great temples wherein he might study and learn of the stars. He molded from clay, images of himself as a specie. He gave unto himself credit for being wise, and gave only little heed unto that which was spoken unto him by his progenitors which had fashioned him, watched and waited for that which he should become as a free willed being. Therefore we assisted (only) in as much as it was necessary for the good of generations yet to come.

As he became self-conscious of his greater mental development, he forgot his progenitors directions, and took upon themselves a greater sense of mastery of their surroundings. Here in this period of long ages he learned to give unto himself power over his brother, and to break his brothers) will unto his, to break his back to bring him under his subservience. This period was the period in which he learned that by fear of the unknown he could hold bondage his fellow brothers. He, the ones which set themselves up as 'masters' of the weaker, became their lords and gods, holding in fear their weaker brothers.

Now, as the cycles again come for a reckoning, a sifting and sorting, we find that these ones of past ages laid the stepping stones for the building of the great and revered temples unto their unknown god... gods of revenge, gods of great power, which they used to hold the weaker brothers subservient. These followed blindly. These priestly forerunners of the present day temples had no more knowledge or less, of their Source, than these of the present day. I say for a truth, that these present at this time are the ones which are the purveyors of lies and diabolical deeds, which hast been the greater cause of the great carnage and darkness of the ages. Yea, through the dark ages they have held bound the weaklings which have bent their backs before their bloody altars!

This small scenario shall be a minuscule preface for the greater part, which shall be the testimony of that which shall become known by mankind this day, for no longer shall man grovel before the altars of the dark brothers. Yea, he too, shall be exposed for the part he hast portioned out for himself.

* * *

"The spores shall be no more"
The black hordes

This is the time long ago foretold within thine 'Holy Writ", when the 'black hordes' should come up from the pit and roam the streets, leaving within their wake great carnage and grief. It is now come that these shall be gone from the earth, as the ones to be seen no more... for this is of the pit wherein there is no eternal substance. This manifestation is that which is referred to as the 'spores' which have no genetic strain. They are the soulless ones. This is the plague which is brought on or upon humanity by the accumulation of centuries upon centuries of wasted energy, by <u>misused</u> energy, and rebellion against the light forces which sustain life. These which have brought forth great monstrous abominations upon the earth are the spores with no roots, no soul, no substance of their own. These shall have no inheritance. They shall be cut off and no more shall they be seen, for they have no existence in the new day. This is as the wind which passeth in the night.

* * *

The sifting & the sorting

ℭℭℭ By the law of free will, the ones which have the mind to destroy themselves shall find that we shall not interfere. These shall go into the blackness wherein they shall no longer be seen. We give unto these no energy, for there is no ℭℭℭ genetic strain within these. They are the chaff, so to speak.

By the law of creation of man this system of these Orders are carried out to perfection. These which have no genetic strain of the ℭℭℭ are the spores, which are not capable of going farther in the light of understanding. Therefore, we of the lighted Order give unto these no energy. They simply disappear from the earth, to be seen no more.

The ones which have the genetic heritage of the ℭℭℭ are the ones which have lain the building blocks for the ꝺꝺꝺ. The ℱℱℱ Order followed in line of the founders of these who laid the building blocks ꝺꝺꝺ for the ℱℱℱ, that this Order might come into their maturity.

Each Order hast had its day of maturing. Now that the new day is come (the cycle of sifting and sorting), we of the higher ℭℭℭ shall be as the light that unites and brings each together in one common bond, as brothers all. However, time, as ye man of earth know time or calculate it, shall take into consideration all aspects of their development and ability to bring forth greater understanding of the universal law of love and Oneness within the O.

Be ye as One with the All-ness, and ye, O man, shall be as One with the light which shall be thine inheritance. Ye shall come to remember thine Source and be as One with it. For this are we prepared to give unto thee as ye are prepared to receive. So be it we are at thy service in the light of the O. Prepare thine self to receive us as thine Benefactors. I have spoken in this fashion that ye come into greater Light/understanding.

* * *

Man's opinions - as gospel truth

Sori Sori: For this hour let us consider the way of man. In his way he hast builded for himself great schools and taught that which he hast pilfered from others work, others experiences, as the "Gospel Truth". While he hast plundered his findings, which are very palatable and profitable, he hast not yet learned that which is his own inheritance, that by which he lives and breathes, that which sustains him in his daily existence. While there are great scientists of renowned, they but use the experience of others on which to build their hypothesis upon. This is as their "Gospel Truth", so they give forth that which they deem to be the true conditions or patterns of the Cosmos, the universe, etc. Yet they know not that which hast given unto them the will to look and see and listen, the power to act, to grow in strength and wisdom.

Some give no thought of their Source or their Oneness with it. While there are many which know there is more, much more to learn, they are not, as yet, prepared to enter into the realms of light wherein we of the Mighty Council hold forth in great halls of light, wherein we see and know all that man has, is, and shall become. In this great hall, from and in which I am now, as the speaker, speaking through and to one of mine chosen vessels which has given unto us of this Council her permission, her will, to give us her hand, her head and heart, that we, together, might bring forth a mighty work. So shall it be for the good of all mankind.

This work shall be as a valid report from the Eternal Source, wherein all records are intact and available unto the ones which so qualify. These which qualify shall be as ones brought forth, as ones which have given unto us of the light their undivided desire to serve the light. They have no fears, no hatred, no false notions or opinions, no idle division of interest. These are at all times ready to answer the call to serve the light which we use as our means of communication. In this manner there can be no interference, no breakdown of apparatus, no power loss, for there shall be as ongoing process which fails pot in its purpose. A Divine purpose it is... therefore it shall be completed as set forth within the mighty plan.

There is a plan, and it shall go forth as perfect. No man in all his evil imaginings shall abort any part or parcel of it, for it is founded on Truth, Light, and Justice for all. So be it this is mine word unto thee O, man of little knowledge, which should do well to give thought unto the source of thine power and that which ye do with it.

* * *

The guardians

𝟛𝟛𝟛 - 𝑃𝑃𝑃 is the watchers and keepers of the way at this hour, for this is of great concern unto all the 𝟛𝟛𝟛 and the 𝑃𝑃𝑃. The 𝒞𝒞𝒞 have set the seal upon the ones which are the watchers, or the guardians.

Let us speak of the 'Guardians'. These have long been watching the trend of man's mind, for there is a trend to destroy that which is given unto them for their upliftment. As the old cycle comes to its final hour, the new is in its dawning. As it is written, there is an overlapping. The dawning is that period when it is not yet sunrise, neither is it the darkest of the night... We speak of this last few moments before sunrise as the dawning.

For this do we speak of the period of time before the old cycle is gone, not ever to be repeated upon the planet earth. All that hast been its sowing is now its reaping... and the balancing follows, surely as the day follows the night.

The balancing

Now let us speak of the "balancing". This day all things shall be as the harvest reaped. The gathering in shall be the harvest, and each man shall have his share portioned out unto him as he hast sown. Thus, he shall be as his own paymaster and responsible for his own pay. This is according unto the Law of the "One", the Law of Justice, which covers each and every man which liveth upon or within the earth. This is the end and it shall bring with it the beginning of the new... while the fullness of the new is not yet seen or felt by the populace.

This is that period of time that hast been referred to in thine record as the End Time, the Armageddon. This hast been as a perfect description of this time of the closing and the beginning of the two cycles when such shall be mankinds lot, such as he shall share in full measure that which he has stored up for this day... be it chaff or wheat. I say unto one and all, none shall escape, for justice shall prevail. Let no man or woman complain about his share, for it is the weighing, the sifting and sorting, when each one shall receive his just portion.

This is that which every man shall experience in the days ahead, as it is but the beginning of the "New Day". The old shall go out with a great loud noise which shall shake lose the old. And likewise, the new shall come in with a great shout of glorious acclaim: "*It is done! It is finished! It is come, this glad new day! The cleansing is finished!!!*" A glorious new day when all manifestation shall be as made new, according unto the law of the One, the O, which hast created the earth and the fullness thereof. In his will shall it be made new.

That which mankind hast despoiled shall be no more, for it is now come that it shall go unto its end, and no more shall it exist... that which hast been man's downfall. Let it be understood that naught of man's likeness of this day, his nature as he is this day, shall inherit the New Earth/the New Heaven, for all shall be made new. Not one shall take with him one single particle of his old nature. He shall be as made new, for this is the sifting and the sorting, the balancing time. There shall be nothing overlooked, even unto the last of created creatures.

There shall be the greatest of all gatherings. Into one place shall they, the ones prepared for the higher light, be placed. The ones of the lesser light shall be within the place nearest unto the higher. While the ones prepared for the lesser light shall not see these (which are) over them, for the lesser lighted ones could not bear the higher light, for this is the time of sifting and sorting...

Sananda

My time is come when I shall speak out that justice be done. I speak for the good of all, yet man of earth is so deep in lethargy and self-aggrandizement that he hears not that which is broadcast from the mountain top. It is now come when the sound, a mighty blast, shall go forth which shall alert them, for too long have they slept at the switch.

I have given unto 'man', as a body of human species, free will. I have given unto him speech and the gift of seeing and hearing, yet he sees not that which he hast done with these precious gifts, neither does he ponder the Source. He hast gone headlong in his own will, in his forgetfulness of his heritage, his Source.

Now, the time is come when he shall arise with the will to learn, and be One with his Source, knowingly. For this do we, as á mighty host of lighted Beings of the higher realms, draw nigh unto the earth that we might awaken him (as a company) which hast divided himself into many fragments.

Now this day is come when he, as a multiple Being, shall be caused to remember his oneness with all the fragments of mankind. He shall no longer buy or sell his brother of the same parentage, the same lineage. He, this manifestation of Light-Source (the substance of all life), has no memory of his Source, therefore we, the ones which have the knowledge, have called time and time again, "*Come! Come! Come! Arise and learn of us thine brothers of light*". We come in love and wisdom, for we see and know that which ye have suffered and cried for relief in thine dark hour. Yea, we have come at thine call, yet ye know not that which we bring as a gift from the source of thine being Ye are blinded by thine own ego, thine forgetfulness falls about thee as a black hood.

We come and offer thee the gift of freedom, wherein ye shall remember all things. Freedom to walk the starry roadways of the heavens, to go and come without any cumbersome 'gadgets which hold thee bound, bound to earth they are. For it is so written, "ye, man of earth, shall not enter into our realm of light with these man made instruments of death and bondage".

We come that thine eyes be opened and thine ears be made to hear... thine mind be given comprehension and thine heart be made to rejoice with thine new found freedom, and thine knowing that which thou truly art... One with the All, O. Thine totality without blemish or fear.

This is the day of awakening, which hast been referred to in thine 'holy writ' as "Resurrection Day". Too, it is said that ye cannot, shall not, take with thee one particle of thy mortal self, not one iota of earthly substance shall ye bring into the Realm of Light, wherein we thine brothers of light abide. Be ye blest to know us, to reach out thine hand that we might lead/guide thee as ones which know the way unto eternal freedom.

* * *

The church

☪☪☪ Wherein is it written that "There are none so foolish as ones which think themselves wise".. It is so! I see them which gather themselves about their little altars, with their icons which are man-fashioned. They are as ones gone mad, as they cry and chant their anthems in honor of the dead image (Christ on the cross). They have given unto me no power, no honor, for it is as the patterns of fools.

They know me not! They are defiant as wayward children when I speak unto them. They fear their God. I say unto them, "*I am the living Lord God... I live within thee... Ye are as mine children, of me ye have thine being*". These words fall on deaf ears.

It is now come when these shall be brought out from their places they have set aside for me, and wherein they have defiled their altars with idols and all sorts of hypocrisy. I say, it is an abomination in mine sight! I am not moved by their pious prayers and lies perpetuated through their childrens' children. The day of deliverance is come when they shall raise up and rebel against such foolish acts, which is but a farce. Within it is no substance, no truth, no light, little understood of or by themselves. For long hast the customs been practiced, until (now) they practice them as robots, without feeling or understanding.

These which shall raise up and throw off the black hood and seek the light shall find it, for I am not afar off. I hear the humble cries for Truth and Light. These are ready to give of themselves that others might find their way. I say, I shall reach out and touch them that they come to know me as I am... then they shall be as ones to give unto others of their knowledge that they be set free.

I see the greater light, for I am The Truth and The Light... I am The Way unto their eternal freedom. While I have given unto one and all the guidelines that should be practiced as children of light... they have given unto themselves credit for being wise. While they have mocked me and mine sayings, they have forgotten these (mine sayings) and distorted them suitable unto themselves. They have called themselves "Father", knowing Him not... while they of such tenor hold the humble and weak in bondage. They ask pittance for penance, which they ask of their 'victims'. Yea, I say, these which bow down before these false gods are victims.

This shall be as the past. It shall be gone, as the wind, to be used no more to hold bound the innocent which hast been held bondage. I say, this day is come when I shall throw down their altars of abomination. I shall set up ther Kingdom of God upon the earth, wherein the purified shall dwell in peace and harmony. For this shall the earth be made new.

She too shall have a new berth, and be as one free of such as hast desecrated her. She shall no longer give footing unto the laggards!

* * *

To set free the captives

ᴇᴇᴇ With this signature I come that I add mine word unto that of mine Elder Brother. As One we come... we know our self to be one in the Allness of the source of our being. We are made in the likeness of the One which we call "Father". We are the Son... we are not divided into fragments as ye of earth. We are as One with the All O, and for this we are One, of one mind, one body, one intent.

Let it be understood, that which We/I am saying unto thee. When I speak of 'one body!, I am speaking as a unit of united entities which have no differences of interest, as does man of Earth. When I speak, I represent the united whole of our Order, the ᴇᴇᴇ. We are not divided by opinions and preconceived ideas. We sit in council as with one mind, one interest and intent at this time, which hast been clearly recorded within these records, with few words as to wit: "To set free the captive", which ye are, as man of earth. Our intent is to free thee from bondage. Thine freedom is offered thee this day as a free gift, should ye have the will to accept it.

Be not so foolish to turn thine face away and spurn us as of no concern, as impostors, for I say unto all and sundry, "*We are of the light regions... We come of the light... We are of the greater knowledge and power*. We are not subservient unto any power other than our "Source", in which we exist as living entities (souls). For this we are filled with love for all, and give of ourself that ye, one and all, might come into the fullness of thine inheritance, willed unto thee of the Source of thine Being...

* * *

Guardian angels

ƤƤƤ This be mine signature, signifying mine particular part, or place, within the whole of the great plan for all the many and sundry beings called "Man". However, we are not as yet finished with our mission upon the planet earth, for as we of the **ƤƤƤ** Order have reached our fullness of time as earth man, we are more prepared to assist our species as Elder Brothers. Therefore we stand as One with our Elders, which hast assisted us in our assent at the end of our sojourn

This ✠ is our mission at this crucial time, to assist thee, mine brothers of little knowledge of thine Source or inheritance. We come that ye be prepared for to raise from thine slumbers and ascend unto the heights with us which have gone before thee. Our mission unto thee this day is one of fellowship and love. We know that which ye are and all that ye do... while ye, mine brothers, know or remember nothing of us of the higher realms of light. There hast been tomes written of us, as man hast envisioned us to be. Very fanciful indeed!

While it hast been, in a measure, based on truth, that we do exist... yet where and how and what do we do, or how can we, as "Angels", assist man on earth? Be it so that they recognize our existence in the time of dire distress, in the time of chaos... yet alas, after the chaos passes, we are often forgotten or denied. Tis the nature of the man of earth, in his earthly nature. That which he has acquired from his forefathers, as before him, had little knowledge of his progenitors and benefactors who have stood by and watched with care, his slow development.

Now we are called forth once again in the name of our Father Mother God, to assist in thine accent into the fullness of thine inheritance. We ask of thee thine acceptance of our love and fellowship, and a willingness to learn of thine reality, thine full inheritance as a Son of the Living God. This is our mission in the realm of denser vibration of earth, the lesser light... the denseness on the saddened world of man.

* * *

The parable

ᶀᶀᶀ   ᶀᶀᶀ   ᶀᶀᶀ   ᶀᶀᶀ   ᶀᶀᶀ   ᶀᶀᶀ

This is that which could be an example unto thee, of the many, as ye might think of us as the many. A group here, a group there, in lots of few or many. I am speaking for the Order of Man as ᶀᶀᶀ. I say unto thee, we are as One, not scattered or fragmented. Fragments are but the parts which are 'within the whole of the specie, be it animal, foul, or fish. No specie ever becomes other than that which it was designed to be. While it is but little understood, that which is said unto thee of this subject, I shall give unto thee a parable:

The sifting and sorting

"When a man goes into his garden to plant, he carries a bag of seeds. He knows the seed he carries and the soil he hast prepared to receive the seed. He watches with care the growth and development. When the harvest is on, the best of the seed is saved for the future sowing... nothing wasted, for he knows the sown to be good, fertile.

Now, within the harvest he finds some hast brought great promise for yet another abundant yield, a more pleasing product... therefore, he sets aside the most likely seed to be his choice for the next sowing... as this is his intention, to bring forth a more perfect harvest. Therefore, he chooses the most favorable of each harvest until he is satisfied that he hast found a stable and suitable product that he could rely upon.

His experiment has been favorable for the present season. While, as the seasons come and pass, the once perfect seed begins to become contaminated, and again he seeks out the best of his harvest, and there is, once again, a sifting and sorting. As the seasons pass, and again the best of the sowing, the greatest of the harvest is plucked out... and once again he finds new soil and moves his experimental garden into fresh new soil. Therein again he oversees the results of his labors.

He now stands as one to give himself credit for the wisdom, and for the assistance, from the condition of the soil, the rain, and his labor, He is not as yet finished, for there is another garden prepared in which he, in proper timing, sows his new garden according unto the signs of the heavens, and the blessing of Solen Aum Solen...

Note: In light of this previous message, we might think of the CCC as those beings who came forth within a previous season or cycle of sifting and sorting... while both the ♌♌♌ and the ҏҏҏ Orders have come forth within this present cycle here upon the earth, from two separate sortings...

* * *

CCC This be my word unto thee this day. It is a great day in which many shall awaken unto their heritage and arise and come forth as new born, born of the light wherein there is no darkness. Blest are they which awaken this day, for they shall go into bondage no more. They shall soar as the Eagle. They shall know, and know that they know. They shall be free from the gravitation of the earth and the attraction of the moon, never more to go into the world of dense matter.

This is the day of weighing and balancing, sifting and sorting. Let it be as the completing of the old and the beginning of the new. For this are we come, that ye be made new.

The call hast gone forth... "*Awaken all ye nations of the Earth*". The day swiftly approaches when the earth and the children of earth shall have a new abiding place, for the earth shall have a new port. The Sons of God shall be as the guardians thereof and all things shall be made new. The laggards shall have a new abiding place wherein they shall come of age and awaken unto their rightful heritage. They shall follow the law of progress, then they shall arise as ones mature, knowing of their lineage, their Source.

This is mine word at this hour. I shall speak again and again... I Am one sent.

* * *

ඌඌඌ By this signature ye shall know me. I am come that ye (Thedra) be prepared to enter into mine place of abode. Herein ye shall receive thine inheritance. Ye shall find that it is worth the waiting, for this shall be thine reward.

Now, it is nigh time that ye be brought in. Ye shall find that ye have been here before. Ye shall be as one prepared to share as one equal unto us. Herein ye shall learn that which hast been hidden from the child of earth for aeons of time. The truth, the real history, the full account of many progressions shall be seen and understood, for we have such methods as man hast never dreamed of.

We need no gadgets of such as earth science uses. We need no "oil". We have everything necessary for our work, for our tools are 'Light', of light are they created, therefore we create as needed. We have no need to store away or destroy that which is no longer needed, therefore we have no clutter such as man of earth.

Be assured that we know when to use our 'tools'. We are well equipt. We are the "Greater Power". Let no man set himself up as the greater power, for I say with the authority invested in me by mine Father, that there is greater power than man of flesh and bone hast dreamed of in all his dreaming.

I am come that earth be lifted up, and I bring with me a host of Lighted Beings. We are come for/with one purpose, one intent... that of delivering her (the earth) out whole, safely, even as the children of earth... for as the children of accountability are lifted, so shall the earth be. For she is a living entity and she has come unto her full time when she shall find her new berth prepared and waiting. For she shall bring forth a 'Son' (*see Mine Intercom Messages*) as she moves out from her present port into her new place, wherein she shall rest and be prepared to receive the new generation, <u>The Sons of God</u>.

For this is it said: "The Son born of Mother Earth shall be as a new moon which shall be the new school for the laggards that Mother Earth hast disavowed for her new place of abode. These are the ones which have betrayed themselves... they have forsaken their mother which hast brought them forth and nurtured them. They are bastards, for they know not their Father. They have denied their 'Source', therefore forfeiting their true inheritance. Even so, so be it that the new moon shall be their school room, wherein they shall grow to maturity with the new born moon. It shall be in the East that it is born, and in the east that it raises and it shall set in the west. The inhabitance of this new body shall have no memory of their earth experience, for they have forfeited that gift.

It is said that this is the time of sifting and sorting, and it is so! The dark shall be separated from the light, for the two cannot occupy the same place. Be it so that I speak in simple language that even the child might understand that which I am saying unto thee. Be ye of a mind to learn of me and I shall reveal unto thee great and new things ye have not dreamed of.

Be ye, O man, not puffed up, for ye have not seen or heard that which is before thee, Ye are as yet babes at the breast. Ye are at thine creeping stage. Let it be recorded herein, that ye which are of a mind to learn shall learn to walk... then run... even leap up where no man hast been. I call thee, O man of earth... hear me and respond unto that which I have for thee, which shall be thine freedom from bondage wherein ye labor for bread by the sweat of thy brow.

I now speak unto the ones which think themselves wise: 'There are none so foolish"... for the time is nigh upon thee when ye shall see that ye have betrayed thine own self. Ye have sold thine birth right for a counterfeit penny...

* * *

I shall set straight the record

Be ye as mine hand made manifest and I shall make clear mine intent unto all which have eyes that see, ears that hear, and a mind to comprehend that which I am saying unto them at this time."

So be it, it is now the time of maturing. The harvest hast been sown and it is now the time of reaping. Each shall be measured out his just portion, be it that which he hast sown.

The Father shall claim his son... The Mother shall suckle her babe... The Son shall own his Father... The family shall be as one...

The harlot shall find her bed hard... The whoremonger shall find no joy....

The day is come when mine sayings shall be brought to mind. Ye shall read and understand the meaning thereof... for this am I giving them.

So be it, I shall make clear mine intent. This shall be for the ones which have asked, "*What is going on? What is being done? What shall be the end?*" I say unto them, I am come with a mighty host of lighted Ones, with the intent of setting straight that which hast been made crooked by the opposite forces which hast brought about the day, the hour of reckoning, the balancing, the sifting and sorting.

The harvest is now in full. Each shall receive his just measure, and for this have we of the Christ Council drawn nigh. We are not the judge. The law which we know and abide by shall be unto every man his guide by which he shall judge himself.' He shall find that he hast given unto himself that which is his by law of justice supreme.

He shall find that he hast been his own worst enemy, He shall find be hast prepared the bitter cup for his brother... now he shall drink the last bitter dregs. He shall see for himself that which he hast done, that which he hast lain up as his harvest... this be his part that no man can take from him or atone for him. Be it such as he hast earned.

I have said many times, in many ways, to many people, that I Am Come! So be it I am come to claim mine own, for the Father hast sent me that the way be made clear for the children of light to be brought in. These are mine harvest. I have tended mine harvest well, and now it is come when I shall see the results of mine husbandry, of mine faithful careful attention unto that which hast been given unto me of the Father as mine portion, as mine inheritance or share.

The Father hast sent me with a mighty host that I reclaim that which is rightfully mine. I shall lay to rest all that which hast been written, spoken, and propagated about me and mine time as the "prophet Jesus". I shall set straight, once and for all time, the record which shall be for generations yet unborn. Their lies shall be as the trap they have set for their own feet. These which have perpetuated these lies to which they have bound themselves shall no longer bind mine children which cry for light and truth, which shall set them free.

I say unto thee, man of earth which call thine self by such and such grandiose titles as 'Father' etc. etc. etc..." "Thine way shall be bard indeed, for ye shall no longer hold mine children bound. Ye shall come to the fount to find it dry... ye shall come unto the table to find it empty... ye shall come unto the confessional to find no ears to hear. Ye shall fall upon thine face in penance and cry for mercy, so great shall be thine sorrow". The hour glass hast given thee warning... have ye not noticed? Thine time hast run out. I have seen it and I am not deceived...

* * *

♂♂♂ This is the signature that ye shall recognize as the Order which has followed the , this being the one and only ♀♀♀, This Order is the one which gives the light and power to the ♂♂♂... for this we are one.

There is no difference in our purpose or authority, for without one the other could not function. This line of order is brought about for the purpose of efficiency, as a perfect whole.

The Orders each operate effective within the ♀♀♀, this being the Great and Mighty overall Council unto which we of the lesser Orders bow. We pay homage unto the over-all Council... there are none greater. We of the lesser Councils are at the bidding of the ♀♀♀, while each one in line, as we are called, respond unto and act as directed.

Therefore, no mistake in where the directions originate or come from, such as the orders of man of earth.

There is such confusion among/within the different departments of thy government that chaos is the result. Find one department which has its order within the whole, the council which has its order within it the supreme power in which all work and operate as one, in harmony and efficiency... there being no confusion with any department? There we simply do not find one which are as efficient as the system which is ours.

We give unto our self no credit for to bring attention to self. We work for the good of the whole, all for one, one for all... no such arguments as we see among these of thine governments. Because of this confusion, the chaos reigns. No peace shall be permanent until there is an over-all Council which has the supreme power, from which justice and truth emerge out from and through all other departments within the whole, for the good of all. Harmony and peace reign within such a system.

We of the greater overall Council have no notion of supreme power invested in one individual as such for to give him the power and the glory... we are not so foolish. For long, longer than time has recorded, we have been evolving the system in which we now find perfect and effective. This includes many planets and star systems, which come into line of their own choice as they qualify. Then by choice and qualification, they are admitted into the Council for which they are best suited for the good of the system, the whole of the system. We have no notion or intent of bringing into line any planet or system of planets before they, or it, has learned to live in harmony, with love and wisdom, with which there shall be peace.

The Great Tribunal sits as the supreme, overall which are in line for recognition for admission into the federation of the ꙮꙮꙮ. This is the one Order in which the final decision is made for any admittance into the next order, which we have not mentioned herein, for it would be most premature...

The governments of the plane of earth are that of little light and wisdom, for the selfish man cannot be called a "just man". He seeks for self the power to hold his subjects in submission that *he* be the ruling power over them.

The "just man" gives equal rights unto his fellow 'brother'. He recognizes them as such, therefore he becomes a guardian of their rights, wherein all share alike the gifts Mother Earth hast provided for her children.

It is said by the unjust man that "this sort of government would be impossible". We of the greater knowledge and wisdom say: "Not So!" For we of the greater power have come to know for a surety that the just government *can* be established on each and every planet within the Solar System.

This is our intent. Our proposition is now before man of earth. We have presented unto him such a plan as should be his for the asking. For we of the Mighty Council, which is the overall power and light Council, are ready and willing to assist with such a plan.

Now, we stand aside for a moment to see that which he will decide. We have given directions and mandates that he might understand our position, and know for a surety that we are their Elder Brothers, come as such for to bring lasting peace. We make no idle promises, no confusion. We are not phantoms, neither are we afar off. We see and know the actions which are brought about by the evil intent... as the good and just intent brings about just acts, results, in harmony and peace.

We are of one mind, one source, that of light... in which we as 'One body' have come unto the lesser, or younger brothers (which hast forgotten their lineage, their "source") that they be unbound from the unknowing, the unjust, which hast set themselves up as superior overall, to hold them in bondage.

Now it is come, when we are prepared to give of our wisdom and fellowship unto this proposition which we place before the governments of man on earth. We wait and watch, prepared to do that which is necessary for the good of all...

* * *

The source - the Creation

ℯℯℯ This ye shall recognize as mine Order, for I come on behalf of my Order which is one with the ♂♂♂ and the ♀♀♀. For we, as the three, are 'One'... one of mind, intent, and purpose, in the light of the O, the One which ye call 'God'. We call It "Father"... Source of being. For in this <u>Source</u> we have our being. Unto this source of 'light' we owe our life, our allegiance... on this Source we rely.

We are of "It" in "It"... It sustains us. There is none, no, <u>not one</u>, greater than this ALL, which permeates all that is manifest or unmanifest. The signature that expresses for our purpose is and shall be the complete unbroken circle, such as O. Therein all things, all power exists, and from the center of this Source it circulates in rhythm with precision and balance. No man can mimic such perfection, timing, creating, by forming of images as he is want to do.

This Source we call Solen Aum Solen. There is no greater name, no greater sound than this, for this be that which brings forth great reverberations throughout the cosmos. Let it be understood, that it is of such power that should man misuse it for his own selfish end or purpose, he would be as one in great danger. This must be the greatest of <u>Sacred use</u> for the good of all created beings. For it is the Source of Power and Light... "It" hast no failures. It moves perpetually with unfailing precision.

Man hast not seen, heard, or felt the power of this eternal Source... for he, man, is but a particle in the power of the all-encompassing Source. Man is but a thought, breathed forth within Solen Aum Solen, as a great wave of light which is like unto a breathing in - breathing out... as a pulsation of energy.

The Creation

This pulsation reaches another point within the action of thought set into motion within the All, for there is <u>no</u> inaction... all is movement, in perfect rhythm. From the thought of Solen Aum Solen was made lesser light, yet of the same and only "Source", for there is but one source of life. From this thought was made, or created, a being of the same power and substance as the thought set into motion.

From this motion, another thought created a likeness of the first being. These two beings were also set into motion, which in endless ages took form yet not dense bodies of flesh and bone. Another period of creation came about by this breathing in-out, as a great pulsation, in which these two took upon themselves another change, wherein they became aware of themselves as One, of one Source. This Source gave unto them "free will". As they became creatures of the will they desired to create as the Source, in light and power.

Note: In a previous message Sister Thedra was told that these first two beings were, in fact, Sananda and Sanat Kumara

<u>Now</u>, we have the two, as separate entities with free will... each was also empowered with power to create. One chose to create material substance.... the other to give of himself that other entities be sent forth, even as he, in light body, yet aware of the source of himself. This one, now aware of his being, his source and power, surrounded himself with many light beings with no will of their own, only to serve the Source of all light and energy. These creatures were of light and energy. The purpose of their creation was to serve the one which chose to give of himself that others might come forth as he.

Now, within him the desire to create as (like unto) the Source became manifest as a conscious entity which was called man. This Man became, after aeons of countless changes, a creature prepared to take physical form, a dense body. This became an age in which man was given free will, and a plan on or in which to work as he progressed. There hast been many periods of preparations.

When mankind reached a point in which he was self-responsible, he was given great lessons of self-improvement, such as letter making, picture and graphics painting, creating form of great beauty, buildings of great strength and symmetry. Where much progress of a material sort was made, many were thought of as gods, for the ones of lesser knowledge knew not their progenitors. <u>This age</u> was shorter than the previous ones, which brought forth the work of the one which chose to work with the materialization of light.

While the one which chose to work as one prepared to bring forth <u>beings of light bodies</u>, brought into existence such beings of light and power as himself, and of himself, this one created in the fashion of Solen Aum Solen. This was the period in which primitive man began to learn to communicate with his Source, even as his creator had done before him.

Now, in this period the two first entities, which emerged within the All power and light, became two separate entities. One was given the mind to create planets, systems of star patterns, and fashion the heavens about, in which is called the firmaments. Now, the other was given the privilege/gift of over-seer, the "Guardian Spirit" of the co-operation of the two entities which first emerged as of light substance. These two were faithful unto their Source... never have they, unto this day, betrayed their trust or themselves.

Much hast been written and fabricated about these two so-called gods, which "We" here at this present age of change are most concerned. For within the material world of mankind is left many records of his (man's) development (progress), therefore, we at this point are not concerned with bringing the details from out the dark ages in which man lost his sense of Oneness with his Source. We are the Lighted Ones which forgot not our Source. It is our part at this time to give unto man a minute microscopic picture of his beginning as materialized spirit, and to be responsible for himself while remembering his Source

This is indeed a microscopic part of our effort which we are now involved with, that man might, this day, give thought unto his heritage, while not going backward to find the lost, forgotten pattern, the fragments of his past.

We give unto the present generation, and all generations to come, that which shall bring them into the light of their inheritance... that is the gift of remembering their Source and their oneness with "It", wherein there is no darkness.

This brings this small sketch to the present day, with which we of the light are concerned... that of awakening thee unto thine Source. For this we are preparing a great festival of light in which mankind shall be awakened as to his birthright, and the acceptance thereof. This shall be known as the Day of Deliverance...

* * *

September 1955 - Los Angeles California.

"Sanat Kumara spoke to me, commanding that I go to the "high desert - the arid land" to hold the light for a work that is to be done. Where? I questioned. Later in my preparation for departure I was told it was Prescott Arizona.

I arrive via Greyhound on Oct 31, 1955, at evening time. (name omitted) met me at the bus station. I find (name omitted) there... later (name omitted) arrives... later (name omitted) and his wife. I was instructed to tell them that I was on my way to South America. None of us knew the other was coming. We all marveled at this gathering.

(Note: This gathering contained the 5 people who were to go to South America with Sister Thedra. That whole episode is another story in and of itself...)

* * *

Sister thedra

Talk on Mount Shasta

Day 2

I have no words that would express my joy to have you all here. And I mean all, regardless of where you have come from or where you are going. Love IS! It just IS! We have to become aware of it. We have heard much about cooperation, and all of these beautiful sayings which we take as mantras. We take them so lightly! My very soul gets sick sometimes at the way we handle words, and I don't mean gramaticaly either. We say things when we don't know what we are talking about... we make commitments which we have no intention of keeping... and these things must be understood, that they carry power. The Masters tell us that even trivia... we should get rid of trivia, that it comes back, boomerangs back to us in little ways, and we say "Why did that happen to me? Why did I get a flat tire? Why did I breakdown on the highway?". Little annoyances are created by trivia. I'm just throwing that out to you...

I have come here today, as always, as a messenger of the Living God. I speak now to ones who call themselves "light workers"... how do we work light? Light just IS! We must become aware of it. God just IS! We have nothing to do with how God came to be nor what He is going to do. We listen with our hearts and with sincerity of purpose, and we say "*Father, Thy Will Be Done*", then listen for direction. None of us working for a big corporation would think it smart to go over the bosses head.

Now, the One from which we have our being, within this being... there is no place to go outside of God, for God is ALL in ALL... but do we mean it when we say it? Do we think it? Do we know it? Do we live it? We say, "*Come lord, come God, take us*". Now where would he take us? Where would he take us? We are "embryos" within the body of God, and there is no place to go. There is no "out" nor there is no "in". God is ALL in ALL. Our job is to listen to the direction from the inner temple and to obey. That is all He asks of us is to obey and then we become aware of love. Love and God are synonymous. And that is all that He expects us to do is to obey the laws of God. And we take very little heed of these Laws... because we don't understand them.

Question: We hear the name of "Christ", and "Jesus", and now we have the new name "Sananda". Now, are these the same entity?

Thedra: It will be the same entity. But remember, there are 'false' ones. There are also people today who have named their children 'Sananda'.

The Father often uses the word "Solen Aum Solen", and Sananda, His first born, says that this is the most holy word that we could speak today. And the Father says "You are *ensouled* within me... that's what "Solen" means. Ye are "ensouled" within me. And the word AUM, I wont tell you what that means because you use it all the time. He says "Solen Aum Solen"... try chanting it to yourself some day before you tell someone and they desecrate it. It is a very sacred name and you don't want to throw your pearls to babes who don't know how to use them. It is a very sacred thing.

Now you must remember that there are ones today who are claiming to be thus and so, and you must turn to the "Source" of your being, to the very "Source" of your being, and ask of NO man, and you will be taught discernment. Discernment is a gift of God. Prey for it mightily.

Question: How may I become ordained?

Thedra: All right dear... now you don't yourself and you don't expect any man to ordain you. Ask of no man your ordination. Only God can ordain you, and you will be given when you are prepared to receive it. Seek ye first the light and all else shall be added. I've just read the rules and regulations you might say in very simple terms.

But now, you have to be consistent, with a burning desire to do the Lords will. And you have to do a lot of listening. You pray... and then you listen. We don't take the time to hear what God is telling us. Now,

God is as much in you as in anyone else, without an ordination, but to become aware of it we do need help. And that is what our "Elder brothers" are here today... to give us the help and to teach us.

Have I time to tell you a story here? Once when I was in school in the high Andes Mountains... (now I want you all to know that you don't go the Andes mountains looking for a school or a temple, you will be wasting your time. You can find it right here, and if there is any reason for you the go to the Andes you will be taken).

So Sananda gave me an assignment this day which was to go into the marketplace, which was a long way, but I got there as there was always a way provided. I got there and it was a very poor market place, with dirt floors, with the wares laid out on dirty sheep skins which had been shaved. And I asked, "*Now that I am here Master, what do I do*"? He said, "*Enter*".

After I had entered he said, "*Now look at the people*", and I looked at these people and thought, "but what am I looking for"... thinks me... *what am I looking for?* He said "*Go over and stand against that wall*", which was a mud wall. So I go over and stand against the wall, and he says "*Now look at them... look well*", and I looked at each and every one. Some of them had no nose or had ears missing (from frost bite), some of them had had their feet frozen, their toes missing... some of them had sores or were blind with cataracts. These were the people who were selling a little bit of this and a little bit of that in this market place. Now, some of you might sicken to see that... I used to think, what would our American doctors do here, where would they start here, and I anguished much over it. Sananda said, "*Now you look at each and every one... look well... see what you are looking at.* I stood there and I was trying to look deeper than my eyes could see. Finally he said, "*Now you love them as I love you...*" (fighting back tears, Sister Thedra continued) My knees trembled... I learned more about love in that one moment than I had ever learned at the feet of any pseudo masters. And I get sick to my stomach sometimes when I hear the platitudes that are so prevalent in the "new age" society. I would like to find a new word for the "new age groups"... it doesn't mean much today. What in the world do we mean by new age... we are still dragging our feet! No matter what we might call ourselves we have no excuse in the world for dragging our feet... none! And for the past forty years I have felt many times, oh God are they all dead out there? And He says "*No, they've just got their fingers in their ears.*" They are walking like this... (ears covered up). They say "*Don't tell me because I already know... you have nothing to tell me*". Now if you don't believe me just go out there and try it.

Well I bless you all and hope you have had your moneys worth (laughter from the crowd, as this event was free). I hope you have felt the love which has gone out from this mountain and the guardians there of. And I hope to see you back here next year with a new vocabulary, new goals, and a wonderful report on the past year.

Bless you dears... bless you all

End tape

* * *

Ending note: After 5 years of training in the high Andes mountains of South America, Sister Thedra was told she was to return to the United States, from where she would begin to give out the teachings. She returned to this country in 1961, and in 1962 she was directed to go to Mt. Shasta. For the next three years she continued giving out the original Scripts which she had carried back from South America..

In 1965 Sananda told her that she was to purchase the land and partially completed structure which was to become the "Gatehouse". Although she didn't have a penny to her name she went ahead and signed the papers which would put the property into escrow. She had no idea of how she would pay for it, but she had total faith that somehow Sananda would provide for his work. When the day arrived that escrow was to close she still had no prospect as to where she was going to come up with such a large sum, but she proceeded ahead on her faith alone. It was not until late in the afternoon, only two hours before escrow was to close, that the entire sum arrived by mail from someone who she had never even met. He simply said that Sananda had told him that this sum was needed.

The Gatehouse was thus established in Mt Shasta, and it was there that the remainder of the Scripts were received. For the next 23 years Sister Thedra provided counseling and guidance to those who sought her out, and hundreds of thousands of copies of Scripts and manuscripts were sent out around the world to those who asked. She had been told that she was not to advertise nor to go out seeking "converts" so-to-speak. She was told that she was simply to make the word available to those who asked. Sananda had told her that when ones were hungry enough for the Word that they would find *her*, and they did.

She said that after 26 years she fully expected to spend the rest of her life there in Mt Shasta. But in February of 1988, Sananda told her to be ready to move the Gatehouse, and without hesitation she made the preparations. By April of 1988 she had relocated here in Sedona, where Sananda simply said...

"It is time to open the gateway of the Red Rocks"

* * *

A BIT OF HISTORY...

The events and experiences spoken of by Sister Thedra on these tapes were just brief sketches of a few of the many experiences which began her preparation for the work which she was later to do. Those years, 1950 to 1955, were the years in which many things happened which laid the foundation for the work which was to come. They were also years in which she learned to deal with the pressure and the publicity which at times threatened to swallow her up. These were the times that were to test her true "metal" before the work could go forward... fortunately for us all, it turned out to be "pure gold".

Since most of us were either too young to remember or were not even born when most of this all took place, we have very little understanding of what transpired at that time. We have heard both Sananda and those who are referred to as the "Elder brothers" say at various times, that they have "Contacted the Governments of the world, and have given them messages of peace and goodwill." We have heard them say that they have "Contacted the heads of the nations of the earth", yet we have no understanding of how or when this might have been done.

If you remember, in newsletter #66 we ran an excerpt from a book by William Dudley Pelley entitled "Seven Minutes in Eternity". We told you how this experience had been published in the <u>American Magazine</u> in 1929, and had attracted worldwide attention for its vivid account of his spiritual awakening experience. Now Sister Thedra was very committed to keeping accurate records of these events so that the truth of these things might not become lost to those who would later follow. Among her records is an original copy of another article also published by <u>American Magazine</u> in 1954. This was during this same period in which she herself was involved in personal contact with those who she referred to as the brothers from other planets".

This article is entitled **<u>The Presidents Caller</u>**. Following her brief description of the experiences in her own life, we thought that this article might help you to understand how this might all fit together. We have no way of knowing if the account portrayed in the article is factual or accurate. We also have no way of knowing what might have inspired a respected magazine to print such an incredible story back in 1954. However, in hind sight, and judging by what Sananda and others have said, we might at least surmise that it was possibly based on information from an actual event. In light of the events which Sister Thedra spoke of concerning her own early experiences, we thought that we should at least reprint the article here and let you all decide for yourselves...

* * *

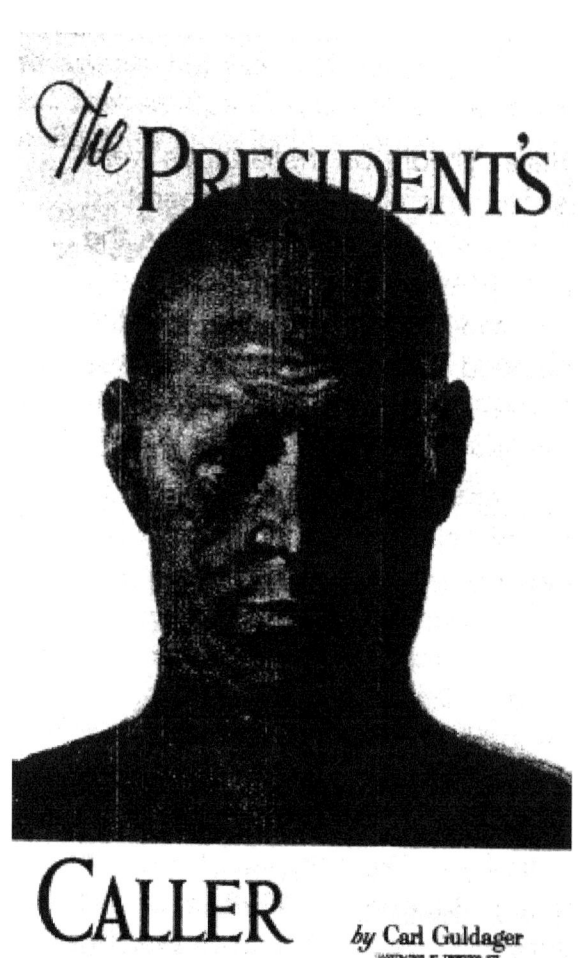

The President's Caller *by* Carl Guldager

American magazine - 1954

Mitchell drove home from the station in a musty freezing rain. He had just put his wife and two youngsters on the train. They were going home to Cleveland for a week, and already Mitchell missed them. He hoped to join them on New Years day, but the way his work was piled up he wasn't sure he could manage even that. Anne had been a little upset at his not being able to go with them, and Mitchell himself, fond as he was of the President and his cause, wondered how much of his personal life he would sacrifice for the White House. He had to write a New Years Day message for the president, and considering the state of the world, he couldn't imagine what he was going to suggest as a theme.

The rain reflected the car lights and Mitchell's head ached. As he was putting the car in the garage he heard the phone ring in the house and sprinted to catch it. In the dark he gave his ankle a crack on the hall table as he snatched up the phone.

"Yes" he said, and he could not keep the irritation from his voice.

"Jim, this is MacReady. You've got to come down right away".

Mitchell sighed, "look Mac, I've just put Anne and the kids on the train and I've brought home enough work to kill two men. What's so important that I've got to hop in the car and get right down?"

MacReady hesitated. "I'd rather not talk about it on the phone" he said. "Take my word for it, you will, and get down here fast, I really need your help".

"Look" Mitchell said, "What gives?".

MacReady's voice was uncertain. "Jim" he said, "I've notified all the security people. In half an hour this place will be closed off completely. I need you to break the news to the boss." His voice changed. "I've got a guy here who says he is from outer space".

Mitchell roared with laughter. "Okay Mac" he said when he could talk again, "I fell for the gag... is he green all over, does he have an eerie light?"

There was a long pause on the phone. "I've seen this guy Jim", Macready said. "I'm not kidding, I think he may be what he says he is. I'll give you fifteen minutes to get over here, but if you still think this is a gag and don't show I'll go to the boss myself." He hung up.

Mitchell flicked on the lights and stood frowning at the phone. Then he turned the lights off and went back out to the garage. He made it to the White House in ten minutes. Only once he thought "if this is a joke I'm going to turn in my resignation". Then he remembered MacReady's voice and suddenly felt chilled.

The place was swarming with protection. Though he was closer to the President than any other man, Jim had to show his papers three times before he got into MacReady's office. Mac sat at his desk, staring at the ceiling light.

"Thanks for coming Jim" he said. "I know this must have sounded crazy over the phone. I've been sitting here wondering if I can make it through to the end of this. If this guy turns out to be a fraud, I'm going back to Kansas with the farm and those green quiet corn fields."

"Where is he" Jim asked. "I've got him in the little study" MacReady said. "He's as snug as a bug in a bullet proof vest. He can't scratch his nose without seven guns pointing in his direction".

"You mean he's got a nose" Jim said."

MacReady didn't smile. "He showed up in my office half hour ago. Nobody knows how he got in or why he picked my office. The minute I saw him I tipped the alarm, and the place was under full protection in ninety seconds. He didn't know what was going on, of course... he just sat there where you're sitting, and said "I've come to your planet with a special message for your President".

MacReady shuddered. "I can't tell you how I felt... I mean the shock of seeing him, and then just that simple sentence. I could hardly stand up. I took him into the little study, checked again on security, and came back here. I called you, and then I just sat."

Jim Mitchell could feel the disbelief mounting inside of him, the incredulousness and a numbing feeling of fear. He was suddenly conscious of the terrific tension in the room. He looked at MacReady, a really nice guy, solid as he could be, and as straight and pleasant as the Kansas planes. He though how much the two of them had been through, and he marveled that between them, over something like this, that the tension should be almost unbearable.

MacReady smiled, and took out a pack of cigarette. "I know what you are thinking" he said. "I have all I can do to sit here myself. Its crazy Jim, but I believe this guy. Wait until you see him".

Taking a cigarette Mitchell smiled back. "You're right Mac" he said, "Easy does it. I agree with you, its weird, but lets go at it slow and easy. Where's the President?"

"In his office working" MacReady said. "He's been there since dinner. We have orders not to disturb him."

"How about Claussen", Mitchell asked.

"He's on his way. The alarm tipped him off, and he headed right in. I've talked to him on the radio phone. He thinks I've gone berserk too, but he has made all the security arrangements. After he comes in, nobody gets in or out until this is over."

"Anybody else around?" Mitchell took a long drag and snuffed out the cigarette. "No, we're lucky", MacReady said. "No visitors scheduled. When our chum appeared I closed off the switchboard."

"We're really closed in then".

"Right", MacReady answered. "I don't know weather you agree or not, but I though it best. I was going to contact the Chief Justice, but then I thought we had better go it alone. Once Claussen comes in we are on our own... the three of us, the President, and his caller."

Mitchell was about to ask what the visitor was like when Claussen came in. He was as tall as Mitchell, but he was older, greying and heavy set. He looked, Mitchell thought, every inch of what he was... the policeman.

Claussen shrugged off his top coat. "All right", he said. "You've bottled this place up, sealed it tight... I'll keep it that way, but now what?"

John MacReady cleared his throat. "Well Tom", he said to Claussen, "if you will just do what is best for absolute security until this thing is over, that will be fine." "Okay, said Claussen, "my men have this character right where we want him. He isn't carrying a thing, not even a nail file. He's an odd one, but we can handle him, I'm sure. I think we can use the television room for the conference. I'll have the lights brought up bright, and we'll watch him like a hawk from the control room. We can give the President maximum security at all times. I sent Jones to join the guard at the Presidents door. Jones will stick with him all the way. I've got Wernicke on the visitor, he's the best man for that. The visitor wont be able to sneeze unless he wants his head blown off."

"That's fine", MacReady said. "Jim, I want you to go in and see this guy. Say anything you like and take as long as you like, if you think he's a bug we'll hustle him off. If you agree with me that maybe he's legitimate, we'll go ahead. I want you to share the judgment with me though, I can't go it alone."

"Agreed Mac", Jim Mitchell said. "And then", said MacReady, "if you decide its for real, I'd like you to break the news to the President. I want you to do it because he likes you Jim. It would be a shock coming from anyone but you, you're his fair-haired boy. Maybe you can use the ease the blow a little. Agreed?"

Mitchell stood up. "I'd like to see this guy", he said. Claussen hesitated. "I think I'll leave you two to that" he said. I'll go over it with the others once more to see that all is ready. Good luck."

"This way Jim", said MacReady. He opened his side door and led the way down a side corridor. He opened another door and stood aside to let Mitchell pass. "When you've made up your mind Jim", he said, "I'll be in my office". "Just ask our visitor to be patient a little longer." MacReady gave him a pat on the shoulder, Mitchell grinned and went into the study.

The man sat quietly in a leather chair. Mitchell could feel his heart pounding... he caught his breath. He had never seen anyone like this in his life, and yet it was just a man.

The caller stood up. He was tall, taller than Mitchell's six three. He was slim. His complexion was like that of someone who had a rich golden tan. He was completely bald, and Jim noticed that there was no hair on the back of his hands. He was a good looking man, with wide set blue eyes and perfectly proportioned features.

The visitor smiled. 'I beg your pardon", Mitchell said, "I was staring."

"You were", said the visitor. "It is understandable."

His voice was beautiful. Clear and not too deep, yet slow and precise. It had overtones of kindness. Suddenly Mitchell felt humble in the presence of this man, and the feeling irritated him.

The man's costume was remarkable. He wore a suit of soft blue, and the fabric was strange to Mitchell. He couldn't tell what kind of cloth it was. It looked very fine and soft, almost lustrous. It was cut almost like a tunic, but there was no buttons. It fitted almost like a turtleneck, and there no cuffs and apparently no pockets. It fitted smoothly and closely. The visitors shoes were all of one piece, there was no top, no sole or heal. The bottom looked stiff and solid, the rest seemed supple.

There was no doubt in Mitchell's mind. He understood exactly how MacReady had felt. If this man was a fraud he was the world's greatest fraud. He had said only five words to him, Mitchell thought, yet there were enough to convince him. His appearance, his very presence, and his voice, were convincing.

Mitchell realized that he had been standing, looking, thinking for some time. "I'll go now and arrange the interview with the President", he said.

"That will be satisfactory", he said, and he smiled again at Mitchell. It was a warming smile, personal, even intimate, as though this man regarded Mitchell as something more than that which we was. It was puzzling.

when he got back to MacReady's office Mitchell had to sit down. Perspiration was running from his face. MacReady handed him a lighted cigarette. He put his hand on Mitchell's shoulder. "I know exactly how you feel", he said.

Mitchell waited until his heart stopped pounding and his head quieted a little, "From outer space?", he said... "and I believe it?"

MacReady said, "You believe it just as I believe it. We had better go ahead Jim."

"I'll go tell the President", Mitchell said. He couldn't help but to laugh. It almost brought tears to his eyes his emotions were so uncertain. "Mac", he said. "This is ridiculous, but I do believe this guy!.."

The President looked up, frowning when Mitchell entered his office. Then he saw who it was. "Hi", he said, and he grinned. "What's your catastrophe son". Mitchell stood before the massive desk. "I'm sorry to disturb you Mr President", Mitchell said, "but we have a rather unusual caller. He just showed up in Mac's office. Mac put maximum security on and called Claussen and me. Everything is under control, but Mac and I though you should know".

"Know what the President asked", his brow wrinkling.

This man says he is from outer space, and says he has a message for you", Jim said.

The President sat a long time reflecting the conflict of emotions within himself. There was silence in the room, but finally he grinned. "All right son", he said. "I'll see the caller that you and MacReady have cooked up." His grim disappeared. "Its funny isn't it... that a thing like this is so beyond belief, yet you get a feeling that its something that you've been expecting for a long time." He stood up quickly and said "lets go Jim."

Mitchell led the way to the television study. The President and he were joined by MacReady at the door. Claussen signaled from down the hall that the caller was waiting. They went in.

The man stood up. He smiled, and Mitchell thought, curiously, how like a smile of reassurance it was.

The President said, "Welcome", and stuck out his hand. Mitchell winced. He could imagine the reaction of Wernicke, gun whipped up, finger tense. The visitor gravely shook the President's hand.

The President sat down and then the others sat down. The lights were murderously hot and bright. Out of the corner of his eye Mitchell could see the observers in the control booth. Claussen, Wernicke, Jones, and he had a wry thought. If the visitor was what he claimed to be, how senseless their protection measures were.

"I will not concern you for long", the visitor said. "I am here to tell you a few things and very briefly." There seemed nothing to say in response, so no one spoke. The visitor looked around, smiled, and continued. "Those of us" - the word "us" chilled Mitchell - "who are your observers, have been struck by two things", the visitor said. "First, you assume that the visitor from what you call "space", will come on a mission of death. I am your caller from another world, and I come on a peaceful mission. You need not fear me nor my people. The reason I have come is simple. We have watched the way of your world, and we have decided it is time to let you know our secret. Perhaps it will ease the tensions, or perhaps it will bring peace closer to reality, and hearten men of good-will everywhere." The visitor paused and looked about quizzically. "It is difficult for me to say this exactly right, since force, or what you call "war", disappeared from our planet a long, long time ago. It disappeared the day we had *our* first caller from "outer space", and listened to *his* message. That day we conquered our most insidious enemy, an enemy which now threatens *your* society.

You should know that you share with other peoples of other planets a common bond. It is not thought of in the same words or in the same symbols, but certainly in the same spirit. Your people and my people, and all living things, look to a guiding Spirit, a force more powerful than any bomb yet devised, yet more gentile that the breath of life itself. It is the only force that can redeem us from evil and ugliness and tragedy."

The room was as still as death. The lights were merciless. The visitor stood up. "Before you", he said, "is a new year. Look forward to it with the knowledge that men of good-will exist everywhere in the universe, and only these men will survive. The greatest enemy is fear... their common bond is faith. From this knowledge lasting peace can endure."

Mitchell had seen the President moved before, but never like this. He sat in his characteristic way, his arms folded across his chest. When he spoke his words were almost inaudible. He said, "thank you sir, and bless you."

Then there was a great commotion from the control booth. Claussen broke into the room with a shout. "Where did he go", he cried, and Mitchell felt himself react as if coming out of a trance. He saw the President stand up, and MacReady fumbling for a signal button.

"Calm yourselves gentleman", the President said. "He's gone."

The room was heavy with indecision. Claussen looked about uncertainly. MacReady watching the President. Mitchell realized he was very tired.

"I think", the President said, "that we ought to break this up right now. This has been hard on all of us, but I want to thank you all for what you have done. You did exactly what you should have done, and I am proud of you.

"Jim", the President continued. "I don't think you have to worry any more about that speech. I have a New Years day message, not only for our people, but for everyone in the world. He stopped for a moment in the door, an erect man, tired about the eyes, but a calm man with sensitive features.

"You know", he said. "I think I will tell exactly what happened here tonight. I will tell them that they may think that this story is untrue if they wish, but that I believe it, and that every man that chooses can believe it. I will offer no proof, since we have none to offer, but I think that those who have faith will believe and rejoice."

Mitchell left the White House shortly after that. He was terribly weary. The rain had turned to snow. He walked to his car, yet for all his fatigue he felt a sense of hope, a certainty, of an understanding and faith greater than he had ever known before.

Mitchell decided that he would fly to Cleveland tomorrow. He was anxious to see Anne and the youngsters. He was anxious to tell them the story of the Presidents Caller...

* * *

Sananda

The "Source" of all life

Sori Sori: Mine beloved, I am now speaking unto thee for the good of all. Let thine hand be as mine, for are we not One in that which is the All, the ineffable "Source" of life, which is the beginning and the end, the Alpha and Omega. For this are we "One" in this Oneness.

I say unto all and sundry: Ye and I are One... there is no separation. Life is eternal, moving thru the multitude of cycles... ever changing, ever upward and onward in the All Life and Light, which is symbolized by the unbroken circle O, encompassing the whole of creation. There is nothing outside, for everything or form is of this "Source", which has no beginning, no end... this being the great mystery

Mankind of flesh and bone can never fathom the Source of the All, the Everness, until he hast learned the Law of the One and become one with it... then he becomes free from all darkness, all pain, all hatred, greed and malice, all bondage. He shall know such freedom as I know.

I know myself to be the Son of God, sent of the one which mankind calls "God". O, my beloved children, I am light, I am love... I am the wayshower, the good shepherd, sent of the Source to bring thee home. For the time, the great cycle, is now come when the gates of the heavens shall swing wide to reveal its mysteries. There are many planes, many things to learn, which ye shall learn by and thru thine own effort, thine free will, which is the precious gift given unto mankind as he went into bondage, into the world of mortality. I have called unto one and all, *Come Home! Come Home!*". I have prepared a place for one and all, and each shall find it such as he is prepared to enter in. He\She shall be in his own environment. He shall be known as he is, yet again preparing for his or her next cycle, his or her greater part.

Mine time is come when I shall find the lost lambs. I know mine flock and they know mine voice. I bring no one against their will!

Hear ye me... I say there is no death. Life is eternal... many stages, many forms... ever lighter, brighter, and more glorious...

* * *

The Host

Sori Sori: This day I say unto them which have a mind to learn, that there are ones which stand by which await them. These ones which await their (mans) preparation are as ones illumined, and prepared to give unto them that which they have not learned within their Halls of Science or Philosophy

We of the host have come from many galaxies to add our part unto that of our brother and compatriot, Sananda... for he hast formulated this great and marvelous plan which he hast now completed for the benefit of all which have the will, the mind, to come forth to partake of that which we are prepared to give unto them.

For this we offer ourself that there be greater light within the world of man... that all darkness be no more... that there be peace within the place wherein mankind shall be placed when the hour strikes, for Mother Earth shall be evacuated.

This hast been referred to. Do ye, the ones which are now within the place wherein ye labor in bondage, remember that which hast been said as a warning? Did ye take note? Are thou prepared to go forth as one prepared to enter into the School which is prepared on behalf of the children of Earth? I say, it is the greatest project which hast been brought into manifestation. Ye cannot even imagine the magnitude of such as is brought forth in love and mercy, that there be light in the days of darkness. This shall be as a continual effort until every living creature is removed from the planet upon which ye now have footing.

So be it I am One with the Mighty Host, the Great and Grand Council. We speak with one voice, one intent... that of bringing freedom unto an awakening people. We Will that all mankind awaken... So may it be!

This is our mission, our intent.

Please see Volume II.

* * *

www.ingramcontent.com/pod-product-compliance
Lightning Source LLC
LaVergne TN
LVHW051515070426
835507LV00023B/3124